Anthony Weir an

IMAGES
of LUST
SEXUAL CARVINGS ON
MEDIEVAL CHURCHES

B.T. BATSFORD LTD LONDON

Why dost thou show me iniquity?
                    Habbakuk

For Martha and Betty

© Anthony Weir and Jim Jerman 1986
First published 1986
This paperback edition published 1993

Typeset by Servis Filmsetting Ltd, Manchester
and printed in Great Britain by
Butler & Tanner Ltd
Frome, Somerset
for the publishers
Batsford Academic and Educational, an imprint of
B.T. Batsford Ltd
4 Fitzhardinge Street
London WL11 0AH

British Library Cataloguing in Publication Data

Weir, Anthony
    Images of lust: sexual carvings on medieval
    churches.
    1. Carving (Decorative arts) — Europe — History
    2. Church decoration and ornament — Europe —
    History
    I. Title   II. Jerman, James
    729'.5   NK5500
    ISBN 0–7134–7404–1

CONTENTS

ACKNOWLEDGMENTS

The list of those who have helped us in our search is long, as our bibliography testifies. It is inevitable that we may inadvertently omit to mention other scholars whose work has been invaluable. To them we give our apologies, and thanks.

We should like to express special thanks to:

Professor George Zarnecki of the Courtauld Institute for his encouragement, for his helpful comments on the first draft of the book, and for use of the facilities at the Courtauld Institute;

Philip Barker, Reader in British Archaeology, Birmingham University, for help and encouragement; Dr Jørgen Andersen and Dr Brian Branston for stimulating our research, and to the latter, and Martin Pover, for the gift of photographs and material;

Henri Renou, formerly of the Centre des Etudes Supérieures de Civilisation Médiévale at Poitiers, for generous help in finding photographs in the archives and for suggesting likely churches;

Professor Serafín Moralejo, University of Santiago de Compostela;

Dr Peter Harbison, Professor Estyn Evans and James Little for invaluable help with the location of the Irish figures and other matters;

Catherine Johns, British Museum; Dr Lucas and Dr Raftery, National Museum of Ireland;

Dr Madeleine Marcheix, Museum of Limoges; Helen Hickey, Enniskillen Museum; Dr W. Schäle, Staatliches Konservatoramt, Saarbrücken; Dr Kay Milton, Queen's University, Belfast;

Sylvia Beamon, Professor Henri Godin, Michael Day, James d'Emilio, John Feehan, Eric Fernie, Dorothy and Henry Kraus, Douglas Palmer, Professor John Williams of Pittsburgh, Doreen and John Yarwood, Vladimir Stodola of Prague; Janet and Colin Bord for the generous gift of photographs; the trustees of the British Museum, the National Museum of Ireland, Colchester and Essex Museum, the Inventaire Général de Bretagne for permission to use copyright photographs;

the staff of the Royal Irish Academy, the interlibrary loans staff of the Queen's University Belfast and of Leicester University, the British Library;

all those people who helped us find our way to obscure sites everywhere;

and last, but not least, for to them we dedicate this book, Martha Weir (for generous financial support, for driving thousands of miles in search of exhibitionists – and on one occasion having her car smashed) and Betty Jerman (for waiting for hours and hours in remote country churchyards). Without their patience and long-suffering, and boundless goodwill this book could not have been attempted.

LIST OF ILLUSTRATIONS

Introduction

La temática obscena plantea una de las mayores incógnitas en el campo de la iconografía románica
Maria Ines Ruiz Montejo

A few kilometres west of the noisy, lorry-laden N1 road from Madrid to northern Spain, up a rutted track from a rough by-road, is the hamlet of Santa Marta del Cerro: a bar, a shop, a few houses, and a church. The church is old and battered, and dates mostly from the twelfth century, built in triumph after this area was seized from the Moors. Past this church, under-neath the carved corbels which support the roof of the semi-circular apse, cattle pass early in the morning, with bells around their necks, filing slowly down to the spring to drink in turn. Strangers never come to Santa Marta del Cerro. No one passes through, for it is a dead end, smaller now than it was in the twelfth century.

The church of Santa Marta is known to few Romanesque scholars. Few villagers notice the

Plate 1 Whittlesford Church, Cambridgeshire.

Fig. 1 Santa Marta del Cerro, corbels: exhibiting couple.

carvings on the corbels high above them and, if they do, they probably do not understand them, for they are a curious assortment: a man pulling his beard; a human-headed snake; an acrobat with his feet doubled behind his shoulders; a stork with a snake in its beak; two birds with interlocked necks; figures of ecclesiastics, one of whom has a barrel on his back; a man playing a viol; a peacock; a leopard; a squatting figure with its hands on its knees; an acrobat with his feet to his ears; a woman with large bared breasts and her hands clasped on her belly; another squatting figure of indeterminate sex, and two squatting figures exhibiting male and female genitals agonisedly (*Fig. 1*).

To twentieth-century eyes these seem like sculptural caprices, carved by exuberant masons out of sheer fun and devilment, and we may be inclined to dismiss them as nothing more than creations of whim and whimsy. But sculptors then, as workers now, did not carve what they were not commissioned to do, nor what they were not paid for. Parish churches in the twelfth century were 'sold' rather as fitted kitchens or houses are today: for so much money you would get so big a building and so much carving. Every sculpted capital and corbel employed a man's time and skill and therefore cost so much – and blank ones were cheaper. Churches like this one, dedicated to St Martha on the little hill (*cerro*) overlooking the plain of Segóvia, were paid for by the rich – perhaps the

pious widow of a reconquistador – and their details were chosen, according to the money available, by the sponsor, the incumbent priest, or a spiritual adviser – perhaps an abbot or prior or private chaplain. Every one of these corbels was chosen with care, and had a message carved expressly for the twelfth-century inhabitants of Santa Marta del Cerro. The cleric with a barrel on his back, for example, pilloried the drunkenness of a local priest, or the weight of his unabsolved sins, or both. The peacock, rarely found as here carved on corbels, had a more complex significance, drawn in part from early Christian symbolism, and in part from fable and medieval Bestiaries. The fearsome raucous cry of the peacock, piercing the night air, seemed like the voice of souls in torment, warning sinners of the inextinguishable fires of Gehenna. Its long tail, on the other hand, was symbolic of Paradise. The many eyes upon it reminded men to be ever watchful, and to be constantly aware of the all-seeing nature of God. St Augustine had said that the flesh of the peacock was incorruptible, so the bird could additionally be representative of the ineffable and eternal splendour of the Holy Spirit.

These small carvings were a lesson in stone for the illiterate villagers of Santa Marta del Cerro. But what of the other carvings? What significance for them had those carvings which to modern eyes are immodest, obscene even?

Three hundred kilometres (186 miles) NNW, in another remote hamlet off the beaten track, where one would least expect to find such a splendid building, stands the collegiate church of San Pedro de Cervatos, one of a number of fine churches in this arid area of Castile. Like Santa Marta, it has a corbel table, with almost 100 corbels on it, vigorously and expressively carved. Of these, one quarter are obscene, far

Plate 2 Saint-Palais, Gironde: corbel table. Note *la femme aux serpents* (*second from left*), an anus-shower, and a clutching pair.

grosser than those of Santa Marta; they include scenes of anal display, and of sodomy. The sculptor at times relegated these acts to apes and other animals, as if he found the subjects too coarse for humans, but he did not shrink from showing megaphallic men, one with his penis in his mouth. On window capitals of this church, acrobats with huge genitals cavort with feet-to-ears females, one of whom shows off her sex in the most outrageously explicit manner.

Between these two churches is Frómista, with its 315 corbels. During the nineteenth-century restorations some corbels were withdrawn as being too indecent, but many of those remaining are arrestingly provocative.

Then there is San Quirce, and San Pedro de Tejada . . . one could go on multiplying examples, and many will be found in the pages which follow. Spanish scholars have suddenly become aware of the great wealth of 'obscene' carvings in the rural churches of northern Spain. But it is not only in Spain that one finds them. Crossing the Pyrenees into south-west France one encounters them again, a great profusion of them, Champagnolles (Charente Maritime) is perhaps second only to Cervatos. The Poitou-Charentes area abounds in such sculptures but does not have a monopoly of them. They can also be found in the British Isles (*see Plate 1*).

In Herefordshire, during the nineteenth century, a vicar of Kilpeck ordered the defacing of a number of corbels which upset his sensibilities. One escaped destruction, the well-known 'sheela-na-gig'. Of the destroyed carvings, enough detail remains for a reconstruction of the original scenes of lovers in amorous embrace.

Scholars have been reluctant to devote time to the study of these carvings, of which hundreds exist, not because of social attitudes and the climate of opinion regarding matters of an improper or indelicate nature, but because they have not considered them important. Corbels, on which most of these unusual designs are cut, are very minor architectural components of a building. They are in some cases high up and difficult to make out (some are even out of sight, but that did not deter the masons from exercising their skill upon them). Some seem to be simple, ornamental designs of knotwork, or foliage, or grimacing masks; yet others appear to be merely fantastic creations, whose message

Plate 3 A sheela-na-gig from Easthorpe Church, Essex (now in Colchester Museum); about 30cm (12in) high by 23cm (9in) broad. The word 'ELUI' defies explanation. (Photo: Martin Pover & Brian Branston)

may be irretrievably lost. Those with which this book is concerned, however, do not deserve such neglect. We believe there is much to be gained from studying them. Their composition and content, their context and date, their frequency and spread can tell us much about medieval masons and their patrons, about medieval beliefs and thoughts, about sculptural ideals and themes, and why these were transmitted and copied over a wide area of Europe within a very short space of time.

One sculptural design which we believe was exploited during this period, about which there has been speculation for at least a century and a half, and which the reader can study for himself without the necessity of embarking for France or Spain, is the British 'sheela-na-gig', one of the few remaining 'obscene' figures in our islands (*Plate 3*). It is a good starting point in our study of how it came to pass that lewd carvings were placed on or in Christian churches, there to resist successfully any attempts to eradicate them during the frequent periods of puritanical iconoclastic destruction of statues and carvings. It is the tenacity with which these grotesque sculptures have clung to existence that has mystified students of the bizarre, and a number of opinions about their possible origin, purpose, and longevity have been expressed.

One view is that they are vestigial idols of some ancient pre-Christian fertility religion, a religion to which agricultural folk in remote country districts still in some way subscribe, especially since, following papal edicts, such objects have been 'Christianised', and imbedded in the fabric of the Church in order to render them tractable, to put them out of harm's way. The religion, the 'Old Religion', which these idols represent, is held to be very old, stretching back to Bronze Age times or beyond, but may have received fresh injections of vitality from the pagan Celtic and Scandinavian settlers (after all, our days of the week, and festivals like Easter are named after pagan gods and goddesses).

Another view, not unconnected with the above, is that these figures, representing ancient powers, are in the popular mind associated with magic. As 'fertility' symbols they have the power to turn aside the forces of evil, the maleficent glance of the Evil Eye. They are protective, tutelary, apotropaic. Perhaps we do not like to admit it, say the adherents of this theory, but most of us cling to superstitious practices. With a wry smile we touch wood, or throw salt over our left shoulder, in order to placate the mysterious forces of darkness. Country folk, who live closer to the earth than town-dwellers, are alleged to feel the need more strongly (or do they simply cling to old customs because they are more conservative?). At least they seem to have done so as late as the seventeenth century in Wales and the granite-bearing areas of Normandy, for houses there were still being 'protected' with phallic emblems, carved on stairposts and fireplaces. The Greeks and Romans made much use of such prophylactic symbols, and the Christian chrism and Agnus Dei can be seen as an extension of the idea. Surely then, it is argued, the sheela-na-gig is to be placed in the same category of apotropaic objects.

If, in the course of this book, we seem to be taking issue with these theories, even apparently dismissing out of hand some of their tenets, it is not because we think they have no part in the creation of exhibitionist sculptures. Who can tell what archetypal atavistic symbolism lurks behind the conscious mind of the creative artist? We shall devote a chapter to a consideration of the folkloric aspects of our subject, and, whenever the need arises, we shall look at the application of any of these theories, whose weakness is mainly that they are not susceptible of proof, and remain little more than inherent possibilities. They tend to be facile explanations of what is a complicated story, and they have often obfuscated attempts at real explanation, leading scholars into making slack, dismissive judgments, some of which we list in the epilogue. More cogently, we consider them somewhat out of place in this book, which we wish to keep within the proper confines of art history. They are best left to folklorists and historians of comparative religion.

We prefer, therefore, to propose yet another theory, one based on harder evidence. We aim to show that sheela-na-gigs and allied exhibitionists are arguably iconographic images whose purpose was to give visual support to the Church's moral teachings. They reflect, albeit in a small way, the subjects depicted on tympana, capitals, friezes and panels – the great dooms and visions of judgment. We believe them to be contemporary and of a piece with other Romanesque carvings, regardless of which other distant origins may have played a part in their make-up. We believe that they dealt with matters of great moment – the sexual *mores* and salvation of medieval folk – and that the importance placed upon them was to leave a lingering memory, so that, long after their primary import had ceased to be recognised, they continued to be protected against destruction. That they kept their strange fascination is evinced by a few post-Romanesque examples, but to what extent this is due to folk attachment, belief in magic, or identification with primeval deities it is not for us to say, for this leads to the sort of speculation we are anxious to avoid.

1 Sheela-na-gig

. . . one of those old Fetish figures called 'Hags of the Castle' . . .

Windele

. . . or Julia the Giddy, or the Girl of the Paps, or the Whore, or the Idol, or St Shanahan, or Cathleen Owen, or Sheila O'Dwyer . . .

Many names have been given at various times and in different places to the indecent carvings which first came into prominent public discussion among antiquaries in nineteenth-century Ireland. The attempts of philologists and historians to trace the etymology of sheela-na-gig in its many Irish and English spellings are admirably reviewed in the first long book to be written on the subject of these carvings: the doctoral thesis for the University of Copenhagen of Jørgen Andersen, published in 1977 under the title 'The Witch on the Wall: medieval erotic sculptures of the British Isles' (Andersen 1977). It gave a catalogue of the then known figures together with a number of chapters of commentary and discussion. Readers curious to know about forms like 'sile na gCioch' could not do better than to turn to Andersen's second chapter. Here we can only say that a great deal of obscurity surrounds the term and its inception. But since sheela-na-gig, the anglicised form of a dubious Irish expression, has gained so wide a currency to indicate the carving which the *Shell Guide to Ireland* (Killanin & Duigan 1967) calls 'an obscene female figure of uncertain significance', we shall continue to use the term (or its shortened form sheela) when we speak of female sculptures. Because our study also takes into account male sexual sculptures, which in France and Spain are more numerous than female, we shall use a more general term when referring to figures of both sexes, namely, 'sexual exhibitionists' or simply 'exhibitionists'.

At the outset we would do well to clarify two terms which have often been used in connection with such carvings. The first is the word 'erotic'. In its purest sense, this word denotes something capable of arousing love or exciting sexual feeling. When applied to a work of art, we expect to sense a sexually-arousing reaction to the piece of work. We cannot think the term is applicable to the exhibitionists we are going to consider. Admittedly these sculptures are sexual and draw attention to the genitalia by a flagrant display often highlighted by the play of the hands; but an equally distinctive feature of the sheela is its repellent ugliness: huge disproportionate head, staring eyes, gaping mouth, wedge nose, big ears, bald pate, herculean shoulders and twisted posture (*Fig. 4*) As Andersen repeatedly states, the sheela is a frightening hag whose message does not seem to be immoral but is rather aimed at dispelling any sexual predisposition the viewer might entertain. We suggest in this book that the function of sexual exhibitionists is not erotic but rather the reverse, that these extraordinarily frank carvings were more probably an element in the medieval Church's campaign against immorality, and that they were not intended to inflame the passions but rather to allay them (*Plates 4, 5 and 6*).

Secondly, we pass under review another popular term, used by us as well as others, when describing such sexual carvings – the word 'obscene'. In the course of this essay it will become apparent that medieval masons did not consider these images to be obscene. Crude, vulgar, not without satirical or sardonic humour, they were executed in the full knowledge that they might shock or give offence. Indeed, that was most probably the intention. But they were not pornographic, or sacrilegious; nor were they inconsequential. In spite of their grossness, their comic exaggeration and impossible postures, they were, in their own small way, serious works. That is not to say that there are never any instances of trivial carvings, the expressions of a mason's virtuosity or humour, but we hope to show that the great majority once formed part of a planned artistic composition, whose several parts combine to create a cumulative effect of high seriousness.

Fig. 2a Insular sheela-na-gigs illustrating the role played by the hands. Type I shows both hands behind the buttocks; Type II only one hand behind; Type III both hands in front; Type IV one hand in front (for a fuller explanation see Jerman, Dundalk 1981). (a) Blackhall Castle, Type I; (b) Doon Castle, Type I; (c) Ballyfinboy, Type I; (d) Clomantagh, Type II; (e) Tullavin Castle, Type II; (f) Lixnaw, Type I.

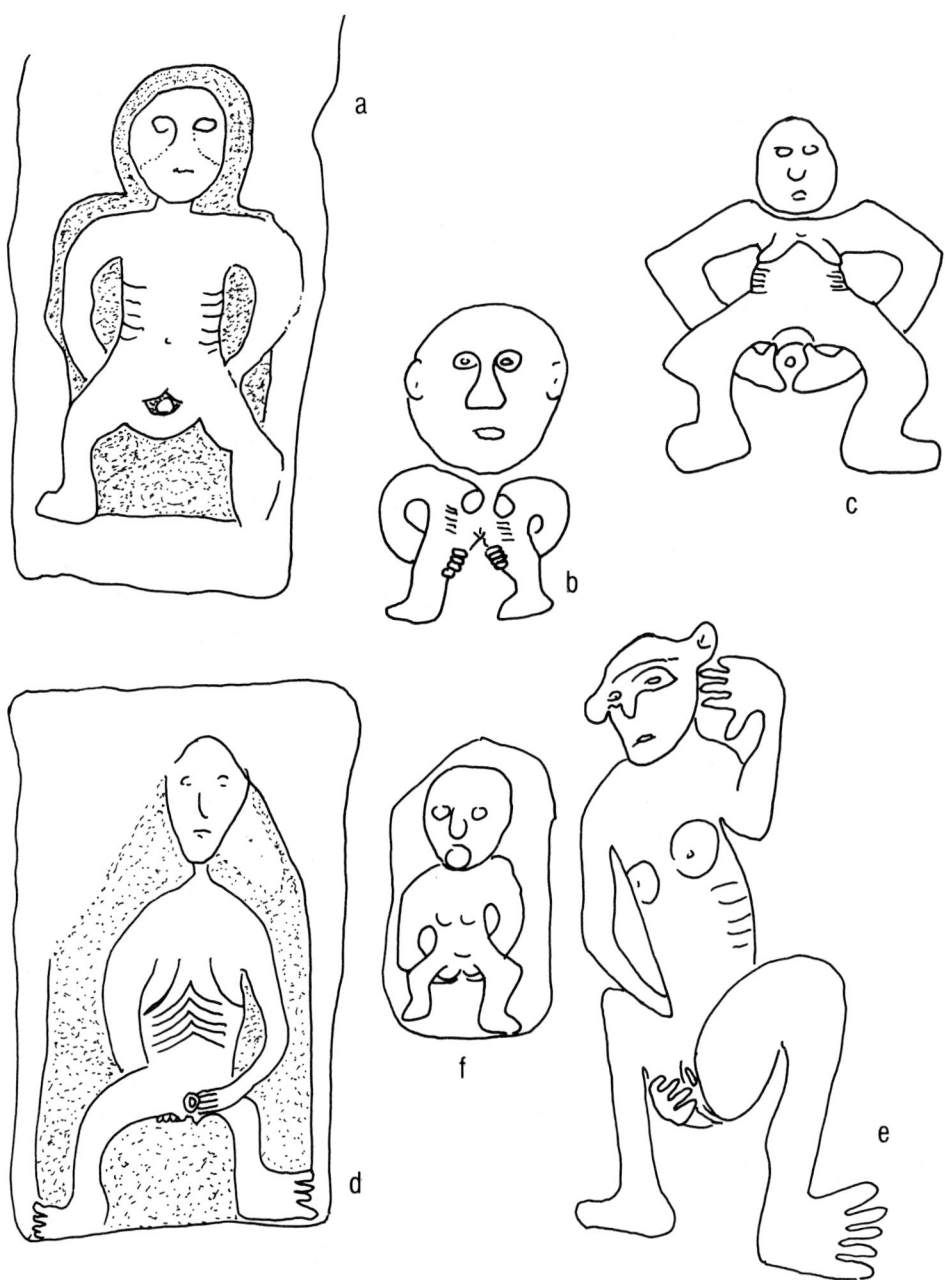

Over the centuries much medieval carving has been thought so crude as to merit destruction, and, where this has happened, leaving behind in isolation the exhibitionist figures, it is understandable that one should be taken aback by the vulgarity of the decontextualised vestiges. If what survives seems to us obscene, the fault is partly within ourselves, since we have become conditioned by our education and upbringing to misrepresent to ourselves the moral climate that prevailed during the early Middle Ages. (The whole question of 'obscenity' in art has been admirably examined by Catherine Johns in her study of the 'erotica' in the British Museum (Johns 1982).)

Fig. 2b (g) Cloghan Castle, Type III; (h) Llandrindod, Type III; (i) Killaloe, Type IV; (j) Ballylarkin, Type IV.

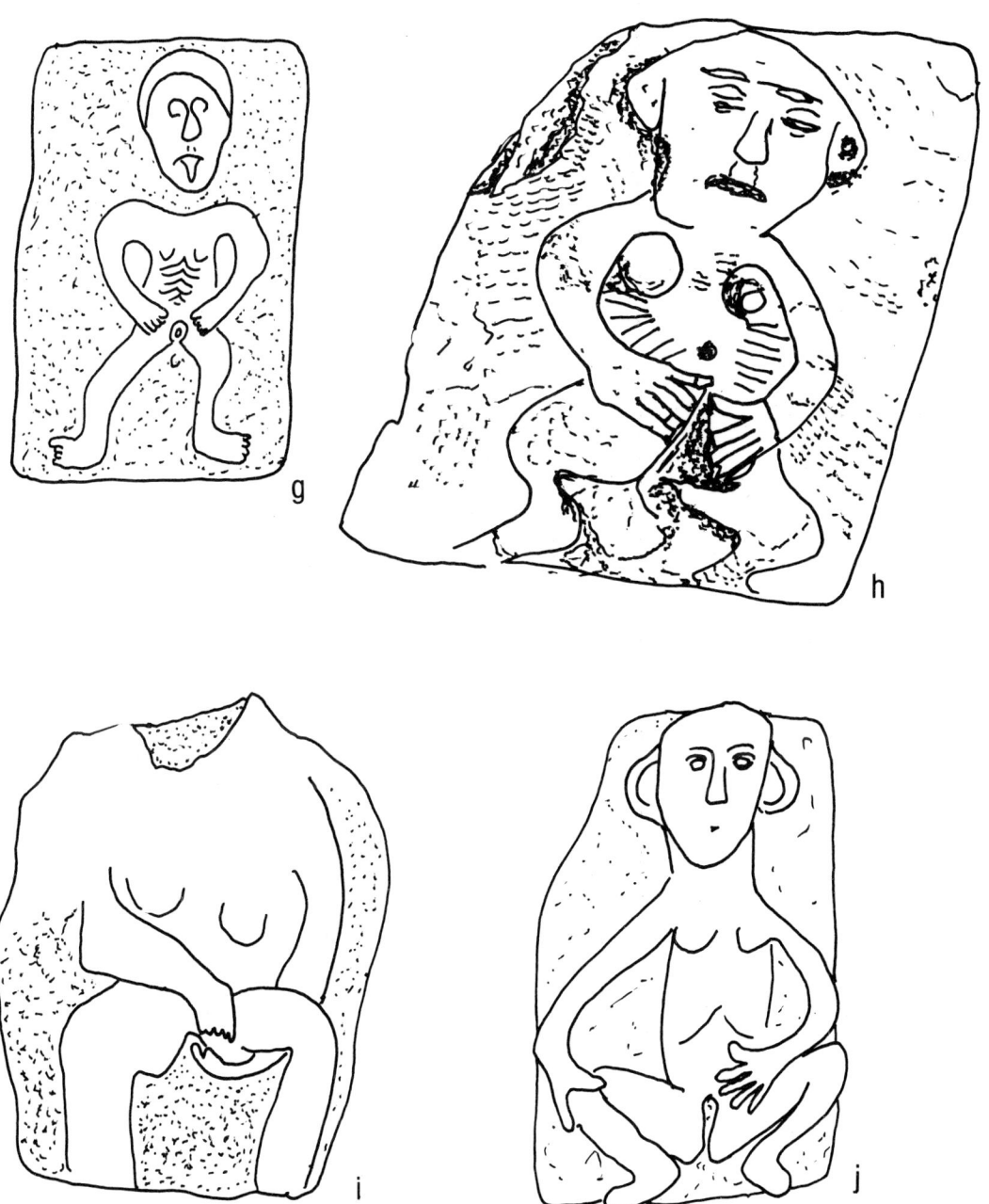

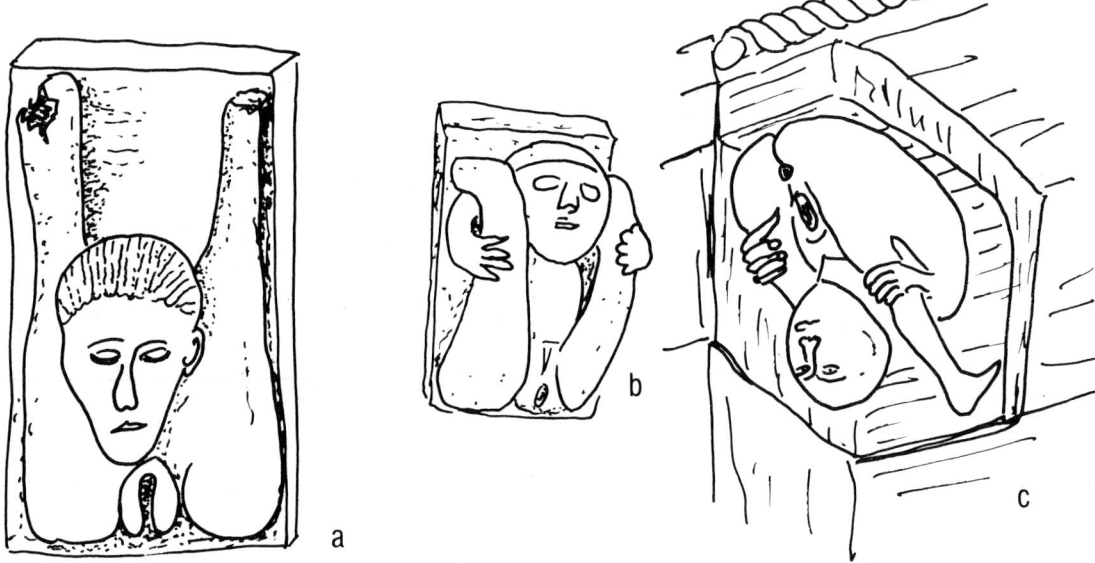

Fig. 3 Some Continental female exhibitionists in the feet-to-ears position: (a) Assouste; (b) Corullón (also displaying anus); (c) Mauriac (upside-down acrobat, also displaying anus).

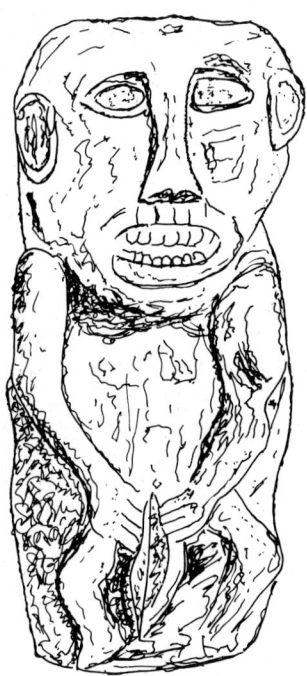

Fig. 4 'Chloran' from Killua, Westmeath, in the British Museum (Witt Collection), shows typical ugliness.

There is no need to give a history of the discovery of sheela-na-gigs by nineteenth-century antiquarians, since Andersen has done this most admirably (Andersen 1977). He supplies a very full bibliography, covering not only all the discussions of the 1840s, but also the very many articles which have appeared, especially since attention was drawn to the notice of a wider public by the first anonymous list in 1894, and the much fuller list and taxonomy by Dr Edith M. Guest in 1935 (Guest 1935). We need only add a little further historical note of evidence that has recently been brought to our attention (Ross 1983). One of the volumes of the Helicon History of Ireland, *The Catholic Community in the seventeenth and eighteenth centuries* 1981, contains a number of references to sheelas earlier than any so far known. These references occur in diocesan and provincial statutes of the seventeenth century:

1   In 1631, provincial statutes for Tuam order parish priests to hide away, and to note where they are hidden away, what are described in the veiled obscurity of Latin as *imagines obesae et aspectui*

ingratae, in the vernacular 'sheela-na-gigs', i.e. at that time priests had begun to take notice of these 'fat figures of unpleasant features' and to remove them.

2 . . . a Diocesan (Ossory) regulation of 1676 ordering 'sheela-na-gigs' to be burned. Bishop Brehan in Waterford was ordering exactly the same thing that year . . .

3 . . . the Kilmore diocesan synod excluded from all sacraments . . . those whom the synod calls *gierador* – they might perhaps be described as 'living sheela-na-gigs'.

This last reference gives support to the evidence that in some country districts 'sheela-na-gig' was a term used to indicate women of loose morals or simply old hags. These regulations also contain further evidence that many sheelas were destroyed or buried, and that once upon a time there must have been a great many more than we can see today.

Another comment may be made at the outset. If Spanish and French antiquaries and writers of the history of art had shown the same curiosity and interest as their Irish counterparts in studying and cataloguing the hundreds of exhibitionist carvings around them (and to this day they still have not done so), then it is our view that a number of misconceptions might never have arisen:

1 sheelas would not have been regarded as purely insular phenomena;

2 their origin would not have been attributed to pre-Christian fertility or other cults;

3 their function would not have been described as mainly a tutelary, apotropaic one;

4 their dating would have been established in all probability as no earlier than the eleventh century;

5 and their study would not have been relegated to obscure journals but undertaken openly, like that of other sculptures of their period.

As it is, we have had to wait over a century and a half for work like Andersen's. Our own belated contribution aims to show that sexual exhibitionists developed, like so many other Romanesque motifs, from Classical prototypes at a date not earlier, so far as we have been able to ascertain, than the eleventh century, and that their *floruit* was during the twelfth century; that they are Christian carvings, part of an iconography aimed at castigating the sins of the flesh, and that in this they were only one element in the

Plate 4 Sheela from Cavan, similar to 'Chloran' (Fig. 4). (Photo: Nat. Museum of Ireland, Dublin)

attack on lust, luxury and fornication; that their horrible appearance is due to the fact that they portrayed evil in the battle against evil; that, in this role of warring against *Luxuria* and *Concupiscentia*, two of the Mortal Sins, they flourished in the sculpture of a well-defined area of western France and northern Spain; that they reached the British Isles by a process we shall describe; that they were supported by a number of carvings which at first sight seem to be unconnected with them, and which are better understood when the connection has been made, and that it is possible that the apotropaic purpose sometimes attributed to them is a later development, stemming from the forcefulness of their imagery and the respect with which they were regarded. In all this, the solutions we offer to problems posed by the sheelas and other sexual figures will be simple ones, of the kind that ought to have been expounded long ago. These solutions, which are free of mystification, and are supported by our illustrative material, ought to be more plausible than much of what has been written on the subject.

We have been blinkered in the past by our restricted horizons in the study of the insular carvings. The solution to the problem of what these figures are and why they occur on churches is not to be found at home but on the Continent. Andersen (Andersen 1977) does tentatively suggest the European connection but, since his study was intended to examine only the insular pieces, he did not pursue it; he did, however, mention some 11 in France (none in Spain), 40 or so in England and over 70 in Ireland. A few have come to light since his work was published – we list them in Chapter 10. He states:

> There seems to be no great mystery about the origin of the motif in the British Isles; it could well have arrived with other motifs to enrich the repertoire of carvers looking generally towards France and the Continent for inspiration.

And, in describing the corbel table of Saint-Quantin-de-Rançannes, he adds:

> It is a context in which we approach the Irish sheelas closely, if we have not in fact found a model for them.

Plate 5 Sheela at Kilpeck, Type I. The fact that it is not entirely human is significant. Either the sculptor was embarrassed (not likely) or he meant to portray the act as beastly. (Photo: J. & C. Bord)

Plate 6 Sheela from Ballyportry Castle. (Photo: Nat. Museum of Ireland, Dublin)

Furthermore, he tells us that he was informed by the Secretary of the *Commission d'Inventaire* for the Poitou-Charente district that there are over 100 exhibitionists in that part of France alone. Our own by no means exhaustive searches have identified over 70 female exhibitionists in France, some 40 in Spain, an even higher number of male exhibitionists in both countries (we gave up trying to count them), and many other figures allied to them by their sexual display or attributes (e.g. coital couples, simple frontal nudes, anus-showers, acrobatic penis-swallowers, testicle-showers, megaphallic men, and so on). Figures such as grimacers, tongue-protruders, beard-pullers, tress-pullers and mouth-pullers often display their sex organs as well and are therefore exhibitionists (especially when megaphallic). Even if these latter figures are not displaying their genitalia, the fact that they are in close association with the exhibitionists, side by side along the same corbel tables or on the same capitals, makes it probable that they were taken by medieval man to have some sort of sexual connotation. They certainly seem to swell the number of carvings that are united in a vast endeavour to create a sermon in stone.

It is the context which defines these latter figures and persuades us that they also carried overtones of sexual significance, and it is because this context has disappeared in many restored churches that insular sheelas have lost their companions, leading people to centre interest on them alone, thus acquiring a distorted impression of their role. In Europe the exhibitionists are a sub-group of motifs which figure on churches where the carving is not only abundant but of excellent quality, and there is so much to study that the sexual sculptures tend to be disregarded as mere curiosities. In the British Isles we can only get a glimpse of the former richness of Romanesque work in the fragments which remain at, for instance, Shobdon in Herefordshire – a good example of a church which was pulled down in the eighteenth century by a well-intentioned squire (fortunately, under the influence of Walpole, Squire 'Dicky' Bateman replaced it by a gem of 'Strawberry Hill Gothick'). Virtually nothing remains of the original Norman church, except for some of the sculptured arches, set up as a sort of 'romantic ruin' in the park at some distance away. They are badly eroded now, treatment having come too late, but a Victorian artist, G. R. Lewis, made drawings of them in which we can pick out some of the fine detail. The Shobdon arches reveal what the context for sheela-na-gigs was once like.

The retention of the exhibitionist carvings alone out of all the iconoclastic destruction that took place in puritanical times is an intriguing question which we shall look at again. It cannot have been out of respect for their artistic merit.

The re-discovery by antiquarians of the Irish sheelas, before there was any discussion of these objects in Britain, led not only to the attribution of a pseudo-Irish name for them, but also to the notion that they must have had a Celtic origin. Yet the only non-Classical pre-medieval female exhibitionist figure so far to be found in Europe is a tiny 'owl-goddess' on one end of a gold bracelet from Reinheim (Saarland), dating to about 400 BC, and even this may have been inspired by Mediterranean or near-Eastern influence. The case for a 'Celtic' origin of female exhibitionists is based largely on an unsubstantiated analogy with the many figures in Teutonic or Celtic art which have a phallic form – pillars, face-pots and the like. But it is to be noted that experts on Roman art all agree that the Celts did not have a native phallic cult, and that any overtly sexual imagery in their art is derivative and due to contact with the Roman world through trade and war (Frere 1967, Wacher 1978). It is not very convincing, in an argument which seeks to establish the origin of female exhibitionism, to point to a very few male phallic stones, e.g. the 'cult' stone at Turoe (if this is indeed a phallic object). The male ithyphallic side of the double-'cult' stone at Boa Island is a better example, but we still have to account for the sex-change. Andersen summarises the 'Celtic' evidence, and discounts it, notwithstanding the authority and eloquence of Ann Ross, Margaret Murray, Tom Lethbridge and others. These scholars noted a number of Irish deities, e.g. the 'hag'-goddesses, and 'war-goddesses in their most hideous form' with vulvas reaching down to their knees, like the remarkable sheela at Oaksey in Wiltshire. However interesting and persuasive their evidence may be, it is the overwhelming European corpus of carvings which dissuades us from 'going a-whoring after strange goddesses' in a desperate endeavour to find an insular solution to what is not an insular problem.

Andersen suggested a quite different source for exhibitionist motifs, but did not pursue the matter. He pointed to the vast heritage of Graeco-Roman art, which itself drew on the diverse cultures of the ancient world of the Mediterranean and near-East, a treasure-house which was to inspire very nearly every medieval subject, however bizarre, from Scandinavia to Spain. As long ago as 1922, Émile Mâle traced the sources of Romanesque art, and few scholars have departed from his main thesis, save in minor details, since (Mâle 1922 and many reprints, and a translation 1978). He showed clearly how Classical themes were metamorphosed into Christian motifs, undergoing subtle changes in the process. In the case of exhibitionists, the change was not so subtle. In the creation of new Christian symbols, an obsession with mortal sin distorted the 'microphallic' Classical prototypes into the all-too-

Plate 7 Sheela on Garry Castle, Offaly.

glaring 'macrophallic' grotesqueries that adorn Romanesque churches. One such pre-occupation with sexual sin can be observed in the 'thorn-puller' figures. The prototype Classical sculpture of a young Roman athlete bending down to pull a thorn from the sole of his foot is naturalistic and microphallic; the Romanesque version of *Spinario* is grossly megaphallic (*Plate 8*). Worse still, the heated imagination of the monks who commissioned a work so revealing of their sense of guilt also produced a female

Plate 8 Saint-Léger-en-Pons: megaphallic thorn-puller or *Spinario*.

version, or *Spinaria*, an astounding composition, which in itself would have been sufficient to furnish a model for sheela-na-gigs (*Fig. 5*).

Such carvings, many of them on façades of churches, could by no stretch of the imagination be stigmatised as pornographic. The very express focusing of attention on the private parts by a revealing position coupled with an exaggerated enlargement of the organs themselves could surely only have had a didactic or minatory purpose. No mason would have been allowed to perpetrate, or been paid for, work of this kind in so exposed a position at the entrance to a Christian edifice, unless his work had been done with the connivance or direction of his patrons (*see Plate 27*).

We cannot stress enough the didactic nature of Romanesque ornamentation. Andersen felt it when he commented on a coital couple at Champagnolles:

> as indicated by the man's testicles this is a veritable act, surprising to encounter on a church, even with the moralising purpose felt behind it, exhibiting erotic activity in a somewhat doubtful light.

He also recognised the implicit inveighing against womankind in the Continental carvings of couples, but did not go a step further and show that the monastic fulminations against Eve were also at the very heart of sheela-na-gig invention. He contemplates a Norman corbel-table and declares of the sheela sitting there: 'it is not known from where she arrived'. We believe that her provenance is to be sought in the anti-feminism of the twelfth-century Church.

We do, however, recognise the existence of some late, post-Romanesque figures, like the sheela over the seventeenth-century stables at Haddon Hall in Derbyshire. Some may be due to a continued or recrudescent interest in the Seven Deadly Sins in the later Middle Ages, as one can see in woodwork on roof-bosses in churches like St Mary Redcliffe in Bristol or Saint-Claude in the Jura, where one can spot a droll comment on everyday life in the carving of a defecating peasant; or in Queniborough Church, Leicestershire, where an ithyphallic acrobat leers down at the congregation.

We shall also have to account for sheelas which appear, unlike their Continental sisters, on flat blocks of stone rather than on corbels, as though not intended for architectural use but

Fig. 5 Bécéleuf: *Spinaria* or female thorn-puller.

only decoration of a particular kind. They do appear abroad on flat metopes (the space between corbels) in France and Spain, for instance at Saint-Hilaire in Poitiers or Saint-Savinien in Melle, where they seem to be the earliest in date. Andersen postulates a 'form of magic behind their employment' in the insular examples; he maintains that they are evil-averting devices, and sustains his argument for an apotropaic function with references to reports of superstitious practices among the 'common people', who 'rub' or touch the stones in order to secure certain benefits, principally pregnancy. We shall examine this question. An apotropaic purpose would account for the ugliness and crude execution of the sheelas. On the whole, our feeling is that folkloric practices are posterior to the importation of the motifs, and that the important moralising tone of the carvings led not only to the preservation of sheelas but also to a popular misconception that they held magical properties. It is significant that folklore about them is local and not universal, and that no folklore whatsoever attaches to the Continental figures. In France and Spain they are accepted for what they are: sculptures among many others of similar appearance; no magical powers are thought to be invested in them, and by and large they go unnoticed by the populace. At the

time our images were being destroyed, buried or hidden, the Continental exemplars were left undisturbed, and they have been there since they were set in place.

Central to many problems posed by sheelas is their dating. Andersen quotes the 1936 Guest article in opening his Chapter XI with:

> From a number of related sheelas in Romanesque settings one is inclined to conclude that the sheela was a product of the 12th. century, originating in western France and Normandy.

He devotes a chapter to 'the Romanesque setting' in which he considers churches which are incontestably of twelfth-century date: Kilpeck, Tugford, Holdgate, Austerfield, Binstead, Rath, Liathmór and the Nuns' Church at Clonmacnois. In his catalogue he adds Bilton-in-Ainsty; and most of the French churches in his list are dated by him to between 1140 and 1180. As all the churches with exhibitionists that we have examined in France and Spain can also be securely dated to the twelfth century or thereabouts, we have no hesitation in claiming that the *floruit* of these carvings lies between 1080 (Saint-Savinien in Melle and Saint-Hilaire in Poitiers) and 1250 (the cathedral of Saint-Pierre in Poitiers) with a zenith round about 1150 (slightly later in the British Isles).

One piece of evidence adduced by Andersen, which we shall probe, is the congruence of exhibitionist carvings with 'beakhead' decoration, another purely Romanesque device, which had its origin in south-west France and rapidly swept up through Normandy into England (and possibly back again through Normandy into northern France). One variant of it, the biting horse's head, has been traced with precision by Françoise Henry, from the coastal area of Saintonge into Ireland. Not only does beakhead and horse's head decoration confirm the date of sheelas, it also provides a clue to the distribution and purveyors of these designs. We shall show how a report of beakhead decoration in northern France helped us to locate a number of unpublished exhibitionists.

During the Romanesque period the Church was mainly under the domination of the monastic orders, and so subject to direction in the matter of church design and ornamentation. There was an obsession among the brothers, who had taken vows of perpetual chastity and poverty, with the Cardinal, Mortal or Deadly Sins, especially those of *Luxuria* (sins of the flesh) and *Avaritia* (sins of the purse). These are the most frequent subjects for portrayal in stone. Whole façades of churches and abbeys are devoted to them, and are supported by auxiliary carvings on friezes, capitals and corbels. The monks' zealousness in pursuing these evils is not without a tinge of guilt, for we read that they were perpetually judging and chastising each other for 'impure thoughts' and, worse, 'impure deeds', by which we understand, even when it is not made explicit, that they sought release from sexual repression in masturbation. This could well account for the preponderance of male exhibitionist carvings, and it is possible that female exhibitionists were a progression, just as *Spinaria* followed *Spinario*. The vehemence of the monks smacks of a guilty conscience, and contemporary literature is full of tales about simoniac clerics, incontinent priests, drunken and gambling vicars. Odo Rigaldi, as Bishop of Rouen, stated in his *Visitations* that some 15 per cent of Normandy priests were guilty of such offences. The Supreme Temptress of the Garden of Eden could never have been very far from

Fig. 7 Kilpeck sheela, after G.R. Lewis. A Victorian 'bowdlerised' version. For the real carving see Plate 5. (G.R. Lewis *Illustrations of Kilpeck* London 1842)

the monks' minds, and masons were directed to use whatever imagery seemed best fitted to combat the frailties of the human race, to depict human behaviour at its worst, and not to be too fastidious in their efforts to vilify Woman, the cause of the Fall of Man. We shall look at some of the writing of influential theologians, whose work was the constant study of the monks, and whose burden was that Woman is unclean, that whoever touches her is defiled. The female exhibitionist is, we feel, the fruit of an unbelievable misogyny (*Figs. 6 and 7*).

Fig. 6 Capital from the collegiate church of Cervatos (south window).

2 Ugly as sin

Miss Sheela-na-gig seems to be coming into fashion, and her topographical range is widening. I am thankful to say that I never saw either her or her brother in connection with any early work, Pagan or Christian, in our islands.

Thus wrote Baldwin Brown, the Anglo-Saxon scholar, to W.J. Hemp, who reported the statement in an article about sheelas in the Welsh Marches (Hemp 1938). Brown's somewhat smug attitude to a subject which seemed to him repugnant is evident, but two matters raised by him in passing are of interest: first, that in his opinion the sheela is not an early artefact of pagan or pre-Christian times, and secondly, that she may somewhere have a brother. He intended this latter remark as a flippancy, and one feels he would genuinely have been surprised to find that Miss Sheela-na-gig does indeed have a brother. His attitude is strangely uncurious for a scholar, and one feels that it was just as well for his modesty that he never visited Whittlesford Church near Cambridge. There he might have witnessed a scene too shocking for his sensibilities.

On a lintel cut to fit over a round-arched Norman window in the tower, just under the clock, where worshippers late for service can scarcely miss it as they glance up at the time, is surely one of the most astonishing compositions in Europe (*see Plate 1*). Here, to the left of the lintel, in full frontal display, sits a squat, splay-legged woman. Her right hand passes under her buttock so that she can insert her fingers into a slit-like vulva. Her gesture, even to our liberated gaze, is brazen. What makes the picture even more astounding is the bearded ithyphallic male crawling his way towards her over the window, evidently at her invitation. He seems to be breathing heavily into her left ear, as well he might. It is mystifying that this work has

managed to survive into the twentieth century, for at first sight it is so gross a spectacle to find on a church that one begins to think it would look indecent even in a bordello. Yet here it has stood for years in full view of the good folk of Whittlesford. Perhaps they have become desensitised to its lubricity through long familiarity.

It is with thoughts such as these that one looks again; doubts assail the mind. For, after all, the woman is as ugly as sin. She is fat, bald, unattractive, and her gesture is repellent. Her partner is no better. He is elongated like a quadruped, and indeed he has been taken by some viewers for an animal. The suggestion that a sexual relation is about to take place is obviously intended to be unpleasant.

Then, at this moment, one begins to realise that the scene cannot be an erotic one. It does little to arouse feelings of sexual passion. It is too offensive. We realise that the carver intended us to see that an act of intercourse between these two figures would be graceless, unamorous, even comic. Interpreted thus the composition becomes easier to understand and to live with; it is no longer a scene of lechery and debauchery, but a sermon whose theme is that human relationships under the spur of lust can degenerate quickly into base carnality. We may feel that the carver, intent on producing a simple, graphic message, has overstated his case – taking a pile-driver to crack a nut. Nevertheless, he has produced an encounter which, far from being, as we thought at first sight, an 'immoral' one, is in fact extremely moralistic.

Surely in this scene, which features a typical sheela, we have a pointer to the role of iconography of such *dramatis personae*. Her function is highlighted by the presence of an aroused male. She is the Whore (not surprisingly one of the names given to sheelas), and even without his aid she would still exemplify harlotry.

A similar conclusion can be reached about single male figures found without an accompanying female. On the east end of the rebuilt church at Abson in Avon, to the south of the east window, is a crawling ithyphallic man, carved with some expertise and knowledge of perspective (*Fig. 8a*). He is moving on all fours from left to right, and his head is turned towards us so that he can look at us through drilled eyes. (This drilling of eyes is found in Anglo-Saxon work, and, when the figure was first reported (Dobson 1940), it was suggested he might be of pre-Conquest date, especially as the Church of the Imps, Pucklechurch, is only a mile away, and behind it are the remains of the hunting lodge at which King Edmund I was slain at a banquet in AD 946. However, drilling of eyes is a common Romanesque practice also.)

At Saint-Savinien, Melle, is a similar figure with drilled eyes (*Fig. 8b*). The church dates to before 1100 (probably about 1080–90), and is now being restored after having served a number of menial functions, including being the town jail. On the corbel table, above the *linteau en bâtière* over the door (a feature which has associations with Auvergne), is a series of remarkable metopes, to which we shall refer again later (p. 80). On one of these, between beast-head corbels, is an ithyphallic man crawling from left to right, carved with some attention to perspective, head tilted to one side; significantly he is crawling towards a couple engaged in sexual intercourse on the extreme right metope. He may or may not be the direct ancestor of the Abson carving, but it is to be noted that both are cut in shallow relief on flat plaque-like stones.

Preserved in the Margam Stones Museum in South Wales is a stone which might once have served as a corbel. It features a pot-bellied male with the same hunched shoulders as an atlas (*Plate 9*). His forearms are held close to the body and his hands are clutching phallic-shaped objects (candles?) pointing to his breasts. An enormous penis rises up to his chest from between two round testicles.

Also in Wales, at Maen Achwyfan, on a tenth- or eleventh-century solid-ring cross, of a type found locally and especially in Cheshire, is a very weathered megaphallic male exhibitionist. Surrounded by loops and a serpent, he has affinities with a slab figure from Gotland (Sweden) which shows a female with a coiffure of

Fig. 8 Male carvings at (a) Abson and (b) Melle.

a

b

Plate 9 Margam (Margam Stones Museum, Glam.) (Photo: J. & C. Bord)

Largely because of its splay-legged attitude (reminiscent of the wild creature astride monsters on a crypt capital at Canterbury [*see Plate 15*], said to be symbolic of lust), the Rath Blathmaic figure is listed by Andersen as a sheela. A sketch by Westropp, illustrated by Andersen, indicates breasts and possibly a vulva to which the left hand is pointing. The figure is presently upside down but only because the stone on which it features, and which appears to be a window lintel, was once the sill (*see Plate 14*).

Other forms of a figure flanked by affronted beasts or theriomorphic men can be seen on the crosses at Moone, Castledermot, Monasterboice and Kells in Ireland. Sometimes the central figure is itself theriomorphic or demonic, as on the market cross at Kells. The theme of beasts attacking a human figure from both sides at once is of great antiquity, found all over Europe and the Middle East, in art of all ages, Christian and pre-Christian (Baltrušaitis 1934 and Moorey 1971). The figure strangling affronted beasts is a form that goes back at least as far as Gilgamesh taming the lions (there is a nice Romanesque version of this on the tympanum of the church at Trévières in Normandy). An Etruscan bronze chariot-plate, decorated with repoussé reliefs, depicts a splay-legged Gorgon with pendulous breasts and a protruding tongue gripping two flanking lions by the neck (*Fig. 10a*). She wears a thin robe and two long plaits

dangling plaits (*Fig. 9a*). She stands on widely-splayed legs and holds a pair of affronted snakes by the neck on each side of her. Above her head is a knot of serpents, not unlike the quadruple knot of snakes below the crucifixion on Muiredach's Cross, of the ninth century, at Monasterboice. Gotland was in the Viking heartland, whither exotic ideas were carried, and whence they were re-transmitted in modified form. The Cheshire crosses display both Celtic and Scandinavian influence. Nevertheless, we shall not seek prototypes of sexual exhibitionists in Celtic, Teutonic or Scandinavian contexts, because we are convinced that their origins lie elsewhere. We mention the Gotland figure for the sake of completeness in our search for prototypes, and because of its similarity to an Irish carving which has often been proposed as a sheela-na-gig, and which can be dated, from its setting, to about AD 1180.

Fig. 9a Slab at Gotland, Sweden. **Fig. 9b** Sketch of Rath Blathmaic figure (see Plate 14).

hang behind her. This bronze, striking in its similarities to many Romanesque and post-Romanesque images (*Fig. 10b*), is an iconographic forebear of the Rath exhibitionist, though exhibitionists between beasts are rare; there is one at Châteaumeillant on a window capital. Non-exhibitionists with flanking beasts are much commoner, as on the Sutton Hoo purse lid, or on numerous Irish crosses which show versions of Daniel in the Lions' Den (the number of lions varies). The Christian version, in deference to the power of the saints, usually shows submissive beasts licking the human being in friendship, as on the cross of Arboe.

Fig. 10a Etruscan bronze plate of *c*.540 BC, decorated with reliefs in repoussé and forming part of the outer covering of a chariot. The female figure is a tongue-protruding gorgon, holding off two lions with outstretched arms; she is approx. 35cm (14in) high (Antikensaamlungen, Munich). **Fig. 10b** Twelfth-century tympanum over the west door at Bully (Calvados).

Another Irish Romanesque carving with attacking beasts is the window-top from the vanished round tower at Tomregon or Berrymount (*Fig. 11*). A remarkable grotesque contortionist displays a vulva(?), while its downward pointing hands are bitten by toothy monsters. Andersen regards this figure as female, with pendulous *labia vulvae*, while Helen Hickey thinks it is male, with dangling testicles but no penis (Hickey 1976).

This brings us back to the question of male insular exhibitionists, for the striking triangular head of the Berrymount acrobat, with its staring eyes, is similar to that of a feet-to-ears acrobat at Aghalurcher (*Fig. 12a*). Since this figure is bearded, the pair of protruberances which appear below must be interpreted as testicles. The figure has no body, but all in all resembles very strongly some sculptures from La Sauve-Majeure. Yet another parallel is a post-Romanesque wood-carving at the Palais de Justice, Rouen, which has no penis either, but two large testicles appearing above the chin, as the thighs flank the head (Adéline 1879) (*see Fig. 49*).

Neither the Berrymount nor the Aghalurcher figures are truly exhibitionist. Their iconographical importance is that they bear a relation to carvings elsewhere. At Boyle Abbey there is a bodiless acrobat with a large triangular head and a circular mouth which recalls the Aghalurcher and La Sauve-Majeure carvings. It has snakes on either side. It is not – or not now – exhibitionist but has a close affinity with exhibitionists by virtue of its posture and the flanking serpents. One might say that they are by the hand of the same mason, one who had seen the French sculptures.

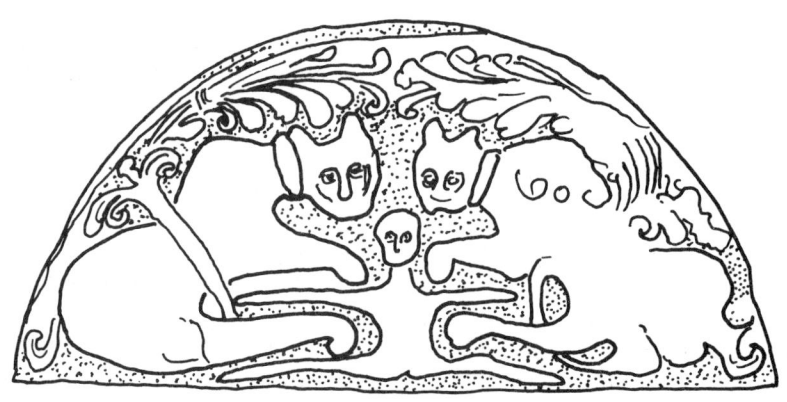

Fig. 11 Tomregan (Berrymount): contortionist figure.

Another near-exhibitionist, from Grey Abbey in County Down, is a penis-less and headless male displaying large testicles, anus and buttocks (Weir 1980) (*Fig. 12b*). It is related to at least two French figures, and may indeed derive from one of them. At Saint-Martin-de-Sescas is an acrobat, seen from behind on a corbel, whose head is between his legs, in the same position as the Grey Abbey figure's enormous scrotum (*Fig. 12c*). The legs are almost identical in both carvings. Slightly off-centre on the left buttock is a hole which is almost certainly a solution-pit caused by erosion; the Grey Abbey figure has a similar hole between his buttocks, deepened by the action of water on the soft sandstone. Similar figures can be seen at Saint-Michel-d'Entraygues, where another headless, penis-less, anal exhibitionist reveals large testicles, and at Bussière-Badil, where a headless figure in the same pose shows a well-marked vulva; at Sablonceaux, an Augustinian abbey, a headless male displays his buttocks, anus and complete genitalia. He too is very like the County Down carvings (*Fig. 12d*).

A curious feature of the Grey Abbey corbel is a pair of human masks on each side of the head (at the point where the Gironde male has his hands). For this, no Romanesque precedent has yet been discovered, save for a crude head at Faurndau in Swabia, which has long plaits or braids and two human masks covering its eyes and cheeks. The long hair may indicate an early representation of the sin of *Luxuria* (lust), which is often signalled by elaborate hair-styles (like the Etruscan bronze and the Gotland slab). The symbolism of woman's hair goes back into antiquity and we shall return to this subject later. Most later Irish exhibitionists have long hair, and the Ballinderry castle doorway figure has two long plaits, each different, one of which is very like those of the Swabian carving (*see Plate 74*).

The Grey Abbey corbel, truly Romanesque in style, is not in a context which can be ascribed with certainty to the Romanesque period. It is one of a number of soft sandstone corbels on the north side of the chancel, supporting an overhang of fifteenth-century date; perhaps one of the corbels is of later date (Phillips 1874, Hunt 1974) but the others are typically Romanesque. Strangely they are part of the fabric of an austere Cistercian foundation of the late twelfth century. Any of these corbels, if transferred to a French setting, would be accepted as Romanesque, the acrobat in particular, and they are strong supporting evidence for the view we shall

Fig. 12 (a) Aghalurcher; (b) Grey Abbey;
(c) Saint-Martin-de-Sescas; (d) Sablonceaux.

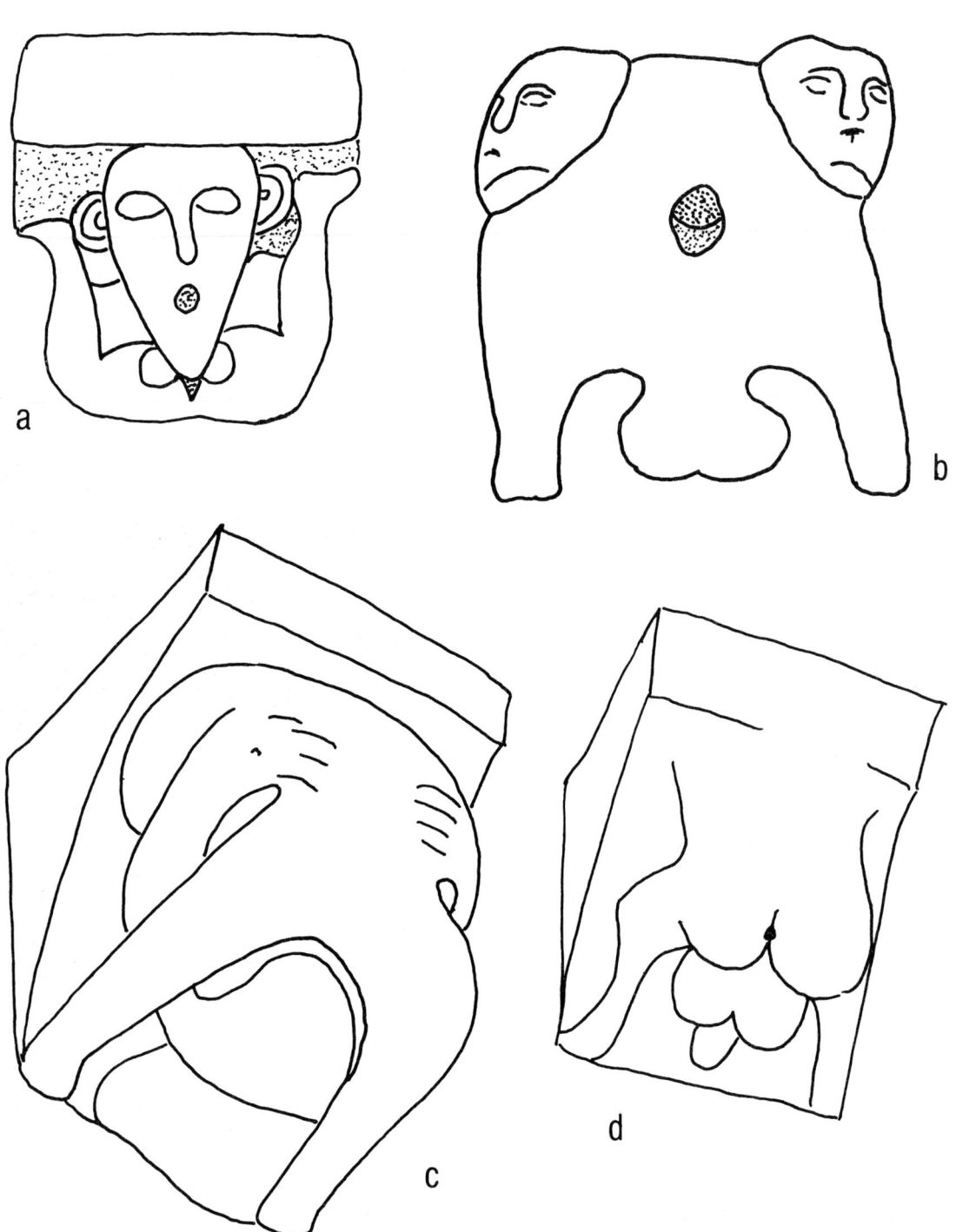

express about the Continental influences in the British Isles and how they were introduced.

The last Irish male exhibitionist for discussion is carved on a gatepost at a former mill in Ballycloghduff (*Plate 10*). The figure has a large round head turned slightly to one side, with almond-shaped eyes under a heavy eyebrow ridge; the pupils are mere slits. The feet are inturned, on unsplayed short straight legs, and the body cannot be distinguished from behind the two arms. The left hand carries a key pointing diagonally to the left shoulder. The right arm, rather longer, is parallel but passes downward and the hand clutches a large, downward pointing penis. There is no scrotum. It could once have had a parallel at Broadford, by the entrance to the church grounds, where there is a key-clutching figure in mirror image, but lacking the lower part of the torso, so that one cannot be sure of its original exhibitionism.

Finally, we should mention a carving in a window spandrel at Smithstown castle, rescued from the filling of a house wall (*see Plate 73*). Male genitalia are neatly carved in the frame of an ogee window of fifteenth- or sixteenth-century date. We shall discuss later its possible use as an apotropaic device; for the moment we should note that a number of French and Spanish churches display similarly disembodied male phallic emblems, for which no apotropaic purpose has so far been documented.

We have tried to show in this chapter that male exhibitionists do exist in Britain and Ireland, although they are not numerous, but no one has associated them with the sheelas. We take the view that, while some, like the Maen Achwyfan stone, may have affinities with 'Celtic' or Scandinavian designs, they are in the main rather to be associated with the female sheelas who, as we shall see, have their origin in south-west Europe. The Whittlesford lintel shows both of them together. We believe that the males, like the females, were introduced into these islands by the same process and the same route.

In passing, we have noted that there is often a trace of apotropaic magic attached to these stone-carvings, but we think that this was a later development, after the exhibitionist carvings had been brought here. We are led to this conclusion by the fact that male figures are rarer than female, yet in apotropaic magic it is usually

Plate 10 Ballycloghduff, on a gatepost.

the male sex organs which are invoked. We find it hard to accept the folkloric view that such magic has lingered on from Celtic times, especially since the Celts made no use of female sexual symbols.

The 'Irish connection' – the term 'sheela-na-gig' being a supposedly 'Celtic' word which was used in the first frank discussions of the many surviving female exhibitionists in that 'Celtic' country – has conspired to arouse the popular notion that these carvings are somehow inspired by 'Celtic fertility magic'. We agree that folk ideas die hard, and that belief in fertility magic may still linger on from ancient times, and that there may even be a trace in the exhibitionist figures. It is clear that the Romans introduced into our islands their phallic beliefs and objects

Plate 11 Amboise: Classical foliage decoration on capitals with a Romanesque 'frieze'. Note the female long-haired acrobat on the right, and the nude man being attacked by amphisbænic winged dragons.

(anything earlier than Roman times is conjecturable) but there is no firm evidence pointing to the Celts. We shall return to the question in Chapter 11.

For the time being, we wish to observe that folkloric arguments verge on the suppostitious, and are in any case somewhat redundant in the face of the Continental evidence. This latter persuades us that, among the influences at work during Romanesque times in the creation of male and female sculptural exhibitionists, apotropaic or fertility magic played negligible roles. We are strongly of the opinion that the origin, purpose and sculptural form of the exhibitionists are to be found in the Romanesque Franco-Hispanic churches, and that this theory can be supported, not only by strong typological arguments but by documentary evidence also.

It may be helpful, in order to set the scene for the ensuing discussions, if we identify some of the characteristics of Romanesque art.

3 The Romanesque background

Romanesque may be considered the first European style

G. Nebolsine;

The term 'Gothic', coined in or before the seventeenth century, was intended to denote a non-Classical style of architecture believed to originate with the Goths and Vandals, the barbarians who had overthrown Rome. Likewise the word 'Romanesque', invented in the nineteenth century, was for a long time a denigratory epithet applied to buildings which were considered to be degenerate forms of Roman Classical style. Both words were at first used only in respect of architecture, and both illustrate the shortcoming of attaching simplistic labels to periods and kinds of art, even in the interest of convenience and for easy reference;

for not only do the meanings of such titles change with fashions and with the passage of time, but they often begin to mean different things to different people. By definition, the word 'Roman-esque' should clearly encompass all those forms of art which take Roman models as their basis. Its use ought not to be restricted to architecture, nor to the eleventh and twelfth centuries, as it so often is. In this sense, to take a few random examples, the crypt of St Wilfrid at Hexham, the oratory of Theodulf at Germigny-les-Prés, the mausoleum of Galla Placidia at Ravenna, the Brescia casket, the Aachen

Plate 12 Gerona: below a vinescroll the Torments of the Damned. Two long-haired females on the left are being attacked by snakes.

bookcovers, and the Cross of the Scriptures at Clonmacnois are every bit as Romanesque as the west front of Lincoln Cathedral, the cloister of Silos, the Gloucester candlestick, the reliquary of Sainte-Foy at Conques, and so on. Yet, even today, much more space is devoted in writing to the more monumental and durable aspects of the style, namely to the great churches.

Of course, Romanesque building before the eleventh century is not abundant. It was only after the last of the invaders had settled down and adopted Christianity, after peace and prosperity began to return, and after the fateful year AD 1000 passed without incident, that, to use the oft-quoted words of the monk Glaber, a white mantle of churches began to clothe the shoulders of Europe. In particular, monasteries were restored, some 400 having managed to survive the tenth century. Now a great rebuilding took place, and there was an architectural renaissance in the Rhineland, in southern France and northern Italy, in Spain and England. Under Benedictine (and especially Cluniac) direction, impressive abbeys and churches, and even cathedrals, arose, all using Classical features – the basilical aisled plan, arcades and roundheaded arches over doors and windows, columns and capitals, cornices and friezes. From the beginning of the twelfth century they were embellished with new-found skills in stone-carving, and a style that had been Roman-esque became Romanesque, developing its own ethos and identity.

The indebtedness of the masons to Classical models became even more pronounced when they turned their hand to sculpture. Unfortunately, pitifully few of the sources which were to serve them as pattern-books have come down to us. Once there must have been an immense wealth of illuminated manuscripts and illustrated books, embroidered and patterned textiles, gold and silver vessels richly-bejewelled, carved and painted altar-pieces, gem-studded caskets and reliquaries and all manner of croziers, pectoral crosses, rings and ivories. The havoc wrought by the Magyars, the Goths and Visigoths, the Huns, the Moors, the Vikings and others was augmented in the Middle Ages by the ravages of ceaseless wars of religion. All these lost treasures we can only enjoy at second hand by turning to the carved stonework which they produced, and for which they were the direct

models. On façades and friezes, capitals and cornices, panels and corbels, we see, caught in stone, patterns taken from Eastern textiles, from Celtic jewellery and Irish manuscripts, from crafted work of many kinds. Gripping and biting beasts, birds and reptiles intertwining their tails or necks, form long processions in the manner dear to the Saxons and Celts, while addorsed or affronted animals juxtaposed with them remind us of the continuous and traditional patterns still found today on Eastern carpets. Mediterranean wave and meander borders run alongside Egyptian palmettes and Greek acanthus; Moorish arabesques and lively inhabited vinescrolls occur alongside plaited knotwork and abstract geometric intricacies. Early carvers took delight in copying the fluted columns and pilasters, the Ionic volutes and Corinthian capitals, the doves and peacocks which they saw on the vestiges of temples or marble sarcophagi, and they perpetuated in colder climes the designs of a sun-drenched pagan world which they knew to have been the cradle of Christianity. Many Classical patterns entered the repertoire of Romanesque artists who had little or no knowledge of the original symbolism involved. They used the acanthus leaf abundantly without perhaps knowing of its Greek significance; and the vinescroll, taken from nature but perhaps also from the text of St John, 'I am the true vine', was perhaps to them only a *rinceau* pattern.

Romanesque art is very much an eclectic art, taking its inspiration not only from Christian subjects but, whenever aesthetically or symbolically satisfying, from heathen sources also, and its expression was as unbounded as its imaginative choice of topics. As they grew surer of their touch and the mastery of their subjects, the masons began to clothe the great mysteries of religion in a symbolic cloak, and it is in this taste for Christian symbolism that we discern the difference between Roman and Romanesque.

Roman statuary had no particular message to convey other than the self-assurance, the suavity and urbanity of the culture which produced it. Accomplished in design, dignified in expression, it is committed to a concern with outward form rather than inward emotion. It

Plate 13 Vouvant: men in torment, under a border of palmettes. Note also the acrobats.

lacks warmth and vitality, and some have even called it frigid. The scenes on Trajan's column, for instance, may at first sight appear to be bustling and full of life, but a second glance shows them to be far too carefully composed to be natural; they remain static, cold, anecdotal. Roman art narrowly misses becoming pompous, so conscious of their official or social position, so meticulous in their posture and toilette are the aloof persons portrayed. All is dignity and decorum. Romanesque art, by contrast, although retaining many features of Roman work (the saints may wear togas, and peacocks nibble at bunches of grapes) and keeping the well-proportioned, naturalistic, clear-cut forms of Mediterranean art, manages to incorporate into these the strange, assymetrical, convoluted, zoomorphic or geometric compositions whose origin is to be found in northern lands. It shuns balance and Classicism, preferring instead the bizarre and gro-

tesque, the misshapen and ugly. We find in it none of the smug self-satisfaction, the serene complacency, the comfortable ease of the Classical patricians and their matrons; instead there is restlessness and tension, anxiety and unease, fear and horror, pain and anguish. Romanesque art does not spring from a world concerned with expressing its well-being and sense of superiority, but from one in which people feel insecure as they journey through a hostile, perilous environment, and it expresses this powerfully. The fusion of northern and southern styles creates tension, which finds release in a dynamic vigour that more than compensates for any lack of grace or Classical decorum. The figures in a Romanesque scene may be ill-proportioned, either squat or elongated, with huge or microcephalic heads; their limbs may be twisted, their features agonised and contorted; they may be executed with style or with a homely primitiveness; but they have one quality which is lacking in Roman art: the power to move and haunt us strangely.

Within the arts of the Romanesque there are distinctive regional and local variations, but

Plate 14 Rath Blathmaic: Irish Romanesque window-sill (now upside down). Note the supposed sheela on the right, sketched in Fig. 9.

they all have enough in common for us to identify it wherever it flourishes:

the significant factor of Romanesque lies not in its diversity but in its essential unity
Nebolsine 1969

This unity derives its driving force, the main-spring of the whole movement, from its religious character, from the Christian doctrine of sin and redemption.

'Terreat hic terror quos terreus alligat error' ('let this horror terrify those bound by earthly sin') is the warning which is carved along the lintel of the west portal of Autun. On the tympanum, the Vision of Judgment, and inside on Gislebertus' capitals, the message is clear and leaves no doubt in the mind of the Christian entering therein. It is his duty to bend his thoughts to the punishments reserved in Hell for the damned, to the devils and loathsome creatures waiting to bear him down to the everlasting fires of Gehenna should he fail to shake off his mortal sins. Illiterate church-goers may not always have understood the precise symbolism of the carvings, although much is explicit and easily-read, but they would have grasped the idea that danger lurked all round them, that the creatures of the unseen world were every bit as relentless in their pursuit as the natural hazards of everyday life in the visible world. The function of church art was to secure awe and apprehension, to define the narrow path, to bring awareness of divine retribution.

'Ingrediens ad templum refer ad sublimia vultum' ('Thou that enterest gaze upon these divine things') is inscribed over the entrance of Mozac, and of course there was also a possibility of rewards in Heaven for the blessed. At Autun, as well as the line of the damned there is the procession of saved souls. Gislebertus was a great artist, and could convey happiness as well as fear; but it is always easier to portray punishment than reward, damnation than redemption, sin than good works. Hell lends itself to portrayal more readily than Paradise, and the masons often took the less arduous course, under the direction of their ecclesiastical patrons who were more set on denouncing the way to perdition than showing the path to salvation.

Romanesque art, then, is Roman-esque only in its outward trappings. The spirit which animates it is far removed from any which may have informed the art of Rome. It is first and foremost a religious art which sets out the teachings of the Scriptures, reinforcing the Christian message with any material which suits the occasion. Decorative aim is second only to the primary didactic purpose. Roman carvings record that which is past; Romanesque carvings record that which is still to come. To this end it employs what comes to hand: biblical texts, commentaries, saints' lives, heroic deeds, mythological or legendary tales, travellers' accounts, events of the natural and animal world, and even fantasy. In the nineteenth century the French poet Rimbaud felt strongly that man walks through a forest of symbols. Medieval man, surrounded additionally by man-made symbols, must have been made even more conscious of the silent voices of the forest in which he found himself.

Louis Réau warns us not to find symbolism everywhere in this art. Much is unintentional and fortuitous on the part of the sculptors, who were often applying a mechanical repertoire of patterns (Réau 1955), and much of the imagery is self-evident, a simple visual representation of Bible stories.

But religious art by its very nature must make extensive use of symbols. It is Bible exegesis for the masses who cannot read, a visual *aide-mémoire* of the Church's teachings. The symbolic representations of the texts can be very simple and narrative, or they can be complex and oblique. No one with even a rudimentary knowledge of the Old and New Testaments can fail to recognise scenes like the Temptation, the Expulsion, the murder of Abel, the Flood and Noah, the sacrifice of Abraham, the whale and Jonah, the children of Israel in the fiery furnace, the raising of Lazarus, the Adoration of the Kings, and the Crucifixion, even though each of these stories receives a different treatment at the hand of individual artists. On the other hand, since these tales also enshrine the more abstract concepts of the bounty and grace of God – the working-out of the divine plan, the faith and obedience of man – they are often treated less simplistically. A man between affronted beasts may represent St Anthony, but between three or more lions he is more likely to be Daniel; two discs and a number of fish indicate the feeding of the five thousand; armed warriors may, among

Plate 15 Canterbury crypt: late eleventh-century capital probably drawn from a Bestiary or other manuscript. A she-devil between affronted beasts. (Photo: J. & C. Bord)

other things, be Crusaders, or figures from the *Psychomachia*, or from a *chanson de geste*, in any event representing the forces of good and evil engaged in combat.

The commentaries on the Book of Revelation by the monk Beatus of Liébana in northern Spain, known as *Beatus* manuscripts for short, gave rise to a more complex symbolism, involving, for instance, the visions of the Apocalypse, with such figures as the Tetramorph, or symbols of the Evangelists. Many a great tympanum is based on an illuminated page from *Beatus*. The natural world, and especially the animals and birds, yielded a dual symbolism in which lions may stand for good or for evil, eagles may represent St John or nobility of character or cruelty and rapaciousness, snakes may symbolise poison or healing, and peacocks may

be a device against the Evil Eye or tell of immortality and incorruptibility. The phantasmagoria summoned up by the imagination gave an even more complicated symbolism, often dualistic also, so that griffins might equally indicate Christ or Satan.

Much of this symbolism, current in the Middle Ages, now passes us by. Who remembers that elephants were stitched on chasubles to protect the priest from the temptations of lust, and were a sign of temperance, or that the cock, usually taken to signify the denial of Peter, was also a sign of Christ resurrected? What do we know now of sciapods, manticores, sphynxes, basilisks, dog-headed apes and the like? Yet they once filled the minds of fearful men.

Of course the Church had more mundane matters to impart. Being dominated by monasticism, which at that time was rich and powerful, it is to be expected that the preoccupations of the monks would find their way into the profuse carvings adorning cloister and chapel. Prominent in their thoughts were the Mortal Sins. Having taken perpetual vows of chastity and poverty themselves, they looked in disgust upon the secular clergy, upon the newly-risen burgher classes, and even upon themselves, for they were sometimes far from blameless. Greed and lust are an obsession with them from the beginnings of Romanesque sculpture. A frequent subject, from Moissac to Lincoln, is the punishment of Dives, the rich man, and the elevation to Abraham's bosom of Lazarus, the beggar at his gates. Visions of Judgment, like that of Sangüesa, dwell with fevered intensity upon the Torments of the Damned.

It is interesting to note, in passing, that, as monasticism loses its ascendancy in the thirteenth century, and power passes to the secular clergy and their bishops, this concern with the crude and explicit tortures of Hell diminishes. Devils and demons are relegated to gargoyles, and the minatory carvings of Romanesque portals are replaced on Gothic buildings by serene prophets and saints. The Gothic urbane vision is more abstract, as befits a materialistic matrix; the minds of the new bourgeoisie and their clergy are diverted from earthly sin and the cut-and-thrust of trade by the soaring spires and vast light-filled naves of the new architecture, pointing towards the rich peace of Heaven. The heavy foreboding gloom of the massive Romanesque church is replaced by a slender, delicate masonry illumined with the sparkling light of high stained-glass windows. Elegant, finely-chiselled, fully-rounded statues announce a more beatific vision, a world of saints rather than of sinners. There is a formal restraint not found in the exuberant carvings of the twelfth century.

Sculpture is profuse in areas where suitable stone is plentiful and of good quality, as in Castile and Aquitaine. The sea air has, it is true, eroded the honey-coloured limestone carvings where they are exposed to the Atlantic winds in Saintonge, yet much remains, as finely chiselled as it was when it came from the masons' lodge, and many Castilian churches boast of delicately-carved capitals depicting embroidery and bird-feathers. Where there was good stone, even quite small country churches were adorned, as well as the major undertakings in the towns and along important roads. One feature common to both was the corbel.

Corbels are a typical feature of Romanesque churches. Skeuomorphic representations of the ends of beams jutting out from exterior walls, they were highly decorated, and can still be seen in their wooden form in the thirteenth-century arcades of Mirepoix in the Ariège. Masks predominate, but there are also acrobats in revealing postures, mouth-pullers and the like. In Classical architecture these beam-ends developed into formal denticulations, or an alternation of metopes and triglyphs. The Romans also modified them as brackets or modillions (still the modern French term *modillons*). A Romanesque church might have any number of these, from five to 300 or more. In some areas they are plain, as in the Lombardic stepped-arcades of Burgundy; sometimes they repeat a uniform pattern, like the 'copeaux' corbels of Auvergne, resembling clusters of woodshavings. But mainly they are richly decorated with numberless designs.

Very little has been written about corbel-carving, although corbels exist in hundreds of thousands (*Plate 16*). In Poitiers' little group of twelfth-century churches there are over 500; at Frómista, on one church alone there are over 300. It is difficult to account for the neglect in the literature of art history of these sculptured features. Any information regarding them is left to footnotes or postscripts. They may be small, high up, even out of sight, yet they usually play a supportive role in the iconography of a church, and a number of their designs are to be found over a wide area. Tracing the distribution and frequency of a particular motif is interesting and rewarding, for it may cast light on the way the designs were passed on. We can learn much about the spread of cultural and sculptural ideas from them. They are, in any case, intrinsically interesting, with their wealth of themes ranging from simple knotwork, or foliage, to groups of humans engaged in multifarious activities.

Plate 16 Lugo Cathedral: barrel-toter and thorn-puller corbels. (Photo: Serafín Moralejo)

They were a challenge to sculptors because of their size and shape, and because of their role. Even when placed out of sight, over an aisle roof or high up in a tower, they were considered important enough to bear rich designs. Because masons may have enjoyed some freedom of choice in the themes for these small pieces (which were no doubt given as suitable exercises to apprentices), some observers have compared them with misericords. As misericords are not normally meant to be seen, carpenters could indulge their whimsy and humour, sometimes modelling a crowned head or a mitred bishop, or perhaps choosing a scene from Aesop, or a legend like that of St George, or, at other times, showing a homely village scene of the ale wife, or the chase. However, misericords differ from corbels in one important way: they are wholly subject to whimsy, having little or no inter-connection one with the other, and not forming part of any one grandiose scheme; they are discrete and random. At St Laurence, Ludlow, it is true that the theme of the alewife can be traced through a number of them, but this is rare. Corbels, on the other hand, although they too may be scattered in random order along a corbel table, are very often part and parcel of a scheme of didactic decoration. They support the important impact of the façade and portal carvings; they bear their own share of responsibility for imparting, by a cumulative process, the moral teachings of the more important carvings, and they add to the feel and general atmosphere of the church.

Carved corbels are rare in Ireland, but England has managed to save a few good series. Kilpeck, one of England's best small Romanesque churches, has some 70 corbels still in a fine state of preservation. Forty of them are masks, but among the others is the famous sheela – a grotesquely human female tearing open her vulva (*see Plate 5*) – as well as an acrobat, a rebec player, a clutching couple, some interesting animals, and the vestiges of two pairs of lovers destroyed by a nineteenth-century vicar who thought them too obscene (their feet position confirms the original design). Not far from Kilpeck, Elkstone, in Gloucestershire, has a couple of corbel tables, on each of which are to be seen defaced stones. At least one of these, a female whose lower abdomen has been cut away, must have been a sheela, for the features which remain are strongly reminiscent of Kilpeck's exemplar.

Studland, in Dorset, assembles on its corbel tables ithyphallic males, coupling pairs, mouth-pullers, tongue-stickers, beard-pullers, and an acrobatic female exhibitionist. Yorkshire's Bilton-in-Ainsty has fragments, still *in situ*, of a once extensive corbel table, now protected by additional aisle-roofs. On the north side of the original Norman nave sits a female exhibitionist and a much mutilated one next to her (the Herculean shoulders are tell-tale); there is a mermaid with long tresses on the south side, and there is a corbel carved in the form of a beakhead (the significance of which we shall examine at a later stage). Holdgate's sheela is so three-dimensional that one presupposes a former use as a corbel, as must have been the case with the figures at St Ives and Margam. We understand from information supplied by Zarnecki that there is a sheela on a corbel, out of sight above an aisle, at Ely Cathedral. Among Ireland's surviving corbels is a buttock-shower at Grey Abbey.

Apart from these examples, and this is a point to which we shall return, most British exhibitionist carvings are carved on flat stones, not unlike the metope carvings of the Continent, and this poses a question – why and to what extent do they differ from Continental carvings? Was their function in some way different?

In this connection it is worth noting a figure in a lunette on the north tower of the west front of Rochester Cathedral (*Fig. 13*). A splay-legged female passes her two hands under her thighs to grasp two large fish. At Brioude, in Auvergne, on an exterior capital of the north-east apsidal chapel, is an almost identical female, while at Parthenay-le-Vieux, on a façade capital, a very similar anguipedal figure grasps two splayed legs which develop fish heads instead of feet. These are churches on important pilgrimage routes, routes which were of paramount importance in the dissemination of sculptural ideas and themes. It is also of interest that in only one place has the Rochester façade been mutilated – the genital area of the fish-holding female has been crudely hacked away during some puritanical iconoclastic vandalism. On either side of her the lunettes hold other symbolic images: two birds tearing a fish apart, and an eagle devouring a serpent. Not far from Rochester, in Canterbury's crypt, on some very early figured capitals of *c.* AD 1080, are some tumblers grasping fish. These capitals seem to be drawn from a Bestiary, perhaps from the monastery's own scriptorium, but it cannot be entirely coincidental that they bear a remarkable resemblance to corbel and capital carvings in the maritime areas of Saintonge and the Bordelais, a part of France in which several of the pilgrim routes converged.

In the foregoing chapters we have alluded to

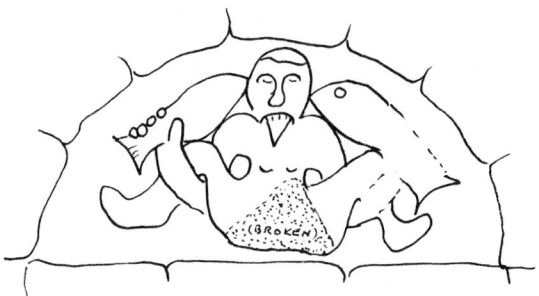

Fig. 13 Rochester Cathedral: lunette on west façade. Vandalised woman holding fish, and sticking out her tongue.

mouth-pullers, tongue-protruders, tress-pullers, musicians and others in the same breath as sexual exhibitionists, and it may seem far-fetched to equate the former (who only seem to be making the kind of rude gesture we associate with naughty children) with sexual exhibitionists. Acrobats and musicians do not at first sight seem connected with exhibitionism. It is true that we cannot always be certain when we look at, say, a mouth-puller, especially if it occurs in complete isolation, that we are in the presence of a sexual carving. By the fifteenth century, when carpenters were cutting tongue-protruders and the like on misericords, it is likely that the symbolism had worn thin and had lost its meaning. But in the chapters which follow we shall examine more closely all these images and their context, and try to show that, in the twelfth century at least, they were loaded with meaning, and that a sexual theme connected them all. We can pre-empt the demonstration a little by pointing out that the Rochester female is sticking out her tongue, as one of the Tugford sheelas does, and that the other Tugford sheela is a mouth-puller. It is because of the close association of these gestures with blatant sexual exhibitionism that we can state with some conviction that their symbolism was mutually transferable, and that medieval man fully understood it. We begin this investigation with the world of acrobats and musicians.

4 The entertainers

Fools make a mock at sin

Proverbs 14

Sculptures of acrobats and athletes are common in antiquity and, from the elegant statues of Egypt, Crete, Greece and Italy, those of our Romanesque performers who have a claim to a degree of realism are directly derived. We see them on the Prior's Door at Ely Cathedral, their backs bent like bows, or arched backward so that their heads touch their heels at Avallon, San Martín de Unx, Kilteel, Vézelay and Santiago de Compostela. Taking up much the same posture, Salome dances before Herod and his court, her hair sweeping the floor behind her, at Alquezar. It has been maintained that the arched posture has a symbolic significance (Beigbeder 1969). Other realistic acrobats and dancers are to be found on the abacus of a capital from La Daurade (now in the Musée des Augustins, Toulouse [*Plate 17*]); at Saint-Rémy, Foussais, Leyre and Saint-Paul-lès-Dax. An elegant female handstands on a bar at Modena, and a bearded male does the same, using the necking ring of the column for a bar, at Massac. There is a superb column of realistic figures twisting around each other at Zurbano.

Such true-to-life figures are not common, however, and, on the whole, Romanesque acrobats adopt near-impossible poses (*Figs. 14 and 15*). Should their posture perchance be a feasible one, as in the case of many feet-to-ears acrobats, then their bearing or features are made to look grotesque. At San Andrés, Avila, a contortionist on an abacus has breasts but

Plate 17 Toulouse (La Daurade): music, gaming and tumbling. Note the Fools' caps.

possessing or even ugly acrobats over the realistic and elegant clearly tells us that Romanesque artists differed from their Classical forerunners in their objectives, that they worked to quite different standards, that they strove to present a different reality, and that they had a different purpose to fulfil. Even though they made extensive borrowings from it, Classical art did not satisfactorily accommodate all their intentions. It is significant that, when they carved purely imaginary subjects like mermaids and centaurs, they treated the details with a considerable degree of realism, but if they were depicting man they made a practice of altering his proportions, contorting his limbs, twisting his features, and stressing his least beautiful attributes. Nor was this the outcome of having to push his shape into the odd surfaces of such architectural features as capitals and corbels, because when they wanted to they were perfectly able to fit any design they wished. It was just that these blocks of stone suited their purpose admirably – to

Fig. 14a Anzy-le-Duc: acrobat using the necking ring as a bar.

Fig. 14b Passirac: megaphallic man assailed by horn-blowers.

Fig. 15 Acrobatic postures at Givrezac (*top*) and Champagnolles (*bottom*).

practically no body, and her legs are elongated so that she can touch her hips with her toes by bending her knees. At Brive a head-to-heels acrobat is bi-corporeal. Bi-corporeal figures abound in Romanesque art, and the double body lends an air of monstrousness to the design. Over the Puerta de las Platerías at Santiago a simian female exhibitionist bends over to grasp her ankles and, in so doing, reveals a large, rimmed vulva. Here and elsewhere, at La Chaize-le-Vicomte for example, the motif of acrobat, ape, and exhibitionist are combined in one figure.

The preponderance of contorted, unpre-

display man and woman in graceless, unnatural, even 'improper' attitudes. They sought to draw attention to the base nature of man implicit in these uncanny contortions, and they were able to make simple, clothed figures like the bent-over females at Matha Marestay or Blaignac, peering at us under their skirts, seem lewd. The acrobat at Saint-Léger-en-Pons bends his legs backwards to place his feet on the crown of his head, but, in so doing, seems, by the violence of his action, to be conveying some urgent message to us. Even the well-executed, realistic acrobats on the Zurbano column are trying to express something, to symbolise the struggle upwards of man, his attempt to throw off his earthboundness; or, conversely, they are stigmatising their own overweening pride in being able to twist their bodies out of shape in this way. We feel compelled to seek a message when we contemplate Romanesque art, for, unlike the Greeks who sought to capture beauty in their statuary, Romanesque artists often deliberately concentrated on ugliness, and for this there must have been a cogent reason; and that reason must have been a religious one: not art for art's sake, but art for man's or God's sake.

So when we witness groups of acrobats engaged in multiple activities, twining their limbs about each other, their legs around each other's necks perhaps, as at Migron, Covet or Saint-Georges-de-Boscherville, or when they take to pulling each other's hair and beards, as at La Sauve-Majeure, then it is plain to see that the artist wished to impart to us some notion of uncouthness, of lack of decorum and spirituality.

The most common expression of obloquy for acrobats is the feet-to-ears position. Dressed or nude, figures in this pose are indecorous, but nude they leave nothing to the imagination; their coarseness needs no stressing (*Plate 18*). Nevertheless, they have a certain wit if they are given an obvious purpose, such as supporting with their feet the superstructure of abacus, lintel or entablature. As atlas-figures, their upward thrust to take the weight of stone above them seems to reflect the Christian idea of man with his burden of sin; and, being themselves upside down, they may further denote *l'homme culbuté*, fallen man, or Simon Magus plunging as it were to his doom (Beigbeder 1969). Feet-to-ears acrobats are one of the few motifs not

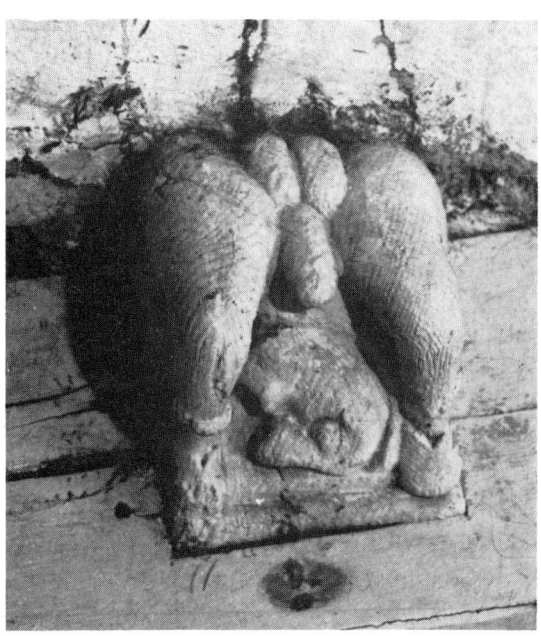

Plate 18 Saint-Servais, Brittany: acrobat. (Photo: Inventaire Général, Bretagne)

derived directly from pre-Romanesque models but they echo the supporting figures known as caryatids, telamons or atlantes; and taken together with Romanesque forms of these, make up, next to human and animal masks, the largest group of corbel and capital motifs. Very often they are carved on capitals so that their heads coincide with the corner of the block and thus occupy the position usually taken up by the volute of Corinthian and Composite capitals. On corbels they appear frontally. Occasionally one finds them on the voussoirs of arches over doors, and at Vouvant a whole archivolt is composed of superb high-relief acrobatic atlantes with bent, splayed legs.

Splayed legs are usual on Romanesque atlantes. Examples of the very rare straight-legged kind are to be found at Sainte-Marie-d'Oloron, on the base of the central column of the portal. Chained together, wearing ornamental boots, knees bent *forward* but not splayed, they are Islamic Saracens, defeated in the Moorish wars, made to do obeisance by supporting the Glory of God tympanum over their heads. Gaston IV of Béarn raised his church on his return from the Crusades after chasing Spanish Moors away from the area. Atlantes are so named after Atlas, who supported the world on his shoulders in North Africa, and it is interesting to see Moors, on the edge of the Moorish world, perform a similar task, a nicety of which the sculptor was perhaps not unaware.

Occasionally we find supporting figures in the shape of saints or prophets; Jeremiah acts as an atlas at Moissac, for instance. But, as they are usually carved on capitals or corbels, their posture is dictated by the shape of the block of stone on which they are carved, and so this tends to be a squatting or *accroupi* position, and this in turn results in a suggestion of indecency. The figures do not have to be nude to give this impression, but very often they are, thus revealing portions of their anatomy which are usually concealed. If they are backward facing, they may clutch their buttocks and reveal their anus. Anus-showing acrobats and squatters are not uncommon. The squatting position is one which lends itself to a number of variations, and the individuals portrayed may pull their beards or tresses of hair, or pull at the corner of their mouths, or stick out their tongues, or play musical instruments, or lift objects such as barrels. They may be surrounded by vegetation, or by animals which whisper into their ears. And in each case the symbolism may vary.

Feet-to-ears acrobats are a development of the squatter, for they simply straighten the leg and thrust it upwards, held by the hand if necessary. Using their feet instead of their hands to support the stone above, they sometimes twist themselves so that, in addition, another part of the body acts as a support. The male acrobat at Barret has bent round so that his testicles form a corbel in themselves; another carving at this church shows an upside down woman, with legs and arms outspread, tangled up with a squatting figure between her legs, whose broken head bites her groin; but there are other carvings here devoted to the iconography of lust, some of which we shall discuss later. In the same *département*, at Biron and Chermignac, similar scenes appear.

At Avy-en-Pons a feet-to-ears acrobat has one foot ending in a serpent's head. Anguipedes, as they are known (figures whose limbs or tails end in heads), are found in antiquity (*Plates 19 and 20*). Illuminators were fond of them, and they abound in Romanesque scenes. Among the

Plate 19 Gisors: detail of triple window now in the Victoria & Albert Museum. Anguipedal woman with long hair.

Plate 20 Poitiers, Notre-Dame-la-Grande. Anguipedal woman in the spandrel. Note the billet-biting beast corbel.

more grotesque of these is a curious mermaid at Rosheim with snake-headed tails, and also a centauress whose tail ends in foliage, and 'un obscenum de petite dimension mais de grande licence' according to Witkowski, one of the first French writers to take note of 'l'art profane à l'église' (Witkowski 1908). The foliate tails or limb-endings are either a development of the anguipede or an extension of the Classical tritons. Auvergne can furnish many examples of human figures whose extremities sprout vegetation, e.g. at Auzon, Brioude, Chauriat, Courpière, Chanteuges, Glaine-Montaigut, Ennezat, Saint-Dier and Thiers le Moutier

(Swiechowski 1973). In England good examples are to be seen at Melbourne; on the door capital a bearded, benevolent looking man sits, entangling his arms in foliage, which become part of the foliage. He is very similar to the squatter at Matha-Marestay. Both seem to be an extension of the exhibitionist, suggesting that *Luxuria* began to develop into 'luxuriance', not only etymologically but also in significance, so that the sexual connotation was diminished and replaced by 'over-indulgence' or 'rich living' (Jerman 1981).

Feet-to-ears acrobats have an affinity with two-tailed mermaids whose tails curl up on either side, with the fins held at shoulder level, often touching the abacus and giving support to it. Like that of the acrobat, it is an attitude which gives the sculptor scope for sexual detail. We return to the subject of mermaids in the next chapter, noting here her symbolism, reaching back into antiquity. She lured men to their doom by her enchantments, her enticing voice, her long hair, her bare breasts, and by her sexual attractions. At least one mermaid, at Zamora, is exhibitionist, and hundreds of others very nearly so. As to acrobats, very many display their well-endowed sexual parts, like the atlas who stares down at us from the right-hand capital of the west door at Semur-en-Brionnais, or a corbel at Frómista, at San Martín de Unx, or from more than one corbel at Mauriac (*Plate 21*).

By virtue of the poses they adopted, acrobats are delineated as objects of opprobrium and derision. It is only rarely that they are granted dignity. On the early tenth-century west door of the Asturian church of San Miguel de Lillo, an acrobat on a long vaulting pole soars over a lion released from its cage and encouraged by its trainer's whip. The symbolism is obscure but perhaps intends us to understand the triumph of Christianity over evil. At any rate no evil is implicit in this acrobat. Such a kind treatment of acrobats is rare, but can be explained in this case by the source of the carving, which was a Roman ivory diptych depicting the start of the games, with a consul throwing his *mappa* into the amphitheatre (Fontaine 1973). In general, however, the attitude of tumblers and contortionists on corbels affirms that it was the carver's intention to pillory them.

No doubt this was in large measure due to the lives such entertainers led – or were thought to lead. Travelling troupes of circus folk, strolling players, and their accompanying musicians and dancers, led wandering, hand-to-mouth, precarious but autonomous lives. The freedom of their ways was greatly envied by those tied by feudalism to one place and one master. Their popularity and acclaim stirred the malice of those who thought themselves less fortunate; their down-at-heel and motley appearance supported the opinion that they were not averse to petty crime in order to eat. Even down to modern times suspicions have lingered on that actors, buskers, and their fellows are not quite *comme il faut*. Even the great Molière was buried with some difficulty, at night, by a reluctant officiating priest.

Naturally, the Church excommunicated

Plate 21 Semur-en-Brionnais: megaphallic atlas, and, to his right on the inside face, a *femme aux serpents*.

them. As Chambers puts it in his opening lines of *The Medieval Stage* (Chambers 1903):

> Christianity, emerging from Syria with a prejudice against disguisings found the Roman world full of *scenici*.

They were consequently legislated against and reduced to performing acts of *mimi*, juggling, rope-dancing, legerdemain, buffoonery and obscenity in one-night stands all over Europe. Because their performances were a source of merriment, satire and bawdry, and appealed to the common people, the theatre aroused deep distrust. Paradoxically enough, the Church was in a difficult position, for the liturgy was a kind of drama; it was out of the liturgy that the medieval Mystery plays evolved, and music and dance had a role to play, music in particular being a necessary part of the ritual. Had not King David himself written music and danced before the Art of the Covenant? He appears in medieval iconography playing his harp, as in the well-known example on the Puerta de las Platerías at Santiago. In south-west France it is common to find the Elders of the Church, copied from *Beatus* pages, playing their rebecs or guitar-like instruments. Music in the service of the Church was free of reproach. A late twelfth-century manuscript from Rheims (?) illustrates David with his court musicians on the upper portion; below, tumblers, musicians and a huge bear with a barrel provide the contrast between the harmony of divine music and the discord of secular, profane entertainment. The bear often stands for Satan, and a harp-playing bear, mimicking David, fills a medallion on one of the archivolts of Barfreston church. There is also the delightful fable of the poor jongleur who, in lieu of worship, performed his tricks before the high altar, to the disgust of an observing monk, who then saw the Virgin descend to mop the jongleur's brow.

Nevertheless, the Church set its face against the lay artistes, all lumped together for the purpose of ostracism. At San Isidoro, León, a musician sits by an acrobat, and at San Martín de Mondoñedo, not far from Santiago, three musicians on corbels are megaphallic, a sure sign of their base instincts. No doubt jealousy played its part, for the gleemen, scops, minstrels and entertainers of all kinds received the approbation and patronage of the lay aristocracy, and, in spite of the Church's interdicts, they prospered. The upper classes and the common people, in an age which knew great hardships and deprivations, had need of them.

The later jongleurs were to look back to Charlemagne as their great patron. He had given them all the land of Provence in fee, and they flocked to the Angevin and Plantagenet courts in France and England, as well as the minor households of noble lords and royal vassals. They sang the great heroic epics, the *chansons de geste*, and they were to be responsible for the spread of the curious cult of courtly love, yet another reason for the Church's condemnation.

> Ye might know them from afar by their coats of many colours, gaudier than any knight might respectably wear, by the instruments on their backs and those of their servants, and by the shaven faces, the close-clipped hair and flat shoes proper to their profession
>
> Chambers 1903

Thomas de Cabham, sub-dean of Salisbury and subsequently Archbishop of Canterbury, wrote a *Penitential*, analysing the range of human frailty, in which he carefully classified minstrels from an ecclesiastical standpoint: there are those who wore grotesque masks or entertained by 'indecent' dance or gesture, who used satire or raillery – these were altogether damnable; those who used musical instruments to sing bawdy songs at banquets were likewise condemned; but those who sang to musical accompaniment about the lives of saints and princes might be tolerated, and only to these was the term *joculatores* to be applied.

Medieval entertainers were of many kinds. Troubadours or *trobaires* composed the songs which the jongleurs or *joglars* actually performed (the term 'jongleur' derived its 'n' from an unknown source; the English word 'juggler' is cognate). Both composer and performer travelled together. The northern *trouvères* were not dependent for their livelihood on the songs they wrote, unlike their southern counterparts, but were middle or upper class professional people – clerks, merchants, officials, nobles. The southern *jougleurs* sang anything that was popular and also danced, tumbled, juggled, performed acts of magic, and thus came near the role of *bufo*. Specialist performers turned somersaults, walked on their hands, leaped through hoops, balanced on high-wires, and twisted themselves into incredible shapes. Female *tornatrices* did the same. Many local forms of tumbling developed – the *tour français, tour champenois, tour romain*. Then there were the bear tamers, men with toothless lions, dwarfs and freaks, sword-swallowers, Punch and Judy shows, and all the fun of the fair. And, as they performed, mountebanks and pedlars, cut-purses and pickpockets, pimps and prostitutes joined the happy throng to ply their own doubtful trades. What with the tricks and feats of magic, the disappearing purses, and the amazing contortions of the acrobats, it was no wonder that ordinary folk assumed that devil's work was afoot, that these tricksters and wonder-performing *saltimbanques* received their supernatural powers from Satan himself, as their own village priest maintained.

Just as subject to clerical disapproval and prohibition as the acts of the professionals were the participatory sports, rituals and festivals of the people. Miracle plays, drinking bouts, ram-raisings, May games, and the Feast of Fools all incurred odium. The May festival included dance and amorous licence, and the pagan 'Jack-in-the-Green' ceremonies, may-gathering, and all the other rituals listed in Frazer's *Golden Bough*. Ecclesiastical prohibitions laid particular emphasis on the love songs and *cantica turpia et luxoriosa* which women sang outside the church doors.

The winter celebrations were perhaps the most abhorrent. The Winter Feast, once held during the middle of November, was moved to the end of December, so that both the Roman Saturnalia and the New Year Festival of the Kalends of January were incorporated into the Christian festival of the Nativity of Christ; these three great pre-Christian festivals coincided more or less with the date of the greatest of all Christian celebrations, and, not unnaturally, they influenced it very much, as they still do. All sorts of customs were enacted, like the hobby-horse rites which often involved the participants with beast-masks, or the Feast of Fools and the Lord of Misrule (Chambers 1903). The Feast of Fools even became an ecclesiastical event, chiefly in cathedrals but also in monasteries (Chambers). People wore caps bearing asses' ears, perhaps a relic of animal sacrifice or a practice of the Roman period in France. The custom is remembered in the paper hats worn round the party table at Christmas. The traditional fool's cap was eared, and sometimes also bore a coxcomb, and the fool wore bells and parti-coloured garments – all features of the Kalendic Feast of Fools. The wearing of masks was a widespread custom at such ceremonies (Chambers). These festivities survived as Twelfth Night, with the *Rey de Habas*, the Bean-king, i.e. the child appointed to rule over the activities. Mock masses, the worship of an ass upon the altar, and other unseemly acts in churches, were, needless to say, grounds for high ecclesiastical disapproval. Yet they continued at least

until the fifteenth century, and one wonders how willing a part the local priest (whose living and popularity depended on the goodwill of his flock) played in such harmless – but to a Christian utterly blasphemous – merrymaking. It has been suggested (Montejo 1978) that the Church turned a blind eye to carnival during the twelfth century, knowing that under the pressures of life men needed a safety valve, and that, in any case, after a period of unfettered licence they returned more joyfully to the service of God. The goings-on of these medieval festivals has considerable relevance not only to the appearance of masks, beast-masks and acrobats on churches, but also to the carving of exhibitionists. Sexual activities cannot have been infrequent at these times, much to the discomfiture of the clergy.

Masks and heads of humans and animals are probably the most frequent subjects for corbels, but atlas-figures and those of acrobatic entertainers run a close second, also appearing on capitals, many of them exhibitionist in character, displaying their sex or making gestures and grimaces. Some are elegant and beautifully carved, so that it is not always clear if the viewer is to admire or disapprove, and the duality of Romanesque symbolism once more comes to the fore. Outstanding muscular co-ordination – keeping ten balls in the air at once, or bending backwards to place the head between the knees – requires, in common belief, supernatural aid from Hell or Heaven. On the whole, though, we may take it that carvings illustrating such acts on church buildings, were intended to make a moral point: that one must regard the world of entertainment with suspicion, and take care not to be tainted by it. We have the teachings of Saint Augustine to inform us. As widely read and quoted in medieval times as the Bible itself, he continued the tradition of Clement of Alexandria's *Protrepticus*, a work which fulminated against the 'obscenity' of performances on the late-Classical stage. Saint Augustine likewise apostrophised circus acts of all kinds, writing:

'He who said I desire you not to have traffic with devils' (Corinthians I, X. 20) meant that believers must distinguish themselves by their acts from the servants of devils. Devils take pleasure in popular songs, in frivolous display, in the manifold immoralities of the theatre.

(see Beigbeder 1969)

5 Mermaids, centaurs and other hybrid monsters

Why these ridiculous monstrosities, these weird deformed beauties?

St Bernard

Mermaids are ubiquitous in Romanesque art. They are to be found not only in churches near the sea, but also in those well inland (*Plate 22*). One might reasonably expect to find carvings which portray maritime activities or sailors' tales and legends near coastal areas, and it is not surprising, therefore, to see in the Bordelais district of France sculpted men carrying huge fish on their backs, or string courses and bands of decoration made up of what appear to be barnacles or limpets. When, however, one comes across scallop shells in Auvergne, at Chanteuges for instance, then it is possible that the church is on a pilgrim route, the scallop shell being an emblem carried by medieval pilgrims returning from Compostela. In the same area of France many capitals display mermaids, but for

these we must seek some other explanation. Carved in wood on choir stalls and misericords as well as on stone, endowed with one or two tails, their significance is not hard to seek.

Many Classical hybrid monsters found their way into Romanesque iconography, among them a fish-tailed human female whose origin is veiled in obscurity. If we are devoting this chapter to a study of the mermaid and some fellow creatures, it is because of her affinity, in her two-tailed version, with the feet-to-ears acrobats we have just been describing. Using her two fins, raised on either side of her body and held in her hands, to support the abacus in the same way that the acrobat uses his feet, she strikes an attitude that strongly suggests exhibitionism. She is, moreover, always in the company of other sexual figures and allied symbols, so that there cannot be any doubt that the carvers were interested in her for reasons more cogent than mere decorative ornament (*Plate 23*). We may find it hard today to discern any

Plate 22 Fuentidueña: mermaids in inland Spain.

Plate 23 Mouliherne: tress-pulling mermaid and centauress.

symbolism in the beautiful scaly maiden, combing her long tresses and gazing into her mirror, other than a narcissistic vanity; but medieval artists were more aware of the mythology attached to her, and had read about her in one of the most popular books of the day, the Bestiary. They knew the story of her fateful allurements, that she brought sailors to their doom by her beauty and her song. Pierre le Picard, in his late twelfth-century Bestiary, notes that she attracted men by her blandishments and deceptions in order to destroy them, and the theme of luring men to disaster by sensual and sensory means was exactly the sort of thing that appealed to medieval moralisers. St Jerome echoed the Stoic philosophers in regarding her as an image of the seductive pleasures of this world, of sensuality and the love of luxury. At Piacenza the siren of luxury sits enthroned on the main door of the church amid dragons and humans.

In Greek legend the siren, a term which became an alternative for mermaid, was half bird, half woman, with a beguiling voice. The process by which she became the half fish mermaid seems to have started in Assyria and Mesopotamia; at Pasargadae, for instance, a frieze bears the lower half of a creature with a fishtail as well as a leg. At some time in late antiquity the mermaid adopted her present form, as on the Porte Antique at Orange, where her tail loops several times, above the panels celebrating Caesar's sea victories. The half bird siren is remembered, however, at Combronde, Chauvigny, Corme Royale, Lacommande (between a mermaid and a merman, and accompanied by musicians, apes and embracing couples), Barletta, several churches round Soria, Saint-Fort-sur-Gironde, La Sauve-Majeure and elsewhere. At Aulnay she takes on a male face. As bird-women the sirens played a dual role: they tried to seduce Jason and the Argonauts, and Odysseus lashed himself to the mast and stopped up his sailors' ears with wax;

49

Fig. 16 Triton on a Pictish stone, Meigle Museum, Tayside.

on the other hand, they tried to warn Alexander the Great to retrace his steps. In Greek funerary art they symbolised the soul as ravens or crows, as they did in Ireland; in Roman art they were benign beings who consoled the departed with their sweet song. This dualism we shall see reflected in Romanesque iconography.

Somewhere in her genealogy the siren may have been mixed up with tritons, nereids and other watery nymphs. A triton, personifying the river god of the Jordan, assists at the Baptism of Christ at Arezzo, and Jordanus, with some triton attributes, is present at the Baptism on the

domes of the fifth- and sixth-century Neoni and Arian Baptisteries in Ravenna. Pagan deities were even then creeping into Christian imagery. On an eighth-century Class II Pictish stone in the Meigle museum there is a siren with an interlaced double tail, clutching her serpentine hair in both hands, a remarkable object to be found so early in Scotland (*Fig. 16*).

By Romanesque times a number of families in Poitou and along the Loire could claim descent from a viper-fairy named Mélusine (the Plantagenets of Anjou also had a demon ancestress, whence rumours that they dabbled in witchcraft). This no doubt helped to popularise snake- or fish-tailed figures in those areas, but by far the most powerful influence came from the Bestiaries and works like the second-century Physiologus (wrongly attributed by some to St Ambrose). Bestiaries were immensely popular. Honorius d'Autun, Hugues de Saint Victor, Philippe de Thaon, Hildebert de Lavardin, Marbode and others, using early works of St Ambrose, Isidore of Seville and versions of the Physiologus, wrote Bestiaries whose importance lay not so much in the zoological descriptions of animals as in the moral and symbolic lessons to be drawn from them. The authors delighted in exploring the habits and sexual behaviour of animals of every shape and size, from hares to elephants, but found purely imaginary mythical creatures gave more scope for moralising. To the Classical fauna of Mino-

Fig. 17 Le Puy, Saint-Michel-d'Aiguilh, door-lintel: two tress-pulling mermaids, single-tailed.

Fig. 18a Zamora: mermaid exhibitionist.

Fig. 18b Issoire: naked rider on a goat, sign of Capricorn

taurs, Chimeras and Hydras they added the Manticora, the Amphisbæna and the Caladrius, to name but three. As a consequence of the popularity of these 'pattern-books', whole archivolts are dedicated to the fantastic fauna of the Bestiaries at Aulnay, Vouvant, Blesle and elsewhere. Even today they exert a strange brooding, disturbing effect. Once upon a time they must have seemed awesome.

In shallow relief on the lintel of Saint-Michel-d'Aiguilh, le Puy, are two affronted mermaids, single-tailed and holding their hair (*Fig. 17*). It is conceivable that a mason might see how to combine two such figures and make a bi-corporeal composition, with a tail on each side of the capital joining the torso and head on the arris or angle. Twin-tailed mermaids of this nature, pairs of them intertwining their tails, abound in Auvergne – Courpière, Brioude, Chanteuges, Mailhat and Chauriat – but the one-tailed variety is also to be found – Ennezat, Orcival and Thiers le Moutier; and, of course, both varieties are to be found wherever Romanesque art flourishes.

What is her significance? By tradition, and from a reading of the Bestiaries, she was a temptress, a seductive creature of Satan ('the siren and the devil shall abide in Babylon' said Isaiah), a mysterious being; most mysterious of all – and a matter of the greatest interest to medieval man – was her sexual anatomy. Usually it is only hinted at, indeed some mermaids wear a little short skirt to cover their abdomen, but at Zamora it is made explicit, and her vulva is clearly shown (*Fig. 18a*). Her proximity to exhibitionists strengthens the view that she is to be taken as a sexual symbol, another of the *Luxuria* motifs. In France the mermaid is always known as *la luxure*, and official guides to French monuments, using a patter supplied to them no doubt by official sources, point out single-tailed mermaids as *la concupiscence*, and double-tailed ones as *la luxure*, on what authority is not known. Commonly mermaids occupy an eye-catching position, just at head-height on doorway capitals, or on transept-crossing pillars in full view of the congregation at Mass, or on window-capitals. On corbels they tend to be single-tailed.

In the Quart Livre, chapter 38, of *Pantagruel*

there is an interesting passage on the subject of Chitterlings (*andouilles* or tripe sausage) in which Rabelais shows his knowledge of Romanesque buildings:

> Iceulx (les géants antiques) toutesfoy n'estoient que andouilles pour la moitié du corps, ou serpens, que je ne mente. Le serpens qui tenta Eve estoit andouillicque: ce nonobstant est de luy escript qu'il estoit fin et cauteleux sus tous aultres animans. Aussi sont andouilles. Encores maintient-on en certaines académies que ce tentateur estoit l'Andouille nommée Ithyphalle, en laquelle feut jadis transformé le bon messer Priapus, grand tentateur des femmes par les paradis en grec, ce sont jardins en françois . . . Si ces discours ne satisfont à l'incrédulité de vos seigneuries, praesentement (j'entends après boire) visitez Lusignan, Partenay, Vovant, Mervant et Pouzauges en Poictou. La trouverez tesmoings vieulx de renom et de la bonne forge, lesquelz vous jureront sus le braz sainct Rigomé que Mellusine, leur première fondatrice, avoit corps foeminin jusques aux boursavitz, et le reste en bas estoit andouille serpentine ou bien serpent andouillicque . . . la nymphe scythicque Ora avoit pareillement le corps my-party en femme et en andouilles. Elle toutesfoy tant sembla belle a Juppiter qu'il coucha avecques elle et en eut un beau filz nommé Colaxes.

> (In sooth these (ancient giants) were nothing more than Chitterlings from the waist down – I tell no lies – the serpent who tempted Eve was a Chitterling, yet it is written of him that he was wilier and subtler than other animals. So are Chitterlings. Furthermore some academics maintain that this tempter was the Chitterling named Ithyphallus, into whose shape good master Priapus was once transformed, a great tempter of women in paradise as they say in Greek, or what we call pleasure gardens in French. . . . If what I am saying stretches your Lordships' credulity, then go, an it please you (after drinking that is), to Lusignan, Vouvant, Mervent and Pouzauges in Poitou, where you will find solid witnesses of ancient renown, who will swear to you on the armbone of St Rigomer, that Melusine, their foundress, was a woman down to the cockpit, and the rest below that was a snaky Chitterling or a Chitterling snake . . . The Scythian nymph Ora likewise was partly woman and partly Chitterling in body. Nevertheless she seemed so beautiful to Jupiter that he lay with her and had a fine son off her named Colaxes.)

No Romanesque church survives at Mervent (area of Saint-Hilaire-des-Loges) but all the others mentioned by Rabelais are dealt with in this book; they have mermaids, male exhibitionists, and other *Luxuria* motifs. It is important from our point of view to note that Rabelais had established a connection between snakes, mermaids, and the ithyphallic figure of Priapus. The relics of St Rigomer were devoutly preserved at the abbey of Maillezais in the Vendée, another church noted by us. We note also Rabelais' allusion to the sexual encounter between Ora and Jupiter.

At Santiago de Compostela a mermaid holds a fish. One might expect mermaids to be found in association with other denizens of the ocean. Fish certainly feature often in Christian art; in early times as a secret sign, from the acronym $IX\Theta Y\Sigma$ (Jesus Christ, Son of God, Saviour), or in scenes depicting the miracle of the loaves and fishes. In later Romanesque art it tends to revert to its ancient Greek phallic and poly-progenitive significance. A man carrying a huge fish on his back, in a way reminiscent of women on certain Greek vases, processing with phallic fish to some Dionysiac revels, may represent mankind struggling beneath a load of sin (Saujon, Oloron Sainte-Marie, Cambes, Lestiac, Santa Cruz de Seros and Navascués). We have already made mention of the squatting figure holding fish at Rochester. A human-headed fish stands beside a female tumbler doing a handstand at Amboise; at Orcival and Mozac men ride fish, like Oceanus on his dolphin; and a pre-Romanesque woman with long hair is astride a large fish on the fine sarcophagus of Adeloche in the church of St Thomas, Strasbourg. Lastly, devoid of phallic significance but nevertheless endowed with some apotropaic or other magical property, fish (usually in pairs joined by a ligament) appear as the zodiacal sign Pisces.

Mermaids almost always have long hair which they pull or hold. Needless to say, hair is another attribute which carries sexual significance: tresses in the case of women, beards or moustaches for men. This association is brought out strongly in the *Luxuria* carvings where a woman is being punished for her sins of fornication by having her breasts and nether regions gnawed by snakes and venomous reptiles; at the same time her hair is pulled by demons. *La femme aux serpents* is the subject of our next chapter, but without pre-empting that study we can point to a variation of her in the mermaids at La Seu d'Urgel (right-hand capital of the north

Fig. 19a La Seu d'Urgell: mermaid *aux serpents*.

Fig. 19b Playful centaurs, Bénévent-l'Abbaye.

door [*Fig. 19a*]), at Lestiac (chevet capital), at Bénévent l'Abbaye (nave capital) and at Caunay (window capital) whose breasts are being attacked by snakes; other bifid mermaids bitten by snakes can be found at Bari (south door of the façade of Sta. Nicolà; a centaur twined with snakes is close by) and San Giovanni-in-Borgo (a capital now in the municipal museum). A capital of a mermaid with snakes at Haux, near Lestiac, has disappeared but there still exists in the interior a capital showing a snake-limbed anguipede, with a grotesque grinning head, being bitten by snakes which are gripped by flanking clothed male figures; at Bussière-Badil mermaids on a nave capital suckle amphisbænic snakes which bite their heads; a single-tailed mermaid is bitten, though not on the breasts, by snakes at Lestiac; and bird sirens have their hair pulled by snakes on a capital at Saint Antonin.

The exhibitionism of acrobats is plain to see; that of mermaids less manifest, but it is accentuated by the association with tormenting snakes or other reptilian creatures thought at the time to be loathsome and venomous, e.g. tortoises and salamanders, and also by juxtaposition with other phallic signs or, say, acrobats (at Vézelay two contiguous roundels of the famous tympanum of Gislebertus contain a mermaid and an acrobat respectively, both arched back in an identical posture, so that feet or tail touch the head). Mermaids into whose ears serpents are whispering perhaps represent temptation and recall Eve (Auzon, Corsiguano), while

anguipedes whose ancillary jaws bite at the main head may imply that we bring punishment upon ourselves by our own actions.

If any further evidence is required to establish the relationship of the sheela-na-gig with other *Luxuria* carvings, then it must surely be provided by the remarkable corbel of Archingeay (*Fig. 23*). Here an acrobatic female, feet-to-ears, clutching her knees, is being bitten on the breasts by snakes, but at the same time she reveals below a large almond-shaped gaping vulva. It is an astonishing piece that leaves no more to be said.

We shall encounter the Archingeay figure again; now we look at another hybrid. At San Claudio, Zamora, a mermaid accompanies two centaurs who are fighting each other. Centaurs, and centauresses, are also ubiquitous in Romanesque art, though not as numerous as mermaids (*Plates 24 and 25*). Sometimes they are phallic, sometimes benign, and yet again sometimes zodiacal. Like the sirens, mermaids, sphynxes and other composite creatures, they entered Christian art through the Physiologus and Bestiaries in the main, then, like all Romanesque animals, took on a new life of their own. They combined with other creatures to form new hybrids. At Brioude a centaur becomes confused with a minotaur; at Rosheim a centaur and mermaid combine to form the hydrocentaur, with a serpentine or fish tail, and a pair of hydrocentaurs at Albignac wearing pointed hats hold gold bassoon-like instruments in one hand

Plate 24 Cashel, Cormac's Chapel: Romanesque tympanum over north door. Lion and centaur-sagittarius.

and touch each others' noses with the other; at Guxhagen, near Göttingen, a centaur and a hydrocentaur attack one another, whilst flanking centauresses bite the ears of a human-faced minotaur at Bénévent-l'Abbaye.

Centaurs enter into the same compositions as other figures; the Brioude creature spews snakes which bite the heads of the two flanking naked males whose legs it grasps; snakes entwine centaurs at Bari, Brindisi and León, on pre-Romanesque slabs in Pictish Scotland, and on the Irish cross of Tibberaghny (where it holds two daggers), associated with a Manticora (also to be found on the Clonca shaft); centaurs are enmeshed in vinescrolls (La Daurade; St Séver-de-Rustan, next to a miser); two of them kiss each other at Lautenbach and two hold hands at Berrioplano, and at Pleinigen an archaic-look-ing centaur with no arms is stabbed by a man; at Maubourguet a centaur plays a harp on a corbel, thus recalling another motif: the ass playing a lyre (perhaps derived from the Boëthius text: 'Do you hearken to my words or are you as an ass before a lyre?' [*Plate 26*]).

There seems to be no malice in a music-playing centaur, and in this benign aspect we are reminded of Cheiron, teacher of Achilles and Jason, skilled in music and the arts; although, in general, centaurs, as ancient enemies of the Lapiths, and with a reputation for being lustful creatures, must be regarded in the less favourable light. They occur, however, in yet another form whose significance seems to be without evil intent, and this is as a zodiacal sign, the centaur-sagittarius. Descriptions of the zodiac are often appended to Bestiaries, together with Labours of the Months, and the calendrical connection indicated to men the need for honest toil and good husbandry. Major churches, able to afford extensive decoration, display zodiacal signs together with the

Plate 25 Kilteel: another Irish centaur turning round to struggle with a lion.

Labours, but minor churches often had to make do with one or two of either or of each, so that Kilpeck has only Pisces, Elkstone a centaur-sagittarius (of course we do not know how much has been destroyed). At Mauriac the outer archivolt of the west door has an extensive range of zodiacal signs, and Aulnay's west door alternates these with the Labours, while other archivolts praise the forethought of the wise virgins (and castigate the foolish ones) and the victory of virtue over vice. Sermons in stones are here in plenty, based on the text 'as ye sow so shall ye reap' . . .

Huge zodiacal signs grace the exterior of Issoire's chevet, but, interestingly, two of them – Capricorn and Taurus – have riders on their backs (a motif found elsewhere, at San Isidoro, León, for instance), and inside the church a winged figure, known as *La Luxure*, rides an

Plate 26 La Plaisance-sur-Gartempe: ass playing a lyre.

MULIER SUPER BESTIA

animal looking rather like a ram (*Fig. 18b*). Humans riding goats, rams and the like, an expression of unbridled lust, are everywhere a *Luxuria* motif, from Mozac and Mauriac to Worcester (where on a misericord a woman wearing a see-through net-like garment rides a goat). One model for this motif is a St Séver *Beatus* illumination (fol. 152) showing a woman riding a fierce beast, with the caption *Mulier super bestia* (*Fig. 20*). So once again the dualism of Romanesque iconography re-asserts itself in the combination of *Luxuria* with the zodiac.

Centaurs come singly, or in affronted pairs jointly hunting or attacking each other, or they appear as bi-corporeal designs like two-tailed mermaids, sharing one torso and head (*Fig. 19b*). As sagittarii they can fire their bows forwards or backwards over their rumps. They fire backwards on the Hook Norton font, or the Parthenay-le-Vieux capital, apparently at nothing; or they can shoot armed men (soldiers of Christ?) as at Irache; two of them flank and shoot at a robed figure of an ecclesiastic (?) at Valdeomillos, while at San Quirce de Rio Pisuerga, in the same province of Palencia, an ithyphallic centaur shoots a horse, and at Guardo, nearby, the font has a centaur-sagittarius with a quadruped on its back alongside an ithyphallic splay-legged man; at Fuentidueña the centaur has a rider; they shoot at a peacock at Bruyères, at a mermaid at Estella and San Pedro de la Rua, or at birds on their cruppers at Orisoain (birds of prey or human souls?); elsewhere they shoot dragons (Adel), monsters (Brañosera), a winged devil (Agüero), a sea serpent and griffin (Winchester), and at Cashel a centaur donning a Norman-style helmet shoots an enormous lion. It is difficult in all these representations to say that the theme is good overcoming evil (or vice versa), though perhaps we are supposed to infer that the centaur

expresses a dichotomy – its upper half, being human and created in the image of God, always trying to gain the ascendancy over its lower, bestial half. Sometimes one half gets the better of the other, generally the animal parts direct the helpless human half, as at Trogir in Yugoslavia, where ensnared in a vinescroll with a shaggy horned demon it grasps at drapery in desperation; though in the triple window of Gisors, now in the Victoria and Albert Museum, the human part does seem to be controlling the beast, as it shoots a cock, the ancient symbol of virility, fertility and therefore of concupiscence and lust. It has been suggested (Rowland 1973) that the centaur represents lust because the arrow indicates the *ejaculatio seminis*. The centaurs suckling their young at Iffley could be thought to show evil begetting and nourishing evil; on the other hand, is it just a peaceful picture of parenthood? We also remember that St Anthony in the desert was reputedly led to St Paul by a faun, a wolf, and a centaur.

The iconography of the centaur is no less bewildering than that of so many other creatures, and mythical beasts indulging in a variety of acts we can no longer decipher nevertheless add to the richness and interest of Romanesque work. While these indicate a faith suffused with every manner of superstition, we none the less admire the enthusiasm and effort that artists exerted everywhere in the service of God, and of man. If we do find ourselves a little baffled by some of the imagery, we can turn with fellow feeling to St Bernard, whose famous words end this chapter:

> Why these ridiculous monstrosities, these weird deformed beauties and these beautiful deformities? What are these filthy apes doing in these cloisters, these fierce lions, monstrous centaurs, half-men, spotted tigers, fighting warriors, huntsmen sounding their horns? Here one sees many heads on one body, many bodies with but one head; here a quadruped, a fearsome beast with the cruppers of a horse . . . all in all such a mass of bizarre, awesome shapes, which occupy the mind that studies them rather than one's book so that one spends time considering them rather than upon meditation of God's law . . .
> In a letter to his friend William, Abbot of Thierry
> (see Coulton 1936)

Fig. 20 Saint-Séver Apocalypse. 'Mulier super Bestia' (Revelation 17 – 'And I saw a woman sit upon a scarlet coloured beast . . . and the woman was arrayed in purple and scarlet colour, and decked with gold and precious stones and pearls, having a golden cup in her hand full of abominations and filthiness of her fornication. And upon her forehead was name written: Mystery, Babylon the Great, the mother of harlots . . .'). The beast is amphisbænic but does not have the horns of the Biblical text.

6 *La femme aux serpents, l'homme aux serpents* and *l'avare*

Et vidit in alio loco viros ac mulieres, et vermes et serpentes comedentes eos
Visio Sancti Pauli, Latin text of the apocryphal Apocalypse of Paul

The love of money is the root of all evil
I. Timothy

On the right of the tympanum over the left entrance of the Puerta de las Platerías at Santiago de Compostela, supreme goal of pilgrims to the shrine of St James, is a fine carving of a distraught woman (*Fig. 21*). Her hair is long, one breast is bared, and in her lap she holds a skull – her lover's. She sits to the right of the Temptation of Christ, still in the position described by Aimery Picaud, the twelfth-century Cluniac monk of Parthenay-le-Vieux, and author of the indispensable *Pilgrim's Guide*. He says of her:

> Nec est oblivioni tradendum quod mulier quedam juxta dominicam Temptationem stat, tenens inter manus suas caput lecatoris sui fetidum, a marito proprio abscisum, osculans illut bis per diem, coacta a viro suo. O quam ingentem et admirabilem justiciam mulieris adulterate, omnibus narrandam!

> (Nor must we forget mention of the woman at the side of our Lord's Temptation. She is holding in her hands the foul head of her lover, cut off by her husband, and which at his command she must kiss twice a day. O what an admirable and terrible punishment for an adulterous woman, which all should know about!)

This is one of the few passages in the *Guide* where the author waxes lyrical and gleeful. His contemplation of the fallen woman's consternation is a typical monastic example of misogynistic celibacy taking it out on carnality.

In the lapidary museum of the cathedral there are two other stones which once formed part of the archivolt of the north porch (*Fig. 21*). On one is a woman whose breasts are being gnawed by snakes while a toothy monster bites her tongue. On the other is a man entwined with snakes, with a reptile biting his penis. Together with the adulterous woman on the tympanum, these carvings must have made a profound impression on pilgrims. Not that they were witnessing such scenes for the first time, however. *La femme aux serpents* and to a lesser extent *l'homme aux serpents* are to be found in northern Spain, south-west France, Auvergne and elsewhere. They feature on the façade of Lincoln Cathedral, both on Bishop Alexander's great frieze, and on the columns of the restored west door. The frieze includes the Torments of the Damned, in which a miser and an adulterous woman are attacked by snakes. One of the portal columns, restored during Buckler's nineteenth-century work, has two pairs of nude men and women; snakes bite at their genitals. Above them one of a pair of clothed figures has a scrip or purse, such as a miser is usually shown to carry. Unfortunately, we have no idea of what the original columns were like, but these modern versions so impress by the knowledge of Romanesque motifs which the nineteenth-century carver possessed that it is difficult to believe he had no original model to copy. The scraps of columns which survive in the cloister are not of the same design.

Towards the end of the first chapter we drew attention to the monastic preoccuption with the Capital Sins, and especially *Luxuria* and *Avaritia*. These loomed large in the minds of the brothers because of the vows they had taken of perpetual poverty and chastity. Imagery based on these sins, which would not only proclaim their views but make it clear to lay folk how they in turn should behave if they were to assure themselves of salvation, were naturally popular

Fig. 21 Santiago de Compostela (*centre*): woman with skull; Puerta de la Platerías: man and woman with snakes, from the north door, now in the Cathedral museum. The man's penis is bitten by a salamander, and the woman's tongue is pulled out by a monster.

with the monks. Most of the population being illiterate, didactic art would act as an immediate and effective reminder of what had been preached to them. One recollects François Villon's words about his mother:

Femme je suis povrette et ancienne
Qui riens ne scay; oncques lettre ne leus.
Au moustier voy dont suis paroissienne
Paradis paint, ou sont harpes et lus
Et ung enfer ou dampnez sont boullus.
L'ung me fait paour, l'autre joye et liesse;
La joye avoir me fay, haulte deesse.

(An old woman am I and poor, who nothing knows and has nothing read. At the parish church I see painted paradise with harps and lutes; and Hell, where the damned are boiled alive. Of the one I'm a-feared, t'other gives me joy and happiness. Grant me the latter, almighty Lady!)

Not all painting or carving is as easy to understand. At the end of the last chapter we experienced some difficulty in grasping the meaning of the more abstruse compositions involving centaur-sagittarii, and it goes without saying that one must exercise great care and circumspection in the analysis of iconography. We have quoted the warnings of Réau and Mâle, but it is pertinent to quote E.R. Gombrich and the cautionary advice he advances in *Symbolic Images: studies in the art of the Renaissance* (Gombrich 1972). Discussing the statue of Eros in London's Piccadilly Circus, erected as a memorial to the philanthropic second earl of Shaftesbury, Gombrich demonstrates the complexity of the symbolism which attends the statue. It represents a winged god, holding a bow and arrow, symbolic of Charity; but some see him as Cupid, god of love, careless in his aim, and an appropriate figure in this quarter of London frequented by ladies (and gentlemen) of easy virtue. To the V.E. Day crowds, he meant something different, and something different again to New Year's Day revellers. His bow and arrow point to the ground, a pun on Shaftesbury, which the designer strenuously denied. Around the base are ornamental marine monsters, for it was intended to be a public fountain. The Memorial Committee had other ideas, however, so there it stands – a memorial, a pagan god, a symbol, an object of fierce parochial pride. To the designer, a champion of modern English classicism, it was also a revolt against the Victorian 'coat and trousers' school of sculpture. But let us suppose an archaeologist had dug it up out of the ruins of Pompeii, or Cluny. Quite different theories would have been aired about its form, its siting, its symbolism. Gombrich remarked that images 'occupy a curious position somewhere between the statements of language which are intended to convey a meaning, and the things of nature to which we can only give a meaning'.

But what of things of art? In arriving at the meaning of a work of art we must carefully distinguish between the significance it has for us, and the significance it may have had for its creator. Had the Piccadilly statue been a Romanesque work, the equation it conveys to us of Eros = God of Love = Charity might instead have read Eros = pagan god of love = lust = damnation. Gombrich further warns us, with an amusing anecdote, to beware of working out whole codes of meaning in works of art. 'It is the danger of the cipher clerk,' he says, 'that he sees codes everywhere', and he cites the wartime telegram sent by the Danish atomic scientist Niels Bohr, in which he asked about 'Maud'. The recipient was convinced that this stood for Military Application of Uranium Disintegration, whereas Bohr was anxiously enquiring about Maud, his former nanny.

Duly warned, we soberly return to the business of interpreting Romanesque imagery, trying not to see pagan symbols everywhere challenging the Church, or deep meanings in routine vegetable ornamentation. At the same time we must take into account the fact that ecclesiastics did help the masons in the choice of designs, overseeing their work where necessary, and they may have instructed their artisans in the meaning and symbolism of certain compositions; and the masons, for their part, did use the patterns furnished by the illuminated manuscripts of the scriptoria. Equally, of course, we have to remember that masons, their horizons

Plate 27 Mason at work under the eye of a bishop, Gerona.

widened by much travelling, and very knowledgeable about matters pertaining to their craft – mechanics and physics, mathematics and engineering, materials and labour management – were very often better educated than the village priest they were serving; they might suggest to him motifs from a repertoire they had gained elsewhere. In the cloister of Gerona cathedral there are some interesting capitals: one shows masons and sculptors at work dressing stone while an ecclesiastic looks on (*Plate 27*); another has carpenters working with large planes; a third shows Cain killing Abel with a mason's dressing tool; and the fourth a woman suckling snakes in a scene of Hell where sinners are being boiled alive. Here then are two scenes from twelfth-century actuality, one from the biblical past, and one a visionary scene of the world-to come, a typical juxtaposition of literal and symbolic images such as one finds in Romanesque art.

It is of great assistance in the interpreting of past imagery to have contemporary written evidence, although some, unfortunately, is of less service than one would wish. Durandus, writing in the thirteenth century, gives an account of the symbolism of architecture (Frans Carlsson in 1976 goes to similar lengths – Carlsson 1976). Durandus, for instance, would have us believe that the columns of the church are the bishops and doctors who spiritually sustain the church, the bases are the apostolic bishops, the capitals are the words of the holy scriptures, the tiles of the roof are the soldiers who protect the church, and so on. G.R. Lewis, to whom we are indebted for his lithographs of Shobdon and Kilpeck, added a text of Victorian sanctimoniousness which repeats the sentiments of Durandus (Lewis 1842, 1852). We are on surer ground when we examine the symbolism of *la femme aux serpents*, however. Some contemporary texts quoted below leave us in no doubt as to the significance of this motif, and the evidence that snake-bitten acrobats, mermaids, exhibitionists and other figures are extensions of the same idea becomes cumulative. There is a vast genre that takes in the exhibitionist bifid mermaid on the doorway of Santa Maria, Zamora (*see Fig. 18a*), the Archingeay exhibitionist acrobatic female (*see Fig. 23*), the copulating couples inside Carennac or Mauriac, the snake-bitten sinners of Moissac, Beaulieu, Charlieu, Lincoln, and many, many more. Sometimes examples are obscured by an iconographical shorthand but, provided one has the key, their meaning can be reached. The purpose underlying this imagery, in its manifold varieties, is to expose the moral view that sexual laxity is evil and will be visited by the most dire punishments.

One of the links unifying the *Luxuria* genre is the use of snakes and reptiles to suggest revulsion and retribution. It is probably a universal human trait to shudder at the thought of snakes and like creatures touching our bare bodies, especially in countries where there are no reptilian creatures. We may today no longer cringe at the idea of handling lizards and tortoises, since pet-shops have familiarised us with them, but medieval folk believed Leviticus XI, which states that all manner of creeping things, and even moles, ferrets, chameleons, snails and mice are unclean, and that whosoever touches them is defiled.

Yet the snake in antiquity often had a beneficent role, and the Romanesque artists had a rich symbolic heritage on which to draw. Classical carvings show us Apollo struggling with Python, Jason with the serpent, Herakles with Hydra, and the Gorgons with their hissing snake-locks; but, on the other hand, snakes pulled the chariots of Athena and Cybele, they adorned the caduceus of Hermes and were the attribute of Aesculapius the healer; a snake was the oracular Pythoness, and was a protective family Genius. The Old Testament metamorphosed Satan into a snake to tempt Eve, but later it created the miraculous snake rod of Aaron; a brazen serpent was a prefiguration of Christ (Wisdom of Solomon, Apocrypha, XVI, 6, and John III, 14–15). Early Christian funerary art employed Classical serpent designs to illustrate the struggle against the Devil; and northern barbarian art influenced Insular Manuscript art, often employing zoomorphic interlacings, especially of ribbon sea-snakes chasing and biting one another.

The negative aspect of the serpent is the one which prevails in Romanesque art, to the extent that one begins to believe that it was not a mere symbol of the torments the damned could expect, but that it was to be taken literally; men actually believed that real snakes would devour them in Hell, and visionaries wrote accounts of the very event:

> Crapauz, colovres et tortues
> Lor pendent aux mamelles nues
>
> (Toads, serpents and tortoises dangle from their naked breasts)

exclaimed Etienne de Fougères, Bishop of Rennes 1168–78, former chaplain to Henry II of England, and in his youth a poet with a good reputation. His 'Livres des manières', from which this quotation comes, is a didactic poem about contemporary morals.

A monk of Saint Victor wrote:

> la courtisane passe comme le reste. Celle qui divisait sa belle chevelure avec des peignes d'or, qui colorait son front et son visage, qui ornait ses doigts de bagues, la voici devenue la proie des vers et la nourriture de la couleuvre; la couleuvre se roule autour de son cou et la vipère écrase ses seins.
> (quoted by Beigbeder, *Lexique des Symboles*)
>
> (the harlot suffers like the others. She who was wont to part her beautiful hair with golden combs, who painted her brows and face, who bedecked her fingers with rings, has become a prey to worms, and the food for serpents; a serpent winds itself around her neck, and a viper crushes her breasts.)

The agony was not only restricted to whores and fornicators; St Alberic (*d.*1109), one of the founders of Cîteaux, would have it visited upon women who refused to wet-nurse orphans or motherless children, or who only pretended to nourish them; in his *Vision*, child brides and unworthy mothers were also included.

Plate 28 Saint-Jouin-de-Marnes: façade figure.

The couplet by the Bishop of Rennes was not the literary origin of the woman tormented by snakes; he was merely verbalising the import of the many carvings found in European churches which depict such a scene. The literary source goes back a long way, possibly to the *Visio Sancti Pauli*, St Paul's Revelation of Heaven and Hell, texts of which survive in Syrian, Greek, Latin, French, English, Provençal and Italian. The earliest Greek text is fourth-century AD, and at least 21 Latin editions survive in whole or in part. It was an extremely popular and wide-spread work. In the Syriac text, the sun and moon complain to God about man's adultery, fornication, avarice, sorcery and witchcraft; St Paul visits the various heavens and the City of God, and is then transported to the lower deep, where the sun sets, and to the ocean which surrounds the earth, thence to where the fires of Hell burn for ever; and here he witnesses the agonies of the damned, including those of an adulterous priest, a sybaritic bishop, a glutton-ous and adulterous dean sunk up to his chin in blood and weeping in bitterness, as worms wriggle from his mouth; in another part of Hell Paul sees a worm which gnaws at men and women as they roast in a devouring flame. In one of the Latin texts, misers and usurers, both male and female, are forced to eat their tongues, while young women all dressed in black amid pitch and sulphur and fire and dragons, entangled in writhing snakes, with vipers at their throats, endure eternal torment for not being virgins when they married, or for foully aborting or killing their offspring and feeding them to the pigs and dogs with never a sign of repentance; in yet another part of Hell Paul observes worms and serpents devouring men and women, and a bishop being assailed by demons because of his carnal appetite, his meanness, avarice, trickery and pride. One wonders whether Hieronymus Bosch, Brueghel the Elder and Dante were aware of these texts when they each created their picture of the Inferno.

There were other texts, like the seventh-century *Ladder of Divine Ascent*, in which John Climacus (or Scholasticus) discusses the body and chastity, and the 'many-faced snake of sensuality'. Popular in the eleventh and twelfth centuries (and still being translated in the nineteenth, e.g. at Mount St Bernard Abbey, Leicestershire) it was much illustrated, with personifications of virtues and vices, clothed more or less in Classical garb. Its burden was

Plate 29 Deyrançon: woman attacked by snakes and monsters.

Plate 30 Huesca: cloister capital, much eroded *femme aux serpents.*

that the monk, or lay Christian, must climb the ladder of virtue to reach the topmost rung, overcoming sinful desires on the way. The symbolism of a ladder was not new. Jacob's ladder of the Old Testament found a new form in the Surrey church of Chaldon, where it appears as the Purgatorial Ladder or Ladder of Salvation. The idea of a Soul Ladder found favour with the Gnostics and Pythagoreans, and the ladder played a role in Orphic cults (as it was to do later in Freemasonry). There is an interesting terra cotta, found in Italy, of ancient origin, of a splay-legged exhibitionist female, sitting on a pig and holding a ladder in her left hand (see Chapter 10, *Plate 58*).

Probably the most influential of all writings were those of St Augustine of Hippo. The Rule adopted by the Canons Regular was derived from a letter he wrote. We shall examine at greater length in the next chapter his disgust for the flesh. At this stage it is enough to note the terrible morbidity of his attitude to sex.

The Bible itself was rarely a direct source for Romanesque artists, who went instead to the commentaries and other writings of the Fathers of the Church, and it is by a roundabout route that biblical admonitions came to the notice of those responsible for the didactic, sculptural or other decorative programmes of churches. Biblical texts which fulminate against loose women abound, from the taboos established in Leviti-

cus (and which include incest, sodomy and bestiality, on the part of both sexes), through the visionary expostulations of Ezekiel about 'whoredoms', to the description of Rome in the Book of Revelations as 'the Whore of Babylon'. In the Book of Wisdom or Ecclesiasticus of the Apocrypha we read:

> Behold not every body's beauty, and sit not in the midst of women, for from garments cometh a moth and from women wickedness . . .

> . . . Use not much the company of a woman that is a singer, lest thou be taken with her attempts. Gaze not on a maid that thou fall not by those things that are precious in her. Give not thy soul unto harlots that thou lose not thine inheritance . . . Turn away thine eye from a beautiful woman and look not upon another's beauty, for many have been deceived by the beauty of a woman . . .

Naturally, the punishment for those who fail to observe these commandments is 'creeping things, beasts and worms'.

For St Paul, marriage was a last resort for those unable to restrain their sexual impulses: 'it is good for a man not to touch a woman, nevertheless to avoid fornication let every man have his own wife' (I Cor. VII), and he urges modesty, even a dreary drabness on women (I Tim. II, 9–13). As for men, he merely urges them: 'not to commit fornication as some of them committed (in the wilderness) and fell in one day three and twenty thousand' (I Cor. X).

The misogyny of the Bible is incredible, but the Fathers of the Church strove to exceed it. The ascetic ideal, preached in early times in Syria and Egypt, was perpetuated by St Jerome, who repeatedly equated luxury and the flesh-pots with lust, condemning wine drinking and the eating of delicious food, and extolling the benefits of chastity. But the more the Desert Hermits and Saints, and the monks who tried to follow their example, tried to repress their desires, the more they were assailed by terrible dreams and visitations. St Jerome punished his body, as St Simeon Stylites and St Anthony had tried to do, by living the hermit life, and, as a result, dwelt on the temptations that harrowed him:

> How often, when I was established in the desert and in that vast solitude which is scorched by the sun's heat and affords a savage habitation for monks, did I think myself among the delights of Rome! I would sit alone because I was filled with bitterness. My limbs were roughly clad in

sackcloth – an unlovely sight. My neglected skin had taken on the appearance of an Ethiopian's body. Daily I wept, daily I groaned, and whenever insistent slumber overcame my resistance I bruised my awkward bones upon the bare earth. Of food and water I say nothing, since even the sick drink only cold water, and to get any cooked food is a luxury. There was I, therefore, who from fear of Hell had condemned myself to such a prison, with only scorpions and wild beasts as companions. Yet was I often surrounded by dancing girls. My face was pale from fasting, and my mind was hot with desire in a body as cold as ice. Though my flesh, before its tenant, was already as good as dead, the fires of passion kept boiling within me.

Plate 31 Champagne: another eroded *femme aux serpents*.

The monks of Europe, seven centuries later, more comfortably installed in stone-built abbeys, monasteries and priories, copying and meditating on the works of the great teachers of Christianity like St Jerome, underwent the same torments and visions, enhanced perhaps by the greater luxury of their lives and the nearness of the outside world. Many of them wrote accounts of their afflictions, in which demons figure prominently as they had done since St Athanasius' account of the life of St Anthony, almost a quarter of which is a discourse on demonology. Eleventh- and twelfth-century monks were frequently attacked by Satan, their monasteries besieged by the Devil and his hosts. The image we have of the Devil, with bestial face, cloven hoof, horns and a tail, is an eleventh-century creation of south-west France; previously he assumed the form of a beautiful young woman (to St Anthony), an angel with flaming hair (to St Simeon Stylites), even the form of Christ Himself (to St Pachomius). The carvings of Vézelay show hideous images of Satan (born of nightmare, in Mâle's estimation).

Demons and snakes afflict the damned in Hell, then – the Bible providing many references to snakes (and toads) as hellish creatures. Even oblique remarks as 'Ye serpents, ye generation of vipers, how can ye escape the damnation of hell?' show a connection and a sense of horror at the punishments in store. So Last Judgment scenes and other Romanesque carvings depict serpents winding round devils and sinners, often biting at sensitive parts of the body.

At times the snakes encoiling a human, just like the foliage tendrils and vinescrolls in which humans, birds and animals are often caught up and enmeshed, may merely represent the snares and temptations of life, the constant struggle against its difficulties and vicissitudes, with no implied fight against carnality. Beasts which symbolise good, such as the lion with its tail over its back, or the eagle, often fight snakes and can be seen simply as good versus evil. Indeed serpents, coiled or in knots, often occur on their own, imparting an air of evil but nothing more specific. Anthropomorphic knot-figures may be a kind of shorthand for the human entangled in snakes or foliage, implying that the body is subject to earthly restraints and that to be free the spirit must shake them off. It has sometimes been stated that Celtic-type knotwork, interlacings and plaitings may have symbolic significance. One cannot be sure that they are anything more than patterns taken from weaving or osier work. However, the anthropomorphic knot-figures which accompany the splay-legged acrobat or squatter at Corullón, the striking example with a beast's head on the *linteau en bâtière* (Auvergnat-style pentagonal granite lintel) at the little pilgrim route church of Barbadelo, and the even more impressive one on the little-known cross-shaft in the graveyard of Bully's Acre in the grounds of the Dublin Royal Hospital, on the site of an old Irish monastery taken over by the Knights Hospitallers, seem to be more than a whimsical 'doodling', and may once have carried a powerful message concerning the toils and coils of Satan, which we carry within ourselves and are our own burden of guilt and punishment.

Whatever the case, some monks could not wait until Judgment Day and were not willing to postpone punishment until the next world, especially for sins committed within the cloister. Sometime after 1140, Abbot Ailred of Rievaulx recorded an event at the Gilbertine convent of Watton, where a wayward oblate nun fell in love with a handsome monk. 'The winding serpent slithered his way into both their breasts and gladdened the vitals of the man', in consequence whereof they 'sowed the garden of love'. Their clandestine meetings could not long continue without discovery, and the sudden disappearance of the monk confirmed suspicions. The nun was forced to confess her love, and the nuns were so outraged that they suggested extreme punishments: to be skinned alive, burned, or roasted over a slow fire. In the event, she was merely beaten, shackled and fettered and thrown into the convent prison. When her belly began to swell, the nuns decided to send her packing after her lover, the pregnant girl having told them, under duress no doubt, where to find him. Instead of pairing them off and sending them in disgrace into the secular world, however, the monk was seized, thrown on the floor and a knife was thrust into his hand. He was forced to castrate himself. Then one of the more zealous nuns snatched up the bloody organs and thrust them in his mistress' mouth. Abbot Ailred praised not their deed, but their zeal in protecting their chastity (Erickson 1976. Erickson gives a historical account of Christian attitudes to women.)

When St Bernard wrote to his friend the Abbot William of St Thierry condemning the wealth of sculptures in Benedictine churches (see end of Chapter 5) he added: 'For God's sake, if men are not ashamed of these follies, why at least do they not shrink from the expense?'. He describes the deformities in general terms only, and makes no specific mention of Last Judgments, Torments of the Damned, or *la femme aux serpents*, and though his attack is against the luxury of art designed for the 'concupiscence of the eyes', he did not expressly forbid the execution of minatory or educational carving meant for the instruction of the common people. He realised that there were sculptures which would 'excite the devotion of the common people by carnal means, not being able to do so by spiritual ones'. He would not, therefore, have failed to understand nor have discommended the carving of the tortures of the luxurious, the concupiscent, the avaricious, on churches which served as places of worship and instruction for the laity. He probably found himself in the dilemma of having to execrate what he regarded as celebrations of impiety on corbel and capital carvings, while at the same time agreeing with the motives behind them; his attack was, of course, principally aimed at monastic establishments, but at least one Cistercian church (the abbey church of Vallbona de les Monges, Lérida) does have such corbel carvings. It goes without saying that he disapproved of entertainers.

When we turn to the carvings of *la femme aux serpents*, the embodiment of some of the texts we have been considering, we notice that a number of themes have come together to produce this composition. First, there is Woman – the temptress, the seducer, the Devil's instrument; next, the snake – emblem of evil, the incarnation of Satan. These two themes would produce figures of females being bitten in various parts of the body as a warning about the danger of lust. But the characteristic feature of *la femme aux serpents* is that she is being bitten on the breasts, so that she appears to be suckling the snakes, toads, tortoises, salamanders, and so on. In other words she also takes her origin from the Classical figures of Gaia, Terra, Cybele, and other goddesses who embody the idea of bountiful nature, with contributory elements provided by the bare-breasted Cretan snake-goddess or, perhaps even more remotely, by Mesopotamian deities like the Canaanite goddess flanked by prancing goats, holding a palm leaf. Holding such a palm leaf is a Mother Goddess figure on an Exultet Roll. The Exultet Rolls, so-called because the word *Exultet* ('Rejoice') appears frequently in the text, are eleventh- and twelfth-century psalms of praise with musical accompaniment, on which illustrations of Terra (always decently clothed, but suckling various creatures) appear opposite the line 'Let the earth rejoice'. On the Byzantine-inspired Exultet Rolls of Monte Cassino, plumed women sit on hillocks amid palm trees, their hands graciously and generously outstretched as they suckle bulls or bullocks and coiled snakes. A Roll from Bari shows this scene, while another from the Casa Natense Library in Rome depicts Terra suckling a bullock and a stag. Yet others have Terra sitting beneath the Hand of God, suckling lions or does.

Earlier forms of Terra with snakes appear on Carolingian ivories. At the bottom of a book

Plate 32 Saint-Palais: woman suckling toads while snakes bite her ears.

cover of *c.* AD 870, possibly from Rheims, now in the Munich Staatsbibliothek (Swarzenski 1954, 1974; Leclercq-Kadaner 1975; Goldschmidt 1969), is the Resurrection of the Dead, with Roma (or Abraham or God) raising a hand in blessing, flanked by a horned figure of Oceanus, and Terra with snakes holding a cornucopia; above the Resurrection is a Crucifixion under which is the conquered Satan in the form of a writhing serpent. (On the ninth-century south cross at Monasterboice in Ireland, knots of serpents can be discerned above and below the Crucifixion.) Another ivory book cover, in the Victoria and Albert Museum, shows a Crucifixion with a snake writhing below; the Marys at the tomb and other scenes appear, together with Oceanus and Terra, the latter kissing a snake-bodied monster (Goldschmidt 1969). Terra is to be found in the ninth-century Sacramentary of Saint-Denis suckling human beings (Adam and Eve?) below Christ in Majesty (Swarzenski 1974).

One of the few Romanesque carvings of Terra was executed in the late twelfth century on the portal of San Marco in Venice, suckling snakes, with stylised palm fronds waving round her (Crichton 1954). At Benevento she suckles a stag and a bullock (Giess 1959); a twelfth-century miniature depicts Christ accompanied by Terra with snakes and a horned Oceanus on a dolphin (Böckler 1924); Adhémar reports carved examples of Terra at Arles (Adhémar 1937). As late as the end of the thirteenth century, a woman suckling a pig and a snake was painted on the apse of the church of St George at Limburg-am-Lahn with the legend *Terra* (Adhémar) (*Fig. 22*); and on the famous bronze doors of San Zeno in Verona a woman offering her breasts to two children stands beside another offering her breasts to a fish and a winged monster with a saurian tail (Leclercq-Kadaner). A different tradition is exemplified in the ninth-century Byzantine manuscript of Mount Athos where a woman suckles a unicorn (Leclercq-Kadaner, who gives other examples).

The Romanesque obsession with the punishment of lust produced hundreds of carvings of different sorts. We can only show a few here, with emphasis on that motif known as *la luxure* (*Luxuria*) on the Continent, i.e. *la femme aux serpents* (we deal with other forms in the text, e.g. mermaids). They are to be found as far north as Scandinavia and as far south as the Italian embarcation ports for the Holy Land. Some are found in the Rhineland, and one has been discovered in Ireland. Here are some examples (*see Fig. 57*).

With snakes

France

Angers (Saint Aubin), Archingeay, Ardentes, Arthous, Aujac, Aulnay, Barret, Beaulieu, Bénévent-l'Abbaye, Biron, Blesle, Bordeaux, Bourg-Argental, Bozouls, Brioude, Brive, Champagne, Charlieu, Cluny, Cognac, Cressac, Deyrançon, Foussignac, Gourdon, Guitinières, La Jarne, Lavaudieu, Lescar, Lescure, Mailhat, Marignac, Mauriac, Melle, Moissac, Montmorillon, Mouchan, Ôo (Oô), Parthenay (Notre-Dame-la-Coudre, Parthenay-le-Vieux), Preuilly-sur-Claize, Riom-ès-Montagnes, Roquesérière, Semur-en-Auxois, Semur-en-Brionnais, Sémelay, Saint-André-le-Bagé, Saint-Christophe-de-Bardes, Saint-Genès-de-Lombaud, Saint-Georges-de-Montagne, Saint-Jouin-de-Marnes, Saint-Léger-en-Montbrillais, Saint-Palais, Saint-Pons, Saint-Sever-de-Rustan, Targon, Toulouse (Saint-Sernin), Urcel, Valence, Vézelay, Vienne, Vouvant

Plate 33 Toulouse Museum: from Oô, surely the most explicit *femme aux serpents*.

Spain

Estella, Gerona, Huesca, León, Miranda de Ebro, Olopte, San Juan de la Peña (now in the Huesca museum), San Quirce, Sangüesa, Santiago, Sos del Rey Católico, Tudela, Vallejo

Germany

Freiberg (near Dresden), Regensburg, Soest (Santa Maria zur Höh)

Italy

Bari, Turin (Sagra di San Michele)

Ireland

Glendalough

With snakes and toads

France

Angers (Saint-Aubin), Charlieu, Moissac

Spain

La Coruña, Sangüesa

With toads

France

Montmorillon, Targon

Spain

San Martín de Mondoñedo

With monsters

France

Angers (Saint-Nicolas, now in Le Mans museum), Bordeaux (Saint-André), Cluny, Lavaudieu, Lescar, Marignac, Melle (Saint-Hilaire), Saint-Léger-en-Montbrillais, Semur-en-Auxois, Semur-en-Brionnais, Urcel

Scandinavian examples

Väte, Sweden – reminiscent of the Saint-Jouin-de-Marnes figure
Bråby, Denmark (breasts under her arms, like the Birr sheela) suckling two very convoluted, plumed snakes carved on the font
Gosmer, Denmark (a clothed woman with long braids between two lions which gently bite her tress-like breasts
Vester Egede, Denmark, (upside down on the front suckling two decorative beasts with coiled tails)

Fig. 22 (a) Terra, mother-goddess at Limburg; (b) font detail at Vester Egede, Denmark; (c) tympanum fragment in Viborg Museum; (d) long-tressed figure from Urcel.

? unknown provenance, now in Viborg museum, a fragment from Jutland (an armless female, standing on a sphere from which foliage issues, suckles two monsters: is she Terra?)

The motif of *la femme aux serpents* first began to be noticed and written about at the time that sheela-na-gigs were occupying the minds of Irish antiquaries (see Desmoulins 1845). Emile Mâle considered that the motif originated in Languedoc, those at Moissac and Saint Sernin, Toulouse, being the earliest, in his opinion. Others suggested it came from the other side of the Pyrenees, from the narthex of San Isidoro in León, now known as the Panteón de los Reyes, where a naked woman gripping two serpents, which fly to bite her head or hair while two other snakes with beast-headed tails pass between her legs to bite her breasts is dated to 1063 by Shapiro (Shapiro 1977). Certainly *la femme aux serpents* is widespread in Languedoc, northern Spain and western France (a distribution to which we shall have further cause to refer anon), less so in eastern France, and rarely found in the corridor of Lombardy-Provence-Roussillon-Catalonia, which has a distinct Romanesque art of its own and where corbel carving and exhibitionists are rare, *Luxuria* being represented by mermaids (mostly double-tailed). In any case, in this latter area the subject does not receive the same attention as in the west.

Being so widespread a motif it is not surprising that it should produce a variety of forms. The woman may be standing (Champagne, Santiago, Moissac, Beaulieu, Charlieu); squatting (Saint-Léger-de-Montbrillais,

Semur-en-Brionnais, Vallejo); kneeling (Ardentes); recumbent (Saint-Christophe-de-Bardes, Aujac, Cognac) or splay-legged (Deyrançon). She may be accompanied by human or demonic tormentors (Ardentes, Bordeaux, Blesle, Guitinières, Saint-Georges-de-Montagne, Vouvant).

She may also be exhibitionist. We have already mentioned the startling corbel at Archingeay (*Fig. 23*). At Saint-Georges-de-Montagne she exhibits a small round vulva, and she displays at Bénévent l'Abbaye. But perhaps the most astonishing and most overtly sexual carving of all is from the Pyrenean rural church of Oô (now in the Musée des Augustins, Toulouse) (*Plate 33*). Carved in false relief on a large flat stone, like many Irish sheelas, and apparently not destined for use as a capital or corbel, is a nude woman from whose vagina, with its large and bulging vulva, issues a large snake which bites her left breast. The power of this carving lies not only in the shock afforded at the sight of a snake issuing from the *labia majora*, but in the sexual duality bestowed by a phallic snake. There are other examples of female exhibitionists accompanied by male phallic signs: a grotesque female exhibitionist introduces enor-

Fig. 23 Archingeay: *femme aux serpents* exhibitionist.

mous male genitals to her comparatively small vulva at Larumbe; and the sheelas of Dunnaman and Cloghan castles seem to have male organs beneath their vulvas. But the Oô carving in its explicit sexuality can only be rivalled by the *phalloi* that dangle obscenely from corbels at Artaíz, Ardillières, Loupiac, Sainte-Colombe and Vandré (*see Fig. 68*); a post-Romanesque example mentioned in Chapter 2 occupies a spandrel of a window at Smithstown Castle (Weir 1980) (*see Plate 73*).

To anyone unacquainted with the frankness of Romanesque masons in their striving for telling effects and clear lessons, the Oô figure and the stark *phalloi* in these places of worship come as something of a shock. They cannot be passed over with ease (or with the euphemistic sort of explanation employed by the Victorian lithographer G.R. Lewis when he described the Kilpeck sheela as a 'Fool cutting his way through to his heart' – Lewis 1842). These are explicitly sexual images which must have received the approbation of the clergy on whose churches they appear. It is much later in time that we find the village priest becoming sensitive to their possibly lubricious nature and ordering an expurgation, as at Kilpeck, or Riom-ès-Montagnes (where a hacked-away capital gives evidence, enough being left for us to recreate the original). Prurience develops late.

Theologians expounded the view that sinners would be punished through the organs of their lusts; Gregory the Great, for example, quoted Ezekiel and Romans to this effect. The image of *la femme aux serpents* would have been very much in keeping with this view, as were those horrific scenes at Saintes, Biron, Barret, Saint-Fort-sur-Gironde and elsewhere, where monsters hold both male and females upside down, their legs pulled wide apart, as they bite their groins (*Plate 34*).

Luxuria figures were joined by other subjects devoted to the idea of concupiscence exposed and chastised. A complete corbel table still surviving is devoted to the theme at Saint-Palais, where a monster bites a horizontal female exhibitionist; other carvings show a male exhibitionist, a female head clutching its hair, an ithyphallic cat, a monster with two heads in its jaws, a kissing couple, an acrobatic female exhibitionist, a megaphallic male clutching his

Plate 34 Barret: *femme aux serpents* on the right, and anthropophagous monster in the centre.

beard, and a woman suckling toads with snakes crawling into her ears (Valin 1976) (*see Plates 2 and 32*). Alternatively, she stands in a single composition, as on the Vézelay capital (*Fig. 24*); here she tears at one breast in a gesture of remorse as a snake bites her belly.

Vézelay has other *Luxuria* capitals: one has Satan whispering the Latin word *time* ('Be afraid') into a woman's ear; on another he plays her like a musical instrument while a jongleur, his accomplice, adds his song to the music of Hell; other musicians join a woman in the clutches of a lubricious devil; and two demons are in company with a monk, tugging his beard. One of the Tavant frescoes depicts a rare subject – a woman committing suicide on account of remorse.

Luxuria may also be figured with snakes that do not actually touch her. They merely coil round her at Ars-sur-le-Né, Maranges and Jaca (*Fig. 25*); at Olcóz she feeds a snake from a cup.

Fig. 24 Capital at Vézelay: a woman tormented by snakes pulls at her breasts.

She is also found standing between two affronted beasts which bite at her ears in a familiar composition of ancient origin (which has given us various versions of Daniel in the Lions' Den, or Gilgamesh and Lions, or the unknown Swedish man of the Torslunda plaques, found on the Sutton Hoo purse lid). An unusual scene is enacted on a corbel at Pecharromán: a grinning devil carries a naked woman over his shoulder, presumably to Hell, both entwined by a serpent which bites her arm. *Luxuria* is rarely displayed as an aged, grotesque female, but one is to be found at Cambes, where a toothy pockmarked hag leers down from a corbel above the doorway,

and another at Foussais, where she matches a toad on the opposite archivolt.

Luxuria is one of the Seven Deadly, Mortal or Capital Sins – Anger, Sloth, Greed, Gluttony, Pride, Vainglory, Idolatry, Envy, Lust. (The number and composition of the list has varied from time to time.) Prudentius, a Latin poet writing in Spain in the fifth century AD, in his *Psychomachia*, a parable taken and expanded from Tertullian, personified the Vices and their opposite numbers, the Virtues, and depicted them in a deadly battle from which the Virtues emerged triumphant (Katzenellenbogen 1939, Bloomfield 1967). The poem is long and makes dull reading today, but it fired the imagination of twelfth-century sculptors, especially in Aquitaine. Celebrated scenes representing the fight between Largitas and Avaritia, Pudicia and Libido, Temperencia and Luxuria, Humilitas and Superbia, Pietas and Discordia, Misericordia and Invidia, Patiencia and Ira, Modestia and Ebrietas, cover the archivolts of Aulnay, Corme-Royal, Chadenac, Fénioux, Fontaines d'Ozillac, Pont-l'Abbé-d'Arnoult and Saint-Symphorien-de-Broue. The *Psychomachia* was to have a very wide influence from, for example, Auvergne to Herefordshire and Northamptonshire to Bavaria, but the frequency with which it originated carvings in the Saintonge area of south-west France ties in very closely with the occurrence of exhibitionists, a link in the chain of our argument that the latter are to be associated with, if not actually identified with, the *Luxuria* theme. If we take another area, to support this proposition, we find that in

Fig. 25 Jaca, Brive, La Charité-sur-Loire (after Baltrušaitis).

Herefordshire and Shropshire, where there is the highest concentration of exhibitionists in Britain, there are also many scenes from the *Psychomachia*, e.g. the armed warriors of Kilpeck, Shobdon and Eardisley, the Claverley wall-painting. It seems ironic, incidentally, that St Bernard never knew the significance of the 'fighting warriors' he so roundly disparaged; had he known their connection with a very moral work, no doubt he would have tempered his criticism.

Besides the snakes and toads that bite her, *la femme aux serpents* has another salient feature: her long hair, sometimes in the form of snaking tresses, sometimes as *fouriaus* – the silken or muslin bags in which was stuffed the shorn hair sold to milliners by poor women, to be sold for wear by the rich (Goddard 1927; for an illustration see Viollet-le-Duc 1872–75, Vol 3 fig. 5). *Babylonia Meretrix* at Chauvigny exemplifies not only Babylon as castigated by Isaiah, but also the Great Whore of Babylon (i.e. Rome) of the Apocalypse, for she holds in one hand 'the cup of her abominations and filthiness of her fornications'. The 'mother of harlots' wears a voluminous robe, which causes one writer to say that she is 'plus obscène qu'un nu' (Oursel 1975); above her shoulder is the inscription which tells us whom she represents. Without that inscription, however, we could have made a guess about her, for her hair furnishes the clue. Long hair, as we have seen in our study of mermaids, is a sexual symbol (see Leach 1958); the tonsure undergone by nuns and monks marks their return to a pre-pubertal state of virginity and purity. In many Eastern religions a refusal to cleanse the hair, and to allow it to become filthy and matted, is a sign of great holiness, underlining a person's farewell to pride in personal appearance with a hint of self-mortification. For similar reasons, medieval monks did not wash or change their habit, developing, no doubt, thereby an 'odour of sanctity'! Generally speaking, however, in most countries and cultures long hair tends to be equated with strong sexuality, short hair with moderation, and shorn hair with celibacy.

In Romanesque art many corbels portray heads with tresses or *fouriaus* or some other elaborate hairstyle, like that of Argenton-Château, as a shorthand symbol of the sin of *Luxuria*. Eve, the supreme temptress, is often

Fig. 26 Châteaumeillant.

depicted with long hair, e.g. on the font at Hook Norton, where her hair style is identical with that of the Castle Widenham sheela. Long *fouriaus* are fastened to the heads of the snake-bitten female figures of Champagne, Saint-Hilaire-des-Loges, and Sacra de San Michele at Turin; an elegant dancer with *fouriaus* sticks out her tongue impudently at Bouresse; at Nonac a female exhibitionist pulls her long locks; and one finds other tress-pullers at Brem-sur-Mer, Saint-Martin-de-Sescas and Saint-Wandrille.

Hair symbolically and literally provides demons, often themselves with flaming hair, with a convenient handhold for dragging sinners down to Hell, at Nohant-Vicq, Jugazan, Saint-Martin-de-Sescas, Targon and Olcóz. Beasts also find hair an attractive mouthful at Saint-Vallier, Brive and elsewhere. The angel driving Adam and Eve from the Garden pulls them by the hair at Notre-Dame-du-Port in Clermont-Ferrand. Beards also provide handholds, either for devils, or for other sinners.

Perhaps Goliath's hair acts as a mere expedient for David, as he prepares to cut off the giant's hair on a fresco from Taüll, now in the

Plate 35a Tuscania, San Pietro. (Photo: C.E.S.C.M.)

museum of Catalan art in Barcelona. But there is deeper significance in the brilliant Aulnay carving of Delilah snipping off Samson's hair, for thereby she deprived him of his strength and virility – presumably a symbolic reference to the sapping of his strength by more feminine wiles.

Lastly, hair may also express the aggressiveness of sexuality. The Gorgon's chevelure of hissing snakes, a model for many fearsome corbel heads, retained its awful magic power even when the head was cut off, thus underlining the symbolic interconnection of hair, snakes and sex.

The attention we have devoted to *la femme aux serpents* and female *Luxuria* motifs would seem to imply that only women were pilloried for sexual crime and that men were regarded as innocent victims, unpunished for their conniv-

ance and participation in fornication. That is not so. Medieval clergy and their masons were just as anxious to warn the male population of the dangers of hellfire, and female exhibitionists are aimed at them quite as much as at women. More particularly, male symbols of concupiscence outnumber the female, and one of these is appropriately enough *l'homme aux serpents*.

L'homme aux serpents derives, no doubt, from Serpentarius, the Classical figure who gave his name to an ancient constellation. He can be found on Romanesque ivories (Goldschmidt 1923) and in manuscripts (Dodwell 1954, Swarzenski 1974). In stone carving, good examples of *l'homme aux serpents* can be found at Solignac and in Corsica, at Courpière, Riom-ès-Montagnes, Limalonges, La Charité-sur-Loire, Mauriac, Rodez, Thiers, Romans, Tournus, San Miguel at Daroca, and Pavia (where the snake is half dragon). Dated to before 1063, the earliest example is probably that of San Isidoro, León, where he takes the shape of an *orans* monk round whom two huge serpentine beasts coil to bite his head, while he protrudes his tongue, a sign of his concupiscence (see Chapter 9); another orans whose arms are bitten by snakes is at the austere edifice of Bernay, possibly carved before 1070. At Amboise a man entwined with snakes stands beside a *tornatrice* and a human-headed fish; and at Souillac a naturalistic pair of naked men, each with a hand in the mouth of a lion, are wreathed in snakes. A very Classical male entwined by a snake, with an eagle on his head signifying, in all probability, the victory or vengeance of God, features at Sessa Arunca, Naples on a carved stone *ambo* (a preaching pulpit peculiar to central Italy). But the most amazing man with snakes is to be found on the church of San Pietro at Tuscania (formerly Toscanella) in Viterbo (*Plate 36b*). To the right of the rose window of this twelfth-century church there is a long, elegant two-light window which is framed by a low-relief composition. On the sill is the tricephalic head of Satan, who clasps a coiled snake to his bosom, almost as Dante was to imagine him in the *Inferno*. The central bearded face protrudes its tongue, and the two profile faces spew climbing plants, in whose S-loops are framed the symbols of the capital sins. The plants climb the jambs and round the lintel, to be swallowed by another tricephalos, whose central face also protrudes its

74

tongue. Beast heads support the corbel table, and baleful dogs glare down from each side of the rose window. Nothing in Romanesque sculpture approaches this carving in design or execution.

La femme aux serpents is rarely chosen to represent *Luxuria* in manuscripts. We find, instead, for instance, bedded couples, as on the British Museum's copy of the Silos *Beatus* (Williams 1977), just as one finds them in later Gothic carvings at Amiens or Chartres. In the *Psychomachia* (an illustrated copy, with some 46 tinted drawings, was produced at St Albans Abbey *c*.1120, and is now in the British Museum – Cotton Titus D. XVI), *Luxuria* is always clothed in Classical dress; and she is richly garbed in a late eleventh-century treatise on the *Eight Vices* from Moissac. We may surmise that manuscripts were not intended for the general public, but for monks only, so that explicit images were not necessary, and perhaps this is also why few naked women and exhibitionists appear in cloister carvings. In the Moissac illustration, however, *Luxuria* loosens her girdle and a devil removes her headdress, as a man approaches her with evident lustful intent. A monster with two bird-heads curls a tongue round her foot, and with pincers pinches the toe of one of her fashionably long-pointed shoes. To her right *Castitas*, standing on a naked man who is crouching with one leg raised, averts her gaze from *Luxuria*, and clutches a palm frond, like some of the Terra figures in the *Exultet Rolls*. A late eleventh-century manuscript (in the Bibliothèque Nationale) from the abbey of Saint Martin in the diocese of Agen illustrates another symbol of *Luxuria* – a naked woman surrounded by foliage has her hands devoured by beasts. The same motif occurs in stone on semi-exhibitionist carvings at Deyrançon and Berrymount.

As for *l'homme aux serpents*, he too is rare in manuscripts (Dodwell 1954, Swarzenski 1974), but an Anglo-Saxon Gospel book (now in the Vatican Biblioteca Apostolica) shows a bearded squatting male exhibitionist holding his large genitals with one hand and pulling his beard with the other, while birdheaded zoomorphs bite his moustaches and scrotum (*Fig. 27a*). Folio 200r of the *Book of Kells* also has a male exhibitionist, clothed, with spear and shield, but showing his genitals nevertheless.

Fig. 27a *Homme aux serpents* from an Anglo-Hibernian manuscript (Barberini, Lat. 570. Vatican). His ears and testicles are attacked while he pulls at his beard. Pre ninth-century.
Fig. 27b Mailhat: *femme aux serpents*.

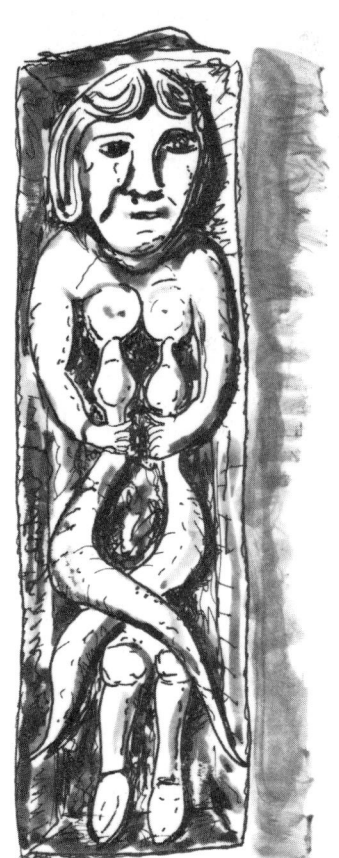

Plate 35b *Hortus Deliciarum,* scene of Hell ('worms and fire torment the sinful eternally'). (Photo: C.E.S.C.M.)

A late twelfth-century illustration of Hell, more elaborate than that of the Silos *Beatus* or the Chaldon fresco, was to be found in the *Hortus Deliciarum,* the Garden of Delights, by the abbess Herrad of Landsberg. This manuscript exists only in photographs as the original was destroyed in the Franco-Prussian war. Folio 253 depicts a Hell in which devils and snakes torment the lustful, and simoniac bishops and Jews are boiled in cauldrons; a monk with a moneybag is led toward Satan by a devil, while another force-feeds a rich man with coins, and a crawling figure stabbed by demons vomits toads. Through flaming holes in the frame of the design heads poke out, and naked bodies strive to crawl – yet another antecedent of the paintings of Hieronymus Bosch. The punishment of the rich in this miniature brings us to the subject of *Avaritia.*

Luxuria is commonly feminine, *Avaritia* commonly masculine, but there are exceptions.

At Dinan the roles are reversed; at Migron and Saint-Fort-sur-Gironde, Greed or Avarice are represented by women; and on the fine façade of Sainte-Croix, Bordeaux, the archivolt of one of the blind arcades is carved with five women tormented by snakes, toads and devils, while another is carved with five figures of greed, holding large rings and likewise tortured by demons (*Fig. 31*). The rings present a problem. Are they meant to portray gold jewellery? The miser carved round the west capital of the portal of Melbourne is holding what at first sight appears to be a ring (*Fig. 29*). Closer inspection shows this ring to be more of a stirrup, and actually turns out to be the handle of his moneybag, the weight of which is dragging him down to Hell. The famous composition on a chevet window at Blesle depicts *Luxuria* suckling a snake which issues from the mouth of a purse-carrying demon, and on the other side of her another devil spews the toad which bites her other breast (*Fig. 28*). He is brandishing a large ring – or purse? At any rate, here we have at Blesle a powerful statement about the connection between *Luxuria* and *Avaritia,* between concupiscence and greed, lust and money. In this connection, too, it is interesting to note that on the opposite capital of the Melbourne doorway sits an exhibitionist-like figure of 'luxuriance', i.e. the next development of *Luxuria,* in which the sexual characteristics give way to the sprouting of vegetation from the extremities, consonant and coeval with the development in language of the term 'luxuriance' from *luxuria* (Jerman 1981) (*Figs. 29 and 30*). Prudentius considered that *Luxuria* and *Avaritia* were partners in crime, money being the root of all evil, and so they usually appear together or near each other in sculptures. They may even combine in the Copgrove female exhibitionist who holds a large ring or purse, and in the Lavey sheela who has a large circular object round her arm (*Fig. 31*).

On the other hand, *Avaritia* is sometimes found alone. The earliest carving of it is probably that of Conques, and from this pilgrimage church the theme made its way into Auvergne, where it found a very sympathetic reception. The Auvergnats have a reputation in France not unlike that of Aberdonians in Scotland, and it seems to stem from the influx into that part of France of usurers, who battened on

Fig. 28 Blesle: *femme aux serpents* with misers on each side. Note the reptilian creature biting her right breast.

Fig. 29 Melbourne: the miser being dragged down to Hell by his purse (compare this latter with that of the Blesle miser).

Fig. 30 Melbourne, on the opposite capital of the north and south doors: a squatting luxuriant figure no longer exhibitionist.

Fig. 31 Bordeaux, Sainte-Croix: designs on archivolts: couple *aux reptiles* and *aux serpents*; misers.

moneyless Crusaders. Brioude was a particularly thriving centre of usury, as a number of Papal Bulls addressed to the Chapter of the town testify. Local stone masons took delight in giving shape to the matter. Swiechowski has distinguished three types of miser in their work: first, Milleartifex, or the devil of a thousand ruses, second, the miser punished for his sin, and third, the miser as a dreadful warning. The first is found at Ennezat, Notre-Dame-du-Port in Clermont Ferrand, Brioude, Saint-Nectaire, Maringues, Mailhat, Nonette and Chanteuges (*Fig. 32*); the second at Orcival; the third at Besse-en-Chandesse and Lavaudieu. At Lavaudieu the miser features on the obverse side of the capital depicting *Luxuria* eaten by two lions; and at Orcival another face of the capital probably shows *Luxuria* in the form of a woman with a basket of jewellery, and a huge snake forming a kind of halo round her head.

A carving at La Graulière, which is a daughter church of Beaulieu, forms a link with the iconography of Beaulieu and Moissac inasmuch as the third series of Auvergnat misers, the minatory sort, appear to be derived from the carvings of the Quercy churches, where associated with the miser is the story of Dives, the rich man who heeded not the leprous beggar Lazarus at his gates. The Moissac narrative is echoed at

Lincoln on the great frieze – Dives is damned whereas Lazarus ascends into the bosom of Abraham. In the Silos *Beatus*, Dives, richly apparelled, is attacked by snakes and assailed by demons who stab him; he also appears in the Chaldon wall-painting.

Avaritia and *Luxuria* were comparatively easy to embody in symbolical form; other sins like Envy, Pride, Anger were less so (*Plate 36*). Drunkenness and gluttony do sometimes find their way into corbel tables; nevertheless, there is overwhelming evidence that it was not merely a question of castigating those sins that were

Fig. 32 Miser (or richly accoutred Dives?) at Chanteuges.

easy to depict in stone. If Greed and Lust seem to predominate it is because the Romanesque period was obsessed by these human failings. There are comparatively few decorated Romanesque churches which do not in some way illustrate the commission of one or both of these sins; quite a number are almost entirely given over to a morbid concern with these alone. In great churches in Spain, for example, we find whole sides of cloisters devoted to themes of sin: the right side of the Portico de la Gloria at Santiago is full of hellish demons and damned souls, with three women suckling snakes and toads; the marvellous doorway of Sangüesa has mermaids, *femmes aux serpents*, a hideous fat snake with a cat's head pulling at a woman's breast, and a monster suckling its young symbolising the nourishing and begetting of evil by evil. And of course everywhere the great Judgment Day tympana take up half of their

Plate 36 Lucheux (Somme): combined *homme aux serpents* and miser.

space with the punishment of sinners.

One predominant thought emerges from this chapter. If sheela-na-gigs and other exhibitionists have survived unscathed in many places, it is because something of their original purport has survived in the folk memory, giving them protection from iconoclastic destruction. Of all the twelfth-century carvings these, by their brazenness, caused them to be regarded with some awe in the succeeding centuries. The respect in which they were held might have been different from that originally intended, but it sufficed to guard them against obliteration.

7 Disgust for the flesh

Make not provision for the flesh, to fulfil the lusts thereof

Romans 14

Male exhibitionists in an evident state of sexual arousal; female exhibitionists openly flaunting their charms as they sit splay-legged to reveal the most intimate parts of their bodies; acrobatic tumblers twisting themselves into impossible shapes in order to expose the secret parts of their persons; men and women in a state of nudity offering the sensitive areas of their anatomy to venomous reptiles – what more daring attacks upon our sensitive twentieth-century modesty can Romanesque sculptors make, we begin to wonder; have we not yet run through the gamut of possibilities?

A glance at the corbel table of many churches will tell us at once that we have more discoveries to make, and that, if anything, there is worse to come. At Nieul-le-Virouil, and in many other churches in its vicinity, we encounter a sexual scene of an astonishing nature (*Fig. 33*). Here on a corbel are a man and woman, their heads turned towards us, his tipped on one side, both of them round-eyed either because they are startled to be caught *in flagrante delicto*, or because they are determined to brazen it out. The man has straddled the woman across his lap, and, as they cling to each other lovingly, he tries to insert into her a phallus as thick as himself; the mason wants us to be in no doubt about this, so, just to make sure we know what the scene is about, he has carved a big scrotum dangling beneath the man's buttocks. The same scene is enacted at each end of the corbel table over the entrance porch and side blind doors at Corme-Ecluse; and again at Champagnolles; and again and again – we shall cite more examples. For the moment we shall be content to examine two more, the first at Passirac (*Fig.*

Fig. 33 Nieul-le-Virouil.

34), where the man inserts a huge tapering penis with the woman's help, as a huge beast rears up behind him to lay its paws on his shoulder, while behind the woman a bi-corporeal creature does the same, these animals no doubt representing evil spirits which attend such acts when they are illicit or lustful, or which prepare to devour them in punishment for their deed. At Saint-Savinien in Melle occurs probably the earliest of these representations in France. On the same band of metopes that figures the ithyphallic crawling man we mentioned earlier in Chapter 2, is a copulating couple in the seated position (*Fig. 35*). Their bodies and legs form a large X.

This X-position will be found a number of times. It no doubt stems from Classical vase-painting, in scenes where the woman mounts the man (Johns 1982). It occurs on a silver plaque,

Fig. 34 (a) Fuentidueña; (b) Sequera; (c) Passirac.

once part of horse trappings, discovered in excavations at Letnitsa, district of Lovech, Bulgaria, which was shown in 1976 in the British Museum's exhibition of Thracian treasures (Higgins 1976); dated to 400–350 BC, it was described in the catalogue (by Professor Venedikov) thus:

> Plaque. Silver gilt. Two women and a man within a rectangular frame. The man is seated on a cushion and has raised the front of his garment . . . the kneeling woman has also raised the front of her garment. The picture illustrates a sacred marriage between two deities. The man and woman are embracing, while behind them another woman wearing a long robe holds a twig in her right hand. The breasts of both women are indicated by small circles . . .

Examination of this piece shows that in fact the man is not sitting on a cushion but on the woman's left foot. Nor are they raising their

garments; the woman's robe forms a semicircular opening into which the man is placing his phallus manually. His testicles are also in evidence. The presence of the third woman may be explained by the polygamy of the Thracians. The plaque is well executed, the figures are elegantly groomed and attired, and the whole picture is remarkably unexceptionable considering what it portrays. This cannot be said of the Romanesque exemplars, because they are a representation that could not be taken for a marriage of deities, but rather that of ordinary mortals in a compromising position. Their lesson is that of the Whittlesford lintel, but the Continental carvers take matters a bit further and show us the couple joined in union.

Such sexual scenes are so explicit that one wonders how patrons, clergy and masons obtained authority for exposing them to public gaze, not in one or two scattered churches, but in a great many. To find the answer we turn to, among others, St Augustine of Hippo.

The Christian, by virtue of Christian teach-

Plate 37 A Type II sheela at Austerfield on a late twelfth-century capital. The face has been obliterated, or perhaps was never intended to be delineated. (Photo: Martin Pover)

ing, has always faced a dilemma in the matter of sex, stated humorously in the old joke 'It's all right as long as you don't enjoy it'. Theologians have pondered questions such as 'Is love concupiscence or concupiscence love?' and 'Is sexual desire always evil?' Since only love of God is pure, love among humans must perforce be impure . . . It was to matters such as these that St Augustine addressed himself. Like St Paul he was a convert and a fanatic. After squandering his wealth, sowing his wild oats, and subscribing to the Pelagian heresy, he became the principal propagandist of the orthodox doctrine against Pelagianism and 'paganism'. His most famous work was *The City of God against the Pagans*, but he also wrote many tracts such as *De Continentia*, *De Bono Conjugali*, *De Sancte Virginitate*, *De Divinatione Daemonum*, *De Nuptiis et Concupiscentia*, *De Conjugiis Adulterinis* and *De Peccato Originale*, from which we can infer that he was pre-occupied with the problem of chastity, or, as we might say today, that he was obsessed with sex. In the second book of his *Confessions* he relates his 'past foulness, and the carnal corruptions' of his soul; how in his youthful dissipation (he was 16 at the time) he 'boiled over in (his) fornications' and with vicious companions 'walked the streets of Babylon and wallowed in its mire'; his vile soul sought out shame itself, shunning mere self-gratifications. He began to organise in his thoughts all the anti-sexual attitudes implicit in the religions whence Christianity had sprung.

Judaism, one of whose most important rites was male circumcision which reinforced the exclusivity of the Jews, was a sexually rigid national religion. Christianity too was an exclusive sect, given a certain political direction by Constantine, and its early 'Fathers' like St Paul and Tertullian, added greatly to its Jewish-derived anti-sexual, anti-feminine bias. Thus St Paul (I Timothy II) could exhort:

> that women adorn themselves in modest apparel, with shamefacedness and sobriety; not with braided hair or gold or pearls or costly array . . . Let the woman learn in silence all subjection. I suffer not a woman to teach nor to usurp authority over the man but to be in silence. For Adam was first formed, then Eve. And Adam was not deceived, but the woman being deceived was in the transgression. Notwithstanding she shall be saved in childbearing, if they continue in faith and charity and holiness with sobriety.

Tertullian, Bishop of Carthage, in his *De Cultu Feminarum* echoed St Paul in urging women not to use finery and cosmetics or try to improve on God's handiwork. As to men, he asserted: 'A Christian remembers his sex only when thinking of his wife'. He equated unrestricted sexual activity with incest, and thus urged chastity, since promiscuity might lead to vast numbers of unrecognised relatives with whom one could be led into unwitting incestuous relationships.

St Augustine, quoting St Paul's words in Galatians V, re-emphasised that the joys of sex inhibit the joys of mind and spirit, a reasonable point of view (*De Continentia*):

> Walk in the Spirit, and ye shall not fulfil the lust of the flesh; for the flesh lusteth against the Spirit, and the Spirit against the flesh; and these are contrary the one to the other; so that ye cannot do the things that ye would . . . the works of the flesh are these: adultery, fornication, uncleanness, lasciviousness, idolatry, witchcraft, hatred, variance, emulations, wrath, strife, seditions, heresies, envyings, murders, drunkenness, revellings and such like.

In *De Bono Conjugali* he went further, to maintain that marriage was not in itself a good thing. Through Original Sin we had inherited the mechanics of procreation, and marriage was no more than a means of accommodating these, in order to procure souls-to-be-saved. In helping to contain concupiscence, marriage conferred no sanctity upon the spouses. The necessity to procreate did not legitimise concubinage any more than sterility might provide the grounds for dissolving a marriage. In Old Testament times, he argued, the proper task of piety had lain in engendering sons even carnally (*etiam carnaliter filios propagare*), and through polygyny in creating a people who would produce Christ and the prophets; but since Christ's death and resurrection things had changed – marriage was praiseworthy only insofar as it created new souls for Heaven.

The erotic, romantic element of love which today we consider to be a basis for marriage is precisely what Augustine termed *concupiscentia*. Men who know not God love their wives in concupiscence, which is an element of lust arising from the Fall, and a sickness which can be present even in Christian union. The guilt of Original Sin is transmitted through sex, an inheritance which justifies damnation in itself. Being born means being damned, until one is cleansed by the saving, mystic waters of baptism.

The whole structure of Augustine's doctrine was built on the belief that, before the Fall, Adam and Eve had the same control over their sexual passion that they exercised over their hands and feet, a theory only tenable in the days before the advent of modern psychology. Control of sexuality, nevertheless, was not an unreasonable goal. Some of today's hedonisms are as dangerous as the more extreme restrictions imposed by the Early Fathers. Both share an unhealthy attitude to sex.

In the Middle Ages Augustine's works were widely read, especially by clergy and monks, and his influence was enormous upon the misogynistic, pleasure-hating, guilt-ridden writers who followed him. In sculpture his teachings imposed themselves in the depiction of 'unholy wedlock' as opposed to scenes of the 'union of the blessed'.

The latter are difficult to distinguish in sculpture. A pair of lovers, holding a chalice and

kissing each other on the Prior's Door at Ely Cathedral, are not a symbol of concupiscence, and they may be copied from an illustrated manuscript of the Song of Solomon. This passionate and erotic poem was interpreted as the Church's love for Christ, and the soul's love of God, and could therefore in no way be construed as an expression of lust. So the pair of lovers denotes the union of two saved souls rejoicing in the Holy Spirit (symbolised by the cup).

As we have already remarked, it is easier to suggest evil than good in art. Sometimes even skilful carvers resorted to crude techniques in order to convey a meaning. In Saintonge the good virtues are distinguished from the evil vices quite simply by inscriptions which describe the conflict between them, as at Aulnay, where each figure bears its name. Or the wise virgins with a happy smile hold up their lamps full of oil, whereas the downcast foolish virgins hold their empty lamps upside down. These are the techniques of strip cartoonists. Without resort to stratagems of this kind, how is the artist to distinguish between lovers who are blessed and those who are damned? Three pairs of kissing clothed figures on the late-Romanesque corbel capitals of Killaloe Cathedral defy precise interpretation – are they pure or impure

Fig. 35a (*left*) Châteaumeillant homosexual encounter; (*right*) Melle, Saint-Savinien, perhaps the earliest example of the X-position.

Fig. 35b (*top*) Sévignacq-Thèze: adjacent corbels; (*bottom*) Saint-Martin-de-Sescas: separate corbels.

lovers? At Châteaumeillant two men kissing are labelled *Hac rusticani mixti*, though even without the label one might have supposed them to be representative of a homosexual relationship (*Fig. 35a*). Scenes of sodomy or bestiality, however, are explicit, graphic, and require no captions at Cervatos, though at San Quirce the sculptor felt obliged to write *Mala Cago* and *Io Cago* over two men in the act of defecating.

The problem facing sculptors was no problem if they saw their work as purely didactic, as messages to be conveyed by the quickest and readiest route; any technique, even the use of captions (albeit in Latin) was permissible. The great sculptor of Vézelay and Autun, Gislebertus, was not above this, even signing his own work in an excess of pride, but on the whole he had no need for lettering; his artistic skills were sufficient not only to convey a moralistic lesson but to create works of pure art. We do not need to understand (indeed many of us perhaps cannot) the import of the carved saints at

Souillac, or St Trophime in Arles, or Chartres, to appreciate their beauty, and sense at least that they have a Christian significance; the greatest accomplishments of Romanesque artists can be viewed without reference to their context – they are complete in themselves.

But however skilled local itinerant masons may have been, they could not always aspire to such high standards, nor was that their intention. On corbels particularly, and on some capitals, they were content to fall in with the wishes of the clergy, and to portray as simply and as dramatically as possible the frailties of humankind – frailties rather than strengths, vices rather than virtues, Augustine's 'unholy unions' rather than 'blessed pairs'. We have to search for the latter. They can be found as pairs of human beings clinging to each other for support in this vale of tears on corbels at Kilpeck, Aulnay and Matha-Marestay. At Rosheim two figures clasp hands and hold each other's tunic down in a sort of chastity pact. Another couple at Loupiac hold each other at arm's length. They are, of course, clothed.

A stage towards a more doubtful meaning is marked by those figures which, in spite of nudity, attempt modesty by covering up their bodies in some way. Like Adam and Eve they know shame, and in an attempt to regain their lost dignity they discreetly hold a hand over breast or groin. At Saint-Sulpice-de-Mareuil in Dordogne a female atlas (now in the Périgueux Museum) supports the corbel table with one hand and covers her groin with the other; and in the same church two squatting figures hold one hand aloft and the other to the groin on one capital, while on another two squatters' genital areas are masked by the enormous hands at the end of the extremely long arms of a third person, a clothed ecclesiastic standing between them. At Sémelay a clothed woman receives a crown from a cleric (?) and stands on the serpent of lust which she has conquered. At Oloron-Sainte-Marie a naked male and female standing side by side hide their genitalia.

A further stage is expressed by the woman at Barret who covers her groin with one hand and her breast with the other, while a serpent attacks the other breast and a demon passes his hand between her legs. Here we are very near to *la femme aux serpents*, but she is attempting to portray shame and remorse, and the carving combines the Temptation of Eve, the punishment of *Luxuria*, Terra, and the expression of chastity or contriteness.

Adam and Eve, of course, are always pictured after the Fall, never before, so their 'holy marriage' always yields to their 'unholy' post-Fall situation. At Saint-Front-sur-Nizonne a nude couple (Adam and Eve?) are frankly exhibitionist (*Plate 38*). With her hands on her knees, Eve squats, displaying a large vulva. Her mouth is open; so is Adam's, but he sticks out his tongue. Holding one hand aloft he also squats, megaphallic. Around them on this rural façade are a large selection of items from the iconography of lust – knots of snakes, a dog chasing a stag, mermaids and a tendril-spewing beast.

At Reignac we get both holy and unholy pairs on the battered north façade, where capitals on the blind arcade show a clothed and chaste pair and a naked couple; on the equally battered west face a naked couple paw each other while a devil, urging them on, grins between them.

An intermediate stage between chaste and unchaste pairs is marked by pairs of exhibition-

Plate 38 Saint-Front-sur-Nizonne: an exhibiting pair.

ists, male and female, side by side, doing nothing more than sitting in full frontal nudity (*Fig. 36*). The earliest of these are on the eleventh-century frieze of the original bell-tower of the church of Saint-Hilaire, Poitiers (*Plate 39*). They sit in hieratic postures, the male with both arms raised, scrotum and penis still in evidence in spite of mutilation or damage. The female, who is bald, places one hand on her head, and the other on her right thigh. They must be the first representation of *Concupiscentia* and, occurring as they do on a church built for pilgrims to visit the relics of St Hilary, they are likely to have acted as models for carvings elsewhere. Naked couples, two pairs of them, are on a pillar base at Loctudy in Finistère (Andersen 1977).

On adjacent corbels at San Pedro de Tejada two well-carved figures raise their clothes to reveal their genitals (*Plate 40*). They are similar to the figures sheltering beneath a shed in the *Très Riches Heures* of the Duc de Berry (the page for the month of February), whom we may style 'post-Romanesque exhibitionists'. The reason for their lack of modesty is that they are warming themselves at the fire, in the way the

Navarrese were wont to do according to Aimery Picaud, and for which he roundly scolds them in the *Guide du Pèlerin*:

> dum Navarri se calefaciunt vir mulieri et mulier viro verenda sua ostendunt

> When the Navarrese warm themselves the man shows the woman and the woman shows the man their privy parts

(Picaud, who does not like the Navarrese, then goes on to say that they fornicate with their beasts – *utuntur fornicatione incesta pecudibus* – and fit them with padlocks so that no one but themselves can use the beasts thus. Furthermore, women are as bad as the men in this debauchery.) (See Jerman 1982 for an exhibitionist figure raising his garment, found at Lammas in Norfolk.)

A cruder but amusing pair is carved on adjacent corbels at Santa Maria del Cerro (*see Fig. 1*); another pair at Perorrubio a few kilometres away; yet another at Jubia near La Coruña. Two upside-down exhibitionists, hands to groin, appear at Echillais but not next to each other. A remarkable pair at Sévignac-Thèze are carved most unusually on adjacent voussoirs of the doorway (*Fig. 35b*), and they are notable for the fact that they have been mutilated: the male's penis has been hacked off, and the female's vulva filled with cement. A strange pair at Savignac-d'Auros shows a megaphallic male pulling back his foreskin and squatting beside a female who passes her hands under her thighs to exhibit her anus.

Fig. 36 (a) An exhibiting pair at Bécéleuf on adjacent corbels; (b) a bashful pair at Oloron; (c) a shameless pair at Loctudy; (d) another pair in the X-position at Studland.

Plate 39 Poitiers, Saint-Hilaire: an early exhibiting pair.

Plate 40 San Pedro de Tejada (see remarks about the people of Navarra by Aimery Picaud).

Plate 41a Cervatos: another view of the window capital.

Plate 41b Cervatos: a pair of corbels.

Plate 42 Mosnac: a couple and a mermaid.

René Crozet lists nine churches in the Saintonge with 'amorous encounters', by which he means tender couples, like those of Sainte-Ouenne and Maillezais (who wear haloes), or the naked couple who charmingly touch each other from behind on a corbel at Saint-Quentin-de-Baron. The apse frieze of Marignac has some charming encounters and chases through the tendrils. But Crozet also lists no fewer than 24 churches in Saintonge with 'obscene couples' of the kind we began to discuss at the beginning of this chapter, many of them in the X-position, for instance at Pérignac and Marignac. One is to be found in England at Studland in Dorset (*Fig. 36*); and it is reasonable to suppose that at least one of Kilpeck's mutilated corbels showed such a scene. A copulating pair figure on an interior capital at Carennac, while an admonishing cleric looks on. Others can be found at Vaux-sur-Mer, Cénac, Marthon, Audignon, Fontaines d'Ozillac, Fuentidueña (*Fig. 34*), Sequera (*Fig. 34*), Sainte-Engrâce, San Martín de Mondoñedo, Cervatos (*Plate 41*) and Marzán.

There are, in addition, many anomalous couples. One pair at Arthous combines the Adam and Eve theme with that of *la femme aux serpents*: naked, they stand side by side wreathed in snakes; she tugs at her breasts while he grips the snakes at chest level. He has no particular sexual attributes but the effect of the pair is that of original sin and an unholy union. They are accompanied by a figure of *Luxuria* suckling snakes, a man being pecked by birds who tear his belly with their claws, a musician playing a *vielle*, a man with a barrel, various animal heads, and two clerics side by side, one holding a censer at groin level, the other a cross at chest level – all on corbels, an unusual position for the two clerics. It is when we study the pair with snakes that we see how close to Romanesque motifs the Lincoln carver came when he restored the columns of the west front.

Plate 43 Maillezais: holy love? Hence the haloes?

Plate 44 Frómista: an exhibiting pair, snakes in attendance.

Of course he had some models in the great frieze above, for a couple in Hell are bitten by snakes, and their hair is pulled by the devil who encircles their legs with his; another couple are entwined with a snake, their genitals are bitten by the birds between them and a devil claws their stomachs; another couple (a nineteenth-century restoration) are in the coils of a dragon which bites the woman's belly while a devil pulls the man's hair. Greed also appears as a figure with a large moneybag hanging from his neck, pawed by two devils and girded by a serpent which bites his penis.

Interpretations of the terms *concupiscentia* and *luxuria* varied between writer and writer in the Middle Ages, and they were loosely inter-changeable with *fornicatio, libido, voluptas* and *incastitas*, so that it is virtually impossible for us to say whether naked, exhibiting couples represent concupiscence, or tortured couples lust (*Plate 44*). In the English language, lust and concupiscence have come to mean much the same thing. Perhaps medieval writers were more able than we are to distinguish between

these terms, and asked their masons to reflect this in their imagery. Whatever the case, it is only after studying numerous examples of their carvings over a large area, that we twentieth-century people are able to overcome the repug-nance which has been foisted upon us by our prim forebears when we gaze on these frank sculptures, and accept them for what they are: the expression of an honest fear of sin and retribution, and a sincere endeavour to bring a message of warning to the common people, applied to church architecture by those whose approach to sex was very different from ours.

8 More priapic figures

Certain lewd fellows of the baser sort
Acts of the Apostles 17

The citizens of the French town of Epinal made a gift to their English 'twin', the Leicestershire town of Loughborough, of a statue, a bronze of a young boy bending over his foot to extract a thorn. It is a copy of a famous Roman carving and bronze known as *Spinario*, the thorn-puller. It represents an athlete doing a little first-aid, and, being a Roman athlete, he is bare. He is naturalistic, that is to say, in the context of this book, microphallic, and quite unexceptionable. The French gift was most acceptable and highly esteemed as any other Classical sculpture would have been; but it tells us a lot about the Romanesque mind that Magister Gregorius, in his twelfth-century description of Rome, described the charming piece as priapic (*mire magnitudinis virilia videbis* he told the would-be tourist). Despite his version, the virile parts of the boy are of no great magnitude, and follow the discreet scale of proportion that Classical artists chose for aesthetic reasons (Rushforth 1919. See also Journal of Roman Studies 1936).

For religion-inspired Romanesque sculptors it was enough that the statue showed a person in a state of nudity; he became at once another object lesson, perhaps symbolising St Paul's 'thorn in the flesh', to wit, concupiscence. There seems to be no other reason for discrediting athletes; their nudity was sufficient cause to believe that they were deliberately exposing themselves. So the carvers carefully noted this aspect of the model, and ensured that their versions would be megaphallic. Exhibitionist megaphallic thorn-pullers can be seen on corbels at Bignay, Saint-Léger-en-Pons (*see Plate 8*), Saint-Léonard-de-Noblat, Monterrey and Segóvia San Millán. Two are carved on

ambos, or preaching pulpits, at Cugnoli and Moscufo in the Abruzzi area of Italy; there is possibly one in Corsica at Murato; and there is one as far north as Tingstäde on Gotland, Sweden (where he is associated with an upside down acrobatic tongue-protruder). Others are at Audignon, Melle, Le Puy and Poitiers (several), Vézelay, Leyre, Matalbaniega, Merlévenez, Vienna and Somogyvar (Hungary).

Even more indicative of the Romanesque tendency to distort the form and content of Classical statuary for moral didacticism is the creation of a female thorn-puller, or *Spinaria*. Quite unnecessary, one would have thought, and suggestive of a monastic overheated imagination. A near-fanatic preoccupation with sex reaches its zenith in the *Spinaria* of Foussais, Béceleuf and Limoges. Lifting her foot to inspect the sole she reveals her vulva and anus (*see Fig. 5*). Wells Cathedral has a thirteenth-century thorn-puller (decently clothed) next to a mouth-puller.

An interesting attempt to show the sexual connotation of the thorn-puller is made by Moralejo (Moralejo 1981) in connection with a megaphallic male carved on an archivolt of the south porch of the cathedral of Orense. Moralejo identifies him with the legendary trickster, one Marcolph (or Saturnus in Anglo-Saxon legend), who outwitted King Solomon. A mythical buffoon, he was very popular from the twelfth to the sixteenth century. In the English version he was 'greatly misshapen and foul' and his wife was said to be 'even more fearful and rude' than himself (Duff 1892 and Welsford 1935). The English Marculf (the name has various spellings) was greatly daring – he showed his backside to King Solomon. Moralejo associated the Orense carving with the little thorn-puller on the north porch of

Chartres Cathedral. He is clothed, wearing a pointed cap, and is non-exhibitionist. The point of connection is that both these figures are in close proximity to Solomon and the Queen of Sheba in each instance. If the case is established for identifying these two carvings with Marcolph, it of course does not mean that the other thorn-pullers must also be the same mythical figure. For female *Spinariae* also exist.

Another priapic figure is that of the 'host' eater or *galette* muncher (*Fig. 37a*). The first of these, chewing a communion wafer and exhibiting huge genitals, represents the blasphemers or those who receive the sacraments with lechery in their hearts; and the second may simply represent gluttons. We have discovered only one male exhibitionist 'host' eater so far, on an interior capital at Bords; the wafer has a cross-and-circle on it. A much weathered corbel at Givrezac also holds a round wafer-like object, but this could be a *galette* or popular French pastry. On a corbel at Champagnolles a grotesque creature with a pig's snout, and an enormous penis and scrotum (strongly resembling a megaphallic male at Santillana del Mar) is devouring a flat loaf, seemingly combining lechery with gluttony. In the same church a megaphallic male with a large stumpy penis is holding what looks like a wafer, and other corbels of this remarkable church are carved with two coupling couples, a feet-to-ears female

with her hands on her buttocks displaying a circular vulva (see Anderson 1977), another female on a transept capital holding her thighs and showing a slit-like vulva, and other carvings of interest. One may also note in connection with 'host' eaters the megaphallic male holding a cake or bun in the shape of a ritual drinking vessel kept in the 'Secret Cabinet' of 'erotica' in the Naples Archaeological Museum. Lopez-Barbadillo, who describes it, also refers to an epigram by Martial concerning vulva-shaped bread rolls (Lopez-Barbadillo in the Spanish version of Marini 1976). Wafer-holding women, clothed, occur at Civray and Saint-Etienne-la-Cigogne, and some in the same area carry the chalice and host. Non-exhibitionist wafer-eaters appear on corbel tables at Arce, Macqueville, Beaulieu and Saint-Quantin-de-Rançannes. In the museum at Vannes a cloaked man showing broken but large testicles and a rimmed anus holds a *galette* or wafer in his left hand. He appears to be a post-Romanesque carving.

Barrel-toters, such as those of Givrezac, Béceleuf and Zamora Santo Tomé, also come into this group of priapic exhibitionist figures, their besetting sin presumably being that of wine-bibbing and drunkenness (*Fig. 37b*). They occur, appropriately, in wine-producing areas. Crozet lists 58 churches with barrels or kegs on corbels in Saintonge alone.

There would seem to be little problem in determining the source of male priapic figures; the very term 'priapic' takes us to Priapus and Classical figures like Pan, satyrs, or the god of gardens and boundaries, Herm or Term. A

Fig. 37a Givrezac: wafer-eater, or galette-eater.

Fig. 37b Barrel-toters at (*left*) Givrezac and (*right*) Béceleuf.

Fig. 38 Merovingian buckle-plate (after Salin).

glance at *Sex or Symbol* (Johns 1982) or at an article about Roman use of phallic symbolism in Britain (Turnbull 1978) gives an immediate insight into material surviving from Classical times which could have been pressed into use by Romanesque artists. As early as the eighth century we find the insular illuminators of the Book of Kells and the Barberini Gospel Book drawing megaphallic men. There exists also from the Merovingian period in France a buckle plate from somewhere in Picardy on which, separated, are a megaphallic male with hands on hips, and an exhibitionist female also with arms akimbo (*Fig. 38*). A second exhibitionist male figures on the flange which joins the tongue of the buckle to the buckle-plate. It is unlikely to have had Christian associations and may simply have had an apotropaic function, or an erotic one. It may have other naked figures on the back (Boulanger 1902–3 illustrates it, together with another buckle plate showing standing figures with breasts and vulvas/navels; see also Salin 1959). Small articles of this kind in metalwork were sources of motifs just as much as Gallo-Roman sarcophagi and the like (Deschamps 1972). Many small votive bronzes in the form of theriomorphic phalluses (themselves endowed with phalluses), or statuettes of dancers and acrobats, phallic horse trappings, have survived from Roman times, together with sherds, if not whole vases, on which are depicted erotic scenes. The Romanesque artist would not have been short of models.

What is interesting is that Romanesque megaphallic figures outnumber the ithyphallic ones, downward-pointing phalluses of large size seemingly more attention-rousing than erect ithyphallic organs. In view of the Romanesque predilection for didactic material, this is not perhaps what one would have expected. One reason has been put forward by Kraus (Kraus 1967, and Heer 1974); discussing some enigmatic figures in the Last Judgment scene on the tympanum of Beaulieu, Kraus notes that three of them are lifting the hems of their garments. They are wearing Phrygian caps and exotic Eastern dress. Kraus identifies them as Jews, preparing to show their circumcision to God on the Day of Judgment. They are ready to present their ticket to Heaven, their magic mutilation, the sign which sealed Abraham's covenant with God.

Throughout the early Middle Ages there was considerable ventilation of problems concerning the Jews on Judgment Day. Would the 'chosen people of God' be cast into Hell if they remained unconverted? Gregory the Great thought so and most writers followed suit. The New Testament stated quite clearly that all mankind would be judged, the quick and the dead, the Jews and the Gentiles (the former by

Plate 45 Poitiers Sainte-Radegonde: interior corbel. (Photo: J.A. Jerman)

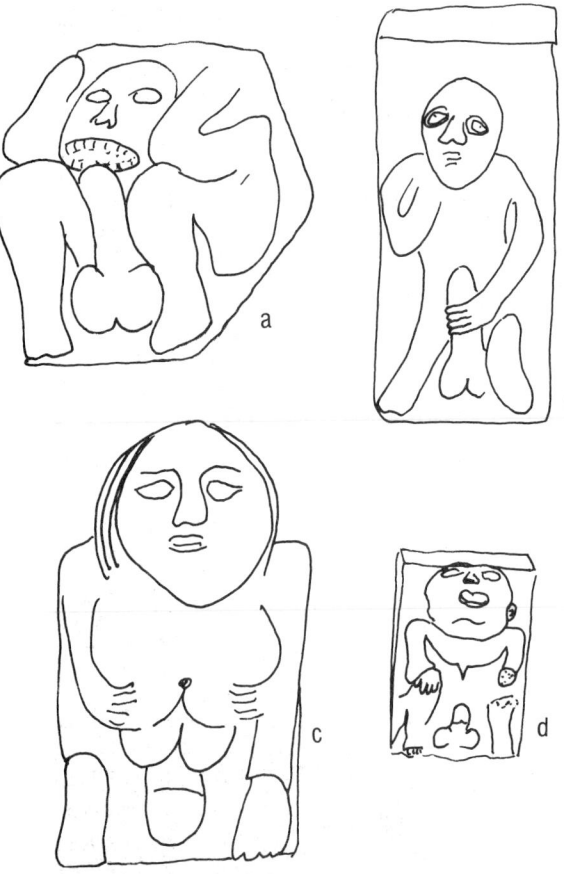

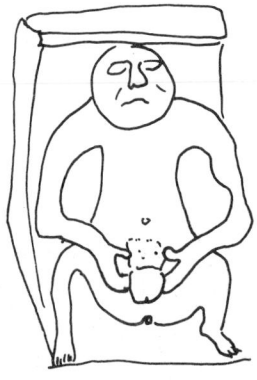

Fig. 39 Various megaphallic males: (a) Solignac; (b) Segovia San Millán; (c) Lusignan; (d) Lussac-les-Châteaux.

Fig. 41 (*top*) Queniborough (fifteenth-century), and (*bottom*) Savignac-d'Auros.

Fig. 40 Montigny-Lengrain, Aisne

Fig. 42 Male exhibitionist at Saint-Hérie, Matha.

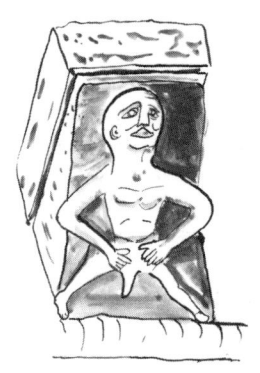

Plate 46 Champagnolles, seen from below.
(Photo: J. Andersen)

the law of Moses, the latter according to the law 'written in their conscience' [Romans II]). Anti-Semitism was strong by this time, having started as early as the fourth century, when St John Chrysostom directed eight virulent sermons against the Jews, accusing them of sacrificing their children to devils, of committing unspeakable outrages which, he implied, were of a sexual nature. From the very early days of Christianity there was a concomitant tendency to de-Semitise the Old Testament and appropriate it for Christianity as a mere series of prophecies of Christ and Mary, and symbolic prefigurations of their acts. Examples of these were Daniel in the Lions' Den as a prefiguration of the Crucifixion and Passion (a very popular pre-Romanesque theme in Spain, southern France and Ireland), and Jonah's three days in the belly of the whale as a prophecy of Christ's death and resurrection. Less reasonable examples included the burning bush and Gideon's fleece (which let the 'dew' through without itself being moistened) as predictions of the Immaculate Conception. St Augustine participated in this process when he excused Jewish polygyny on the grounds of 'historical necessity' to produce the prophets and the House of David which would bring forth the Saviour of the World. The exegetical process itself is encapsulated in the famous Vézelay capital of St Paul grinding in the Mystic Mill of Christ the corn of the Old Testament into the flour of the New Testament.

Up to the beginning of the eleventh century the Jews had operated the trading lifeline for a Europe surrounded by perilous cold seas, by the Arabs and the Arab-controlled western Mediterranean, and by dangerous unsettled peoples in the East; but with the huge economic expansion of the eleventh and twelfth centuries, the Jews were no longer needed as much. Princes and merchants encouraged anti-Semitism to seize Jewish land and money, trade and monopolies. Jews were forced to live in ghettos, pay crippling taxes, wear prescribed clothing, such as the ridiculous funnel-shaped hat, and be subjected to such Christian charity as slapping and stoning at Easter (*Plate 49*). Their property was confiscated, they were not allowed to leave inheritances, and they were restricted to trading only as usurers and old-clothes dealers. They were subjected to continual persecution, pogroms and massacres. Almost half of the £130,000 levy raised in England (the first country to expel the Jews) for the Third Crusade (1189–92) was squeezed from the Jews. The harder they worked to make the money to pay the taxes, the more they were reviled for avarice and usury. During the First Crusade (1096–99) some 12,000 Jews were slaughtered in a few hours in western Germany, and in the Second Crusade (1147–49) a Cistercian monk organised Jewish pogroms, inciting his eager followers to revenge themselves on the 'Christ-killers' before going to do combat with the infidel Moslems.

So Jews were stigmatised as attendants of Satan or the Antichrist. From Christ's words to the Jews who rejected him (John VIII): 'Ye are of your father the devil, and the lust of your fathers ye will do', it was but a short step to seeing Jews as foul and unclean beings who must be destroyed to make the earth a fit place for the pure and clean in heart. In innumerable commentaries on the Book of Revelation, *Luxuria* and *Avaritia* are noted as marks of the Antichrist; so the Jews joined the rich as well as the impure as those for whom the Kingdom of Heaven was unattainable.

A graphic carving illustrating the Romanesque attitude to Jews can be seen in the fine cloister of L'Estany, in Catalonia, where capitals carved with fierce devils and beasts include

Plate 47 Puypéroux: a bi-corporeal beast.

Plate 48 Civray (Saint-Pierre-d'Excideuil):
exhibiting devil reminiscent of the Silos *Beatus*.

one depicting a devil and a Jew (wearing his funnel hat), and another showing a devil with a Jewess, also in pointed hat, spewing a snake (*Plate 49*). In the former, the devil, looking like a wild boar, devours the Jew's beard. These capitals are in a context of sin: two women kissing, a musician and sinuous dancer, a boar and a dog (animals of concupiscence), a cleric clubbing a hare (also an animal with mythical sexual prowess) and a woman combing her long luxurious tresses. In the presence of these carvings we can have no doubt that the Jews were regarded as devilish and damnable.

It is possible, then, that in some contexts megaphallic males may represent Jews. To this day Semites are credited with having large organs, like the Hamites of Africa (Ham, it will be remembered, committed the unpardonable sin of exposing his father Noah's nakedness). A megaphallic Jew would be seen as presenting a 'counterfeit ticket to Heaven'.

Only a few male exhibitionists can positively be identified as circumcised, however Frómista,

Plate 49 L'Estany (Barcelona): monster tormenting a Jew.

Poitiers, Arce, Savignac d'Auros, Santillana del Mar, Givresac and Champagnolles provide examples. The male about to be devoured by a bicorporeal beast at Puypéroux (*Plate 47*), and the Sablonceaux anal exhibitionist are also circumcised. At Droiturier a lugubrious megaphallic ape is shown as circumcised.

One must remember, too, that Islamic law also required circumcision, and Moslems were frequently polygynous, which was equated by Christians as lechery on a grand scale. The churches above-mentioned were all at some time under Moslem domination or influence. Mention of the Droiturier ape also calls to mind the easy association that linked Moors with Barbary apes. Moors were dark, 'barbaric', hence 'bestial'. Male apes are well-known for their frequent, and in extreme cases, continual masturbation, in the cruel and depriving conditions of captivity. In Romanesque sculpture, apes are frequently chained, either together or to a trainer, symbolising the captivity of sin on the one hand and the victory of Christianity over sin, or Islam, on the other (*Plate 50*). Chained apes are common in Auvergne – Mozac, Chauriat, Riom, Saint-Nectaire, Issoire, Besse-en-Chandesse and Thuret for example (see Swiechowski 1973); an ape with its trainer can be seen at Bayeux and another at Saint-Genou. Apes of all kinds are discussed in Janson (Janson 1952).

Apes were regarded as degenerate human beings, and were a handy simulacrum for artists who wanted to depict base human acts vicariously. They could be shown playing musical instruments to illustrate the degeneracy of musicians (a monkey plays the harp on a corbel at Surgères and Plaisance-sur-Gartempe, Nevers and Saint-Parize-le-Châtel in company with an ass playing the lyre); and in exhibitionist pose could pillory all the vices of lust and concupiscence, indeed even the carved head of a simian could serve as a shorthand message for sexual guilt. Squatting apes with hand to groin appear frequently in Spanish churches (San Martín de Unx, Arce, Aibar, Jaca Sos del Rey Católico, Loarre, Rubiães (Portugal) and Oloron-Sainte-Marie); San Quirce has megaphallic apes on the chevet corbels; the cloister of La Seu de Urgell has ithyphallic apes and female apes with slit-vulvas. Non-exhibitionist apes are found widely. Even without sexual display their pres-

Plate 50 San Quirce: chained apes.

ence would be significant to medieval people; the context in which they are found, the company of attacking snakes and beasts, e.g. at San Isidoro and Nuestra Señora del Mercado in León, Saint-Gaudens, Morláas, San Quirce and Chartres would serve to confirm the message.

It is obvious by now that there is no question of male exhibitionists, from thorn-pullers to megaphallic apes, having been carved as a kind of erotica, put up by wayward stonemasons against the wishes of the local populace and village priest. That is not to say that these minatory carvings were always taken seriously. No doubt they raised an occasional eyebrow or smile, but there is no evidence to suggest that they were mere indecencies, and the corbel-table at Cervatos rules out the possibility of 'obscene' subjects being passed off on the ignorant or gullible, or put up in defiance of the clergy, for Cervatos was a collegiate church.

Many churches where exhibitionists in a flagrant state of display seem to the twentieth-century mind to be incongruous curiosities, if not actually repellent obscenities (and, to judge by the nineteenth-century destruction, this attitude already existed among some priests), were abbey churches, collegiates, or Augustinian buildings erected as part of a pastoral mission, and even Cistercian buildings erected in accordance with St Bernard's austere, anti-aesthetic policy (e.g. at Sablonceaux, a large severe building with a handful of carved corbels). These carvings, however whimsical, amusing, discordant or uncomfortable they may seem now, were at the time to be taken seriously. We cannot dismiss them out of hand as of little interest, as otiose sculptural graffiti.

9 Rude gestures and ruder postures

Against whom do ye make a wide mouth and draw out the tongue?

Isaiah 57

At Sablonceaux, a strict Cistercian establishment, there is a corbel on which a male displays his anus (*see Fig. 12a*). Male (and female) anal exhibitionists are another sub-theme of the *Luxuria* story, and quite a number of them are to be found. Sometimes they are merely rude, but sometimes they are more extreme, as in the case of the San Quirce figures we have already mentioned which show men in the act of defecating. This act, surprising to find on a church wall, had an equally surprising longevity, for woodworkers, plasterers and makers of church roof bosses were still carving this scene in the fifteenth century. Formerly known as 'caccans' (the use of Latin points to the erstwhile prudery with which art historians approached this topic), the defecating peasant, with clothes tucked up and trousers down, is to be seen on the

choir-stalls of the cathedral at Saint-Claude in the Jura, carved by a Swiss artist between 1449–1465, and opposite, on a poppy-head, is an ape, pulling his buttocks apart to display his anus. 'Men at stool' is the term given by Cave in his study of English roof bosses to this composition (Cave 1948). There seems to have been a recrudescence of interest in the Mortal Sins in the later Middle Ages which was responsible for the prolongation of such images.

Males exhibiting their anus and their genitals can be seen at Mauriac, Lusignan, Chelles, Artaíz, Cahors, San Pedro de la Rua at Estella, Jubia, Saint-Michel-d'Entraygues, Vallbona de les Monges, Montils, Perros-Guirec and Grey Abbey Co. Down (*Fig. 43*). Those whose sex cannot be determined, but some of which may be female, are at Saint-Quantin-de-Rançannes, Saint-Sauvant, La Rochette, Champagnolles and Bruyères-Montbérault, and there are others, including some we have already encountered in previous chapters. The acrobatic, feet-to-ears posture, exemplified by some of these, lends itself of course to anal display, and the Mauriac examples, one at Santiago, another

Fig. 43 Anus-showers at (a) Bors-de-Baignes; (b) Givrezac; (c) Saint-Coutant-le-Grand

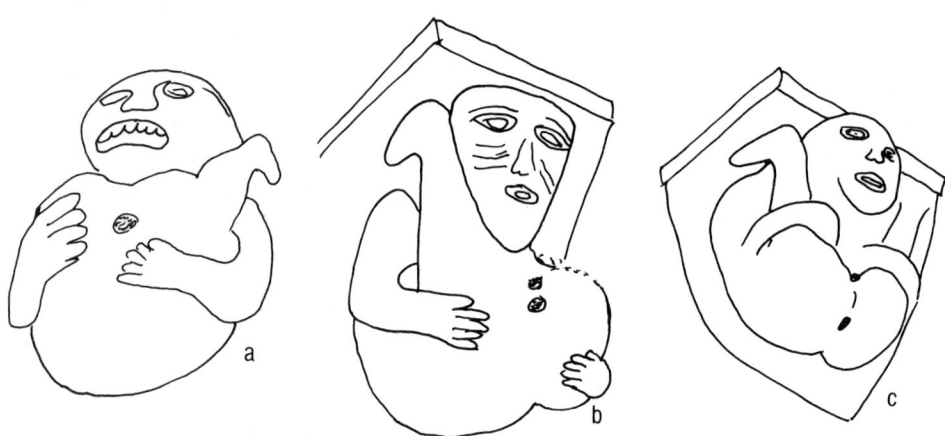

Fig. 44 Tongue-pullers at (a) Conzac and
(b) Pérignac; (c) penis-swallower at Chauvigny.

at Mens, and yet another at La Villedieu-du-Clain, show this most clearly. Cervatos, as one might expect from this extraordinary church, outstrips all others in display of this kind, and one corbel shows a man pulling apart the buttocks of another. At least one sodomitic union is also portrayed.

Two simians in sodomitic union are carved on a capital at La Chaize-le-Vicomte; the one being mounted holds a curious circular object with three concentric grooves (a musical instrument?). Sodomy was the most heinous crime in the Middle Ages, its punishment often far exceeding that doled out for manslaughter or murder. St Augustine considered it the vilest of acts, amounting to a sin against the Holy Spirit because it was so contrary to nature. The Greek and late-Roman predilection for homo-erotic love naturally produced a savage response from the Christian Church. Like baby-eating and impossible orgies, it was attributed to all minorities – the Romans attributed it to the Christians, the Christians to the Cathars (thought to come from Bulgaria, hence the term 'bugger') (see Cohn 1976). The Bulletin Monumental (Vol XIV) had this to say, in awed tones, about a carving at Sémelay:

> on voit sur un des chapiteaux du choeur les épouvantables et dégoûtants details de la sodomie.
>
> (on one of the capitals of the choir can be seen the horrifying and disgusting details of an act of sodomy.)

Scenes of sodomy are rare, but equally *outré* are the acrobats who bend themselves double in order to place their penis in their mouth. Very often this posture is relegated to animals. They can be seen at Mauriac, Maillezais and Chauvigny (*Fig. 44*); and at Astureses (Orense) a variation is that of a beast swallowing two of its legs and its tail, leaving two large testicles displayed. Scenes of bestiality are restricted to animals attempting to rape human beings (another punishment of sinners?). A much eroded carving on the archivolt of Macqueville is reported to have been an example. Clearer instances are at Aulnay, and at Kilkea Castle, which as well as possessing a sheela has an ithyphallic beast in the X-position with a bearded human, attempting an act all the more striking for being impossible. The carving is on a quoin, and, as in the case of many Irish figures, may not be in its original position.

Ithyphallic beasts, as a comment on the 'base nature' of the sexual instinct, abound in Romanesque sculpture, though they are not as common as human exhibitionists. An initial of a pre-Romanesque manuscript preserved in the Bibliothèque Nationale ends in the hindquarters of a leonine beast. Its tail curls up over its back, forms a knot, then drops down to reappear projecting between its legs, makes another knot, then terminates in a vine leaf with an unmistakeable resemblance to male genitals (Micheli 1939). There is no need to be so devious, however. Any male mammal in a state of sexual excitement shows its genitalia conspicuously. Besides the ithyphallic apes we have described there are ithyphallic equines at Besse, a centaur at San Quirce de Rio Pisuerga, cats at Saint-Palais and Sangüesa, a dog at Annaghdown, a pig with human genitals at Uncastillo, a pig at Jubia and at Cervatos, and ambiguous monsters at Foussais, La Sauve and Studland. At Alloué and Vielle-Tursan, sows exhibit large vulvas.

On a corbel above the Puerta de las Platerías, Santiago, a beast appears to be inserting its tongue into a man's anus, a scene paralleled in the same city, at Santa Maria del Sar, by a man doing the same thing to an animal. At San Michele, in Pavia, a dragon sticks its snout up a person's backside; and two flanking beasts with long tongues lick a man's groin at Saint-Avit (see Fig. 49). Most curious of all carvings depicting relations between humans and beasts is in the cloister of Millstatt in Austria. On the base of two columns is a woman supporting one of the columns on her back. Straddled over a beast, she inserts her tongue into its anus while it bites the other column with large toothy jaws (Sheridan and Ross 1975).

With these impressive inventions of the medieval mind hell-bent on portraying the punishment of the damned, we end our review of the more extreme fantasies and turn now to some very common motifs of Romanesque iconography which were to continue well into the later Middle Ages. First, two designs to which we have already made allusion, the mouth-pullers and tongue-protruders (with a variant, the tongue-pullers [Fig. 45]). We shall attempt to show that, far from being simple rude gestures, they were often associated in the minds of medieval folk with sexual ideas. Until recently in Quebec it was considered not merely rude but an outrageous act to stick out the tongue, which, in its ability to rouse ire, could be compared with the phallic fica sign in Italy and South America (our two-finger sign is a derivative; see Chapter 12). The root of these insulting gestures must lie deep in the past in some sexual observation. Isaiah LVII provides a clue:

> But draw near hither, ye sons of the sorceress, the seed of the adulterer and the whore. Against whom do ye make a wide mouth and draw out the tongue? Are ye not children of transgression, a seed of falsehood, enflaming yourselves with idols under every green tree?

According to the Scriptures, then, tongue-pulling and tongue-protruding are the gestures of a wicked adulterous generation. The text appealed to masons, who underlined its message by applying the gestures to exhibiting squatters,

Fig. 45 (a) Megaphallic tongue-puller at Barahona; (b) female tongue-sticking exhibitionist at Tugford and (c) her mouth-pulling companion (one on each side of the entrance, inside the church).

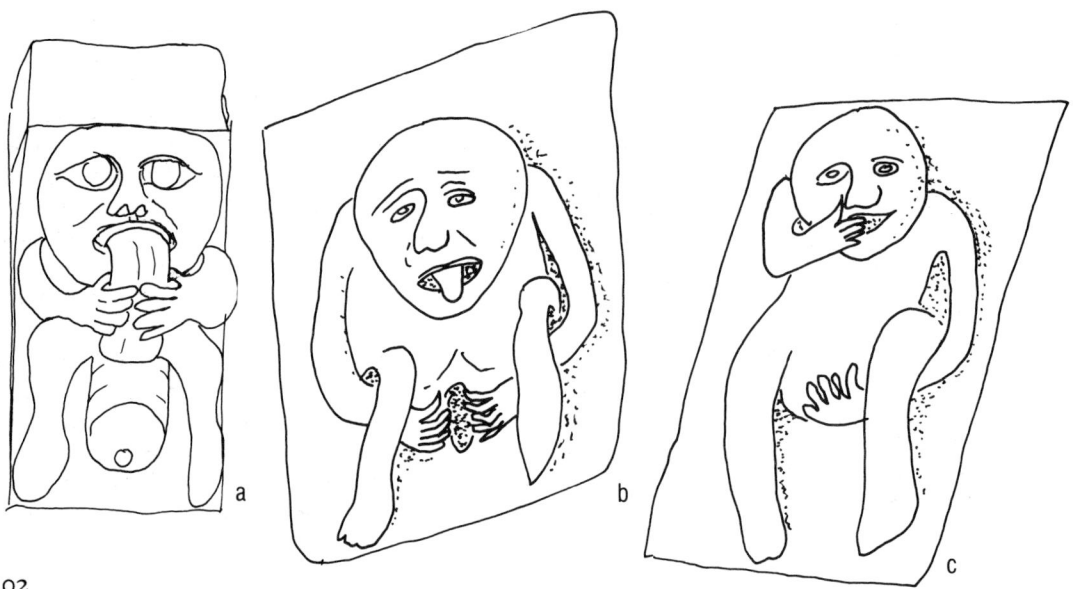

thus making patent a palpably direct association with sex.

We have on a number of occasions noted that an exhibitionist or other sexual figure is sticking out its tongue, for instance the sheela at Tugford (and that its companion on the other side of the door is pulling its mouth), the male of the exhibitionist pair at Saint-Front-sur-Nizonne, and the female holding fish at Rochester. This is not unusual, and it occurs widely from Cashel to Tingstäde in Sweden, Rio Mau in Portugal to Paulinzella in Germany, Barfreston to Cheb in Czechoslovakia.

The phallic significance of the tongue needs no inquest (*Fig. 45*). Protruded, it has today become only a mild insult, but the tongue, like the genitals, was once a target for hellish beasts (*Fig. 46*). *Luxuria* suckling snakes at La Charité-sur-Loire is on one face of a capital, and on another face is a figure whose tongue is attacked by a snake. On the left arcade of the Angoulême façade is a horrific scene of a wretched, ragged sinner on a flying monster, being dragged off to Hell by a ferociously gleeful demon who holds a long hooked or barbed stick which passes behind the double columns to catch his tongue.

The Classical origin of tongue-sticking could be the Gorgon-mask, like that on a clay relief from Syracuse (Boardman 1973), which found its way into the theatre as a grimacing mask worn by actors. At Anzy-le-Duc, St Michael fighting the Devil has a Gorgon's head and a lion's body. The Egyptian god Beš is also portrayed with his tongue protruding. Pan appears with tongue outstretched, complete with pan-pipes and a serpent round his arm and

Fig. 47 Tongue-pulling devil, and mouth-puller at Poitiers Cathedral.

shoulder, on a Hellenistic ivory relief of Isis Pharos from the pulpit of Henry II at Aachen (Wessel 1965). Gorgons with tongues occur in English manuscripts (Dodwell 1954). Romanesque tongue-sticking men unusually appear as sheep-carriers in Auvergne at Brioude, Saint-Nectaire and Issoire, and do not represent here Christ and the lost sheep, but Hermes Criophoros, a symbol of evil, just as other pagan gods like Vulcan and Venus became Satan and *Luxuria* at Autun (Świechowski 1973; and Grivot & Zarnecki 1961).

Examples of tongue-stickers are: the Irish sheelas at Cloghan, Cavan and Burgesbeg; an upside-down acrobat at Fole (Gotland) and a tongue-sticker next to a thorn-puller at Tingstäde in the same area; the thorn-puller and tongue-sticker together at Grandson in Swit-

Fig. 46 Chaldon Church, Surrey. Details of the twelfth-century wall-painting of Hell, with tongue-protruding devils.

zerland, and two images of Satan on the Chaldon wall-painting. In France many examples can be found, as at Cunault, Chauvigny and Montmorillon (several); at Abillé, beside a long-necked megaphallic male; at La Villedieu-du-Clain, where a wimpled female sticks out her tongue near an anal exhibitionist; at Bouresse, a dancer wearing *fouriaus*; and several in Poitiers in the Cathedral of Saint-Pierre.

A variation is the tongue-puller. At Pérignac a tongue-puller stretches a tongue right down to his feet; at Conzac a seated anal exhibitionist pulls out an enormous ribbon-like tongue (*see Fig. 44*); one member of one of the couples on the corbel table of Besse pulls the other's tongue; and a devil pulls out a long tongue with both hands at Poitiers.

Many beast-heads protrude their tongues, often in the company of sexual exhibitionists, and these may have phallic significance, or at any rate imply savagery or evil.

Tongue-protruding naturally lived on into the Gothic period, and misericords and roof bosses can be found illustrating this grimace (Cave 1948; Remnant 1969; Sheridan & Ross 1975).

Mouth-pulling, i.e. inserting the fingers of one or both hands into the corner of the mouth in order to pull it open sideways, may also be phallic in origin, resembling as it does the gesture of the sheela (*Plate 52*). It is found in company with other gestures and postures, e.g. a little figure on the roof screen at Willingham, whose tongue hangs down over the genital area; or the megaphallic male at Poitiers near the tongue-puller. Examples are: Fontaines d'Ozillac, where a superb feet-to-ears female exhibitionist on a corbel over the doorway pulls her mouth (*Fig. 48*); a megaphallic male at Puente la Reina; Vallbona de les Monges (among anal exhibitionists, barrel-toters and a mouth-pulling pig); Solignac, Fontevrault (on the kitchen), Marthon and Oloron-Sainte-Marie. Mouth-pulling figures which deserve special mention are to be found at Aulnay and Matha Saint-Hérie, whose significance will be discussed in Chapter 11, when we look at the dissemination and distribution of Romanesque motifs.

Plate 51 Saint Joan de les Abadesses: bi-corporeal beard-pullers.

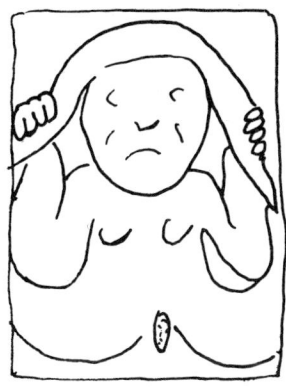

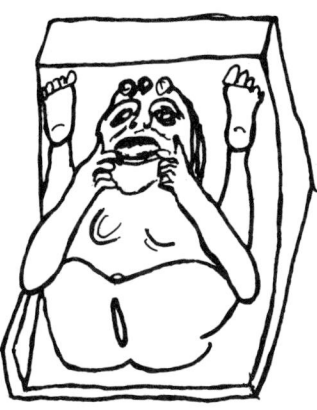

Fig. 48 (*upper*) Tress-puller at Nonac; (*lower*) mouth-puller at Fontaines-d'Ozillac.

Plate 52 Oloron-Sainte-Marie: mouth-pullers. (Photo: C.E.S.C.M.)
Plate 53 La Sauve-Majeure (now in the Metropolitan Art Museum, New York): acrobatic beard-pullers. (Photo: C.E.S.C.M.)

Often mouth-pulling faces, without bodies, are a shorthand symbol whose significance is only clear when the masks are found, as at Bruyères-Montbérault, along the same cornice or corbel table as anal-exhibitionists, and the female exhibitionist. Mask mouth-pullers are common (*Plates 54 and 55*). Examples are at Parthenay-le-Vieux and Charlieu (a corbel now in the lapidary museum); in Ireland at Ardfert, Balrothery, Cashel and Drakestown (Weir 1977, 1980); in the Victoria and Albert Museum – a corbel reputedly carved in the 'Herefordshire School', and a little mouth-puller and a tongue-sticker can be picked out on the façade of Cerne Abbas church. They are also found on roof bosses and misericords.

Another very interesting motif with a wide distribution is the face from whose orifices issue snakes or, more commonly, vegetation. For the sake of brevity we have called these 'foliage-spewers' (*Plate 56*).

Plate 54 Castletown, Dundalk: mouth-puller.

A head spewing foliage or snakes may possibly have symbolised blasphemy, heresy, scandal or evil in general. A snake-spewer, once an impressive and early capital, sits in a side aisle at Saint-Hilaire-le-Grand in Poitiers; the head with its mouth turned down at the corners, remarkably like the head of the Cavan sheela, spews several snakes. The motif recalls the Saint-Séver *Beatus* page which shows a beast and a man spewing toads, and which was probably the model for the demon spewing a toad who torments *la femme aux serpents* at Moissac. Snake-spewing found its way into tenth-century Anglo-Saxon manuscripts.

Foliage-spewing is much commoner than toad- or serpent-spewing, and is one of the very most popular medieval motifs from the twelfth century onwards, carved on bosses, misericords, bench-ends, and other furniture. Often they are confused with 'Jack-in-the-Green' or 'Green Man' motifs, and indeed the distinction often becomes unreal. We shall examine the folkloric associations in a later chapter. Here we should note that foliate and floriated heads have a direct line of descent from the Classical heads of Medusa, Oceanus/Neptune, and Hellenistic leaf-masks of Dryads or Silenus (Basford 1978), and the earliest in our islands are the Oceanus mask on the Mildenhall silver dish, and the head of Sulis Minerva at Bath. Abroad, masks with

Plate 55 Thirteenth-century mouth-puller at
Finchingfield, Essex. (Photo J. & C. Bord).

vegetation sprouting from mouth, nose and ears
are found from the second and third centuries
AD in the Rhineland, in the Middle East, and in
Rome. The first Christian one is probably that
at Saint-Hilaire-le-Grand, Poitiers, on the
tomb of Sainte Abre, daughter of Saint-Hilaire,
which is decorated with other motifs from
Gallo-Roman tombs such as dolphins, vases and
a bust. Basford points out that the work is,
nevertheless, novel: its leafage does not look
back to Hellenistic leaf-masks, but seems to set
the pattern for future Romanesque heads. The
tendrils issue from the nose to form two scrolls,
one on each side of the head, itself surrounded
by leaves. Already the head is no longer that of a
Classical god, but looks forward to the manuscript masks of the tenth to twelfth centuries,
when these take on a demonic look.

We have the documentary evidence of
Rabanus Maurus, Abbot of Fulda, an influential theologian of the eighth century, that,
according to Ezekiel and Job, leaves represented
the sins of the flesh or wicked, lustful men
doomed to eternal damnation (Basford 1978).
Whatever the origin or the early symbolism of
the foliage-spewing mask it very often takes on
an evil look, and as a linking device, joining
together medallions made up by the tendrils
issuing from it, it lurks in the background of

Plate 56 Foliage-spewing feline and near-exhibitionist at Melbourne, Derbyshire. (Photo: J. & C. Bord).

Romanesque *Luxuria* scenes, or vice and virtue combats, or even in the joyous chase of lovers through the vegetation. It is this association of the mask with lust themes which leads us to believe that, for medieval man, it was not just a decorative device but signified, in shorthand, sin and its punishment. We shall see that its use in English decoration follows very closely that of the exhibitionists.

Beard-pullers are comparatively rare, and the motif, which does not have any Classical antecedents, was not popular after the twelfth century (*Plates 51 and 53*). As a secondary male sexual characteristic the beard, representing virility, enters the iconography of lust through scenes like that of Maranges: a megaphallic beard-puller is in the company of *Luxuria* suckling snakes, a winged, grimacing demon with a purse hanging on his chest, a figure bitten on the mouth by a serpent which coils round it, and contortionist dwarfs. Megaphallic beard-pullers occur at Barahona, Saint-Palais, Cénac, Limoges, Santo Domingo de Silos (bi-corporeal), and two more (also bi-corporeal) at Sant Joan de les Abadesses, Gerona. Acrobatic beard-pullers can be found at Bresdon, and Oloron-Sainte-Marie, the latter bearing a strong resemblance to the mouth-puller of Aulnay and Matha Saint-Hérie. A beard-puller and an anal exhibitionist adorn corbels at Guarbecque in the Pas-de-Calais; there is an-

Fig. 49 Later medieval wooden carvings showing coarse humour at (a) Rouen and (b) Bourg-Achard (after Adéline); (c) beard- and tongue-pullers at Oloron-Sainte-Marie (after Baltrušaitis); (d) animal biting man's testicle and megaphallic demon standing on a 'soul' at Villers-Saint-Paul.

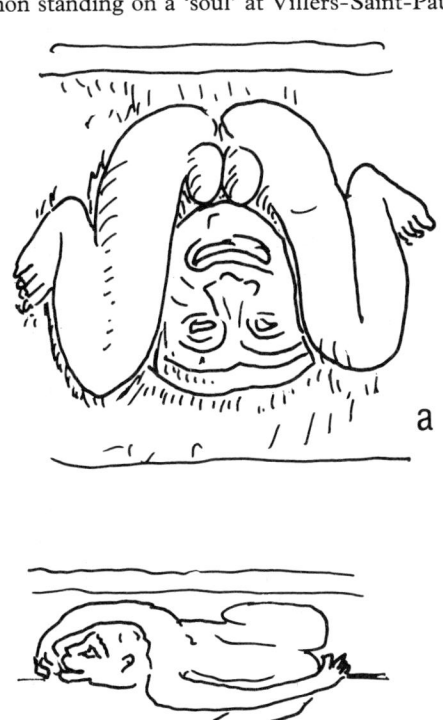

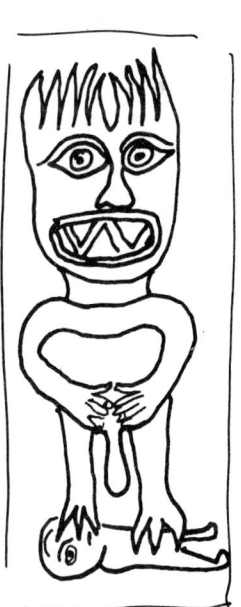

other at St Augustine's Abbey in Canterbury; and more at Lucca Cathedral, and Santiago (above the Puerta de las Platerías).

Mâle illustrates a capital from Saint Hilaire, Poitiers, carved from a design in the Saint-Séver *Beatus*, which shows two partly bald old men tugging each other's beards and hair in the presence of a woman. It could be construed as the folly of old men's lust, or the power of women's sexuality to set men against each other. Related to this carving is a piece from La Sauve-Majeure, now in New York, which shows a pair of fighting acrobats pulling each other's beard (*Plate 53*). Two clothed upright figures on one face of a capital are related to wrestlers (or embracers?) on another face at Anzy-le-Duc. Wrestlers and struggling figures naturally denote the vices of anger and discord (*Ira* and *Discordia*), and beard-pulling associates them with concupiscence.

Of course some figures may merely represent professional *bateleurs* or itinerant wrestlers who entertained for money, and who therefore incurred, like other entertainers, considerable odium (Svanberg 1970); other bearded figures may have no evil significance whatsoever but represent the Patriarchs or other holy gentlemen.

Mutual beard-pullers feature in the *Book of Kells* (folio 253v), and men pulling their own beards are on folio 2b. Some similar Gospel Book illumination supplied the model for the two seated men pulling each other's beard on the base of the south cross at Monasterboice. Also in manuscripts we find a variant in the moustache-puller (Barberini, already mentioned [*Fig. 27a*]). The presence of birds biting or pecking at these, as at the legs of the *Book of Kells* figures, indicates that a sinner being plagued is the subject of the design. At Lucheux two diminutive devils pull the imposing moustaches of a dignified bearded head. Another figure is cut in relief above the door of Brem-sur-Mer, associated with an impressive tress-puller.

Tress-pullers we have already encountered in mermaids and *la femme aux serpents* or *Luxuria*, and we have discussed the sexual significance of hair. This is highlighted by the female who sits splay-legged, exhibiting a large vulva, at Nonac, and pulls at her long tresses, near a coupling pair and a megaphallic wafer-eater. A hair-puller sticks out her tongue at Saint-Palais; another

hair-puller (*Fig. 48*) is at Lichères, and an interesting variant is the bearded male at Hérent, in Belgium, who pulls his long hair. The *Book of Kells* on folio 8r has a head pulling his hair and spewing interlace.

Lastly we come to the mask or head which appears to be swallowing (or spewing) a column. It is widespread, and often appears on the spokes of Romanesque wheel windows, e.g. at Barfreston and Patrixbourne. Its meaning is obscure, but the old French local name for them, *grand' goules* (or *grandes gueules* in modern French), indicates that local people accept them as menacing jaws of devilish fashioning, ready to swallow unwary sinners. They may represent gluttony, or unnatural appetite; their sharp teeth certainly suggesting menace. It is doubtful if they have sexual significance, but they do occur in the same context as other figures we have been examining, and thus contribute to the overall sinister, brooding aura that, even in the clear light of Aquitaine and Galicia, seems to emanate from these sculptured stones.

10 More female exhibitionists

The Sheila-na-gig appears to be peculiar to the British Isles and is not found on the mainland of Europe. In France its place is perhaps taken by the two-tailed mermaid who holds her tail in either hand, and whose attitude is therefore reminiscent of Baubo.

Murray 1934

In his first and last chapters, Andersen (Andersen 1977) recalls the early attempt of Margaret Murray to trace the source of sheelas by considering the mother-goddess figures of the Middle East, which she placed in three categories, the last of these being the Baubo figurines. She assumed in all this that the sheela was an idol:

> That the Sheila-na-gig was regarded as divine, or at least as having divine attributes, is shown by the fact that the figures are almost invariably found on Christian churches

hence her use of the capital letter for Sheila.

Since the 1930s we have had 50 years of further investigation during periods of sporadic interest in the sheelas, and our knowledge has widened considerably. In this book we have postulated a different origin and purpose for female exhibitionist carvings, but it is nevertheless worth reinvestigating briefly the Baubo reference made by Murray and Andersen.

Andersen illustrates a Baubo figurine, now in Copenhagen, and discusses the enigmatic myth of this obscure personage as retold by Clement of Alexandria. He rejects Murray's genealogy and says:

> The Baubo is an interesting parallel to the sheela, although not in any way directly connected with her.

He may be right in this, but it is possible that Clement's writings were widely known, for, being born c. AD 150, he was one of the earliest Christian writers. He was extremely knowl-

Plate 57 A Baubo terra cotta in the British Museum. (Photo: B.M.)

edgeable about Greek and other pagan myths, about philosophy and religions, and was able to see Christianity as an advanced philosophy. Origen, perhaps the most influential writer after Augustine, was one of his pupils (he castrated himself in order to be able to work among women). Eusebius completed his *History of the Christian Church* about AD 325, the most important early history of the Church, and it is due to him that we know as much as we do about Origen and Clement. The writings of these three men would be eagerly studied even when their views were later abandoned. There is a strong likelihood that the legend of Baubo recounted by Clement would come to the notice of many monks and ecclesiastics.

The word 'Baubo', used to describe certain antique, exhibitionist, splay-legged female figurines, is as mystifying as the term 'sheela-na-gig'. Clement's account of her follows:

Dèo (Demeter) wandering through Eleusis in search of her daughter Koré, sits down at a well in deep sorrow. Baubo receives Demeter as a guest and offers her a (ritual) gruel, *cyceon*, but Dèo disdains to take it and refuses to drink it, deep in grief as she is. Somewhat put out, Baubo believing herself scorned and slighted, uncovers her private parts and displays them to the goddess. At this sight Dèo is brought out of her deep sorrow, and delighted at the spectacle, accepts Baubo's offering.
These are the mystic secrets of the Athenians! These are also the mystic secrets of Orpheus' poems and I will now quote to you the very Orphic verses, so that the mystagogue himself can verify this shamefulness:

'Baubo lifted her *peplos* to show the obscenity of her body; the young Iacchos, who was also present, laughing at the sight, waved his hand under Baubo's bosom; Demeter then smiled, smiled in her heart, and accepted the cup which contained the gruel.'

Protrepticus II

Clement, who is thought to have been initiated into certain cults, is here obviously trivialising and distorting an important ritual in the Eleusinian Mysteries. He proceeds to rail against the absence of shame among the Greeks in displaying sexual organs and symbols; he expresses outrage against Greek 'sensuality' in the form of images of little naked girls, drunken satyrs, and erect phalloi; and he attacks 'pagan licentiousness'. In other words, he is preparing the ground for the Christian view of sex which will permeate the carvings of the Romanesque masons.

The British Museum possesses a small terra cotta figure, some 11cm (4½in) high, in the form of a crouching female figure, which may be about to give birth, or merely be plump. She squats with legs drawn up to display navel, swollen belly and circular vulva. She has large round breasts which match the top-knots of her elaborate headdress. Both hands are raised on either side of her (obliterated) face, and in her left she holds a vessel. It is an Egyptian figure of the Ptolemaic period, i.e. about the time of Christ. The British Museum's *Catalogue of Terracottas* compares it with a similar figure found in Italy, mounted on a boar and holding a ladder (we referred to it in Chapter 6), and identifies it with Baubo or Iambè (*Plate 58*).

Iambè, Baubo and Demeter are the chthonic triad of maiden, nymph and crone, according to Graves (Graves 1955). But some accounts identify Iambè with Baubo, as she is supposed to have made Demeter smile at the house of Celeus. Demeter, goddess of fertility, instituted thereafter the Mysteries of Eleusis. The Baubo or Iambè figurines might possibly be fertility objects, but how they came to be associated with the myth, and hence obtain their name, is not clear. Picard argues that there is no connection between the splay-legged figures and the Eleusinian Mysteries (Picard 1920). He suggests that Baubo is a female counterpart of a hypothetical Baubon, rather as Freya is the female counterpart of Freýr in Scandinavian mythology, and was invented to explain earlier *Blemya* figures (originating in Egypt and Crete), which had no head but whose vulva formed a mouth, and whose eyes were on their

Fig. 50 (a) Baubo in the Copenhagen Museum (after Andersen); (b) mother-goddess, and (c) toad-goddess (after Gimbutas).

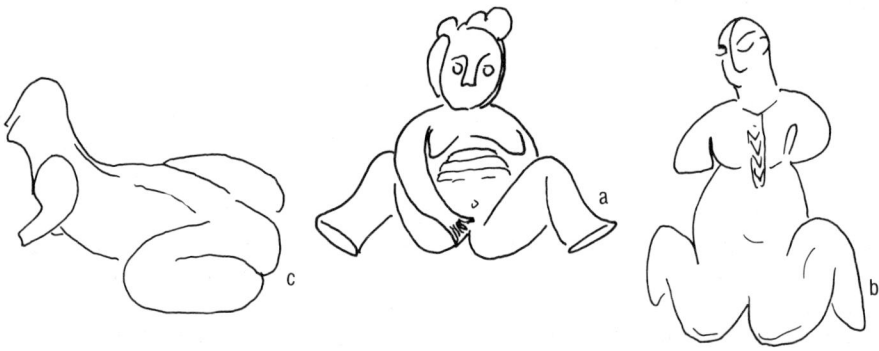

Plate 58 Figures in the Staatliche Muzeum of Berlin.

belly (see Reinach 1912, 1922; Baltrušaitis 1955; Kauffman 1975 for illustrations). They could well have been personifications of the vulva (Murray's 'personified *yoni*'), and the word 'Baubo' may have meant 'vulva'. Whatever the case, splay-legged figurines have become known as Baubo, many of these being found in Hellenistic contexts in Egypt (*Plate 58*).

Reinach points out that Constantine Psellos (*c.* AD 1018–1078), an influential Byzantine politician, monk and writer, drew heavily on Clement of Alexandria's account of Baubo's exhibitionism in his descriptions of quasi-theatrical productions which aimed at pouring scorn on pagan beliefs and practices. A corbel on the church of San Vicente, Ávila, and two figures from Como and Milan, show women lifting their robes to reveal their private parts in the way described by Clement. These suggest that the Baubo episode was known in medieval times. St Augustine knew of Clement's account also. There could, then, be some justification for Margaret Murray's suggestion that the tale of Baubo in Christian writings, and the figurines themselves, played a possible part in the creation of the female exhibitionist carvings. In our last chapter we shall refer to a description of folkloric practices in the Abruzzi area of Italy by G. Pansa. In this account he has something to say about Baubo, namely that:

1 chronologically speaking she follows Iambè;

2 the name 'Iambè' is still used today in parts of Greece to describe a queer old hag (just as, according to Guest, 'sheela-na-gig' was used in remote districts of Ireland);

3 Iambè or Baubo, in offering the ritual drink, introduced into the Eleusinian Mysteries an ancient rite performed by women in the nocturnal feasts of the Egyptian Bubaste (Herodotus);

4 since the Eleusinian Mysteries were fertility ceremonies, and so close to the hearts of country folk whose livelihood depended on the soil, they were never quite ousted by Christianity. In fact the Christian clergy adopted some of the esoteric mystic rites and, to this day in the Abruzzi, priests take part in, and bless, a number of phallic ceremonies, and that

5 the use of phallic amulets and jewellery is still current among country people in that part of Italy. Among these is the 'frog' device, which some have taken to be another form of Baubo.

Pansa also notes that the first person to identify the terra cottas with Baubo was Millingen (Millingen 1843).

It would seem, from all this, that a number of

distant influences may have played a part in the development of sheela-like exhibitionists; one cannot exclude a number of other sources like the Etruscan chariot-plates showing a splay-legged Gorgon with pendulous breasts and a protruding tongue (Bloch 1961), or the Merovingian belt-buckles, or Gallo-Roman Venus figurines. It makes for very interesting speculation, but the amount of evidence is not large.

Leaving aside these interesting genealogical questions, we offer now a list of the female exhibitionists known to us. A number of catalogues have been compiled in the past, Andersen's being the most recent and most

Plate 59 Sainte-Radegonde, Poitiers.

Plate 60 Llandrindod sheela. (Photo: Martin Pover and Brian Branston)

comprehensive with regard to the British examples. We have a few more to add to his list, and a rather larger number of Continental ones.

We do not know of any in Scotland, though Andersen and others have put forward three grotesque figures at Iona (Strathclyde), Rodil (Isle of Harris) and Taynuilt (Strathclyde) as sheela-like.

For the sake of the convenience of students who may wish to go and see any of the figures in the following lists, we shall depart from our practice in the rest of this book and give in brackets the county (or geographical location), *département* or *provincia*.

LIST A ENGLAND AND WALES

Ampney St Peter (Glos)
Austerfield (S. Yorks)
Bilton-in-Ainsty (two figures) (Yorks WR)
Binstead (I.O.W.)
Bridlington (E. Yorks)
Buckland (Bucks) (*Plate 67*)
Buncton (Sussex) (see remarks below)
Church Stretton (Shropshire)
Copgrove (Yorks WR)
Croft-on-Tees (N. Yorks)
Easthope (Essex; in the Colchester Museum)
Fiddington (Somerset) (M.A. Aston, *Somerset Achaeol.*)
Haddon Hall (Derbyshire)
Hellifield (N. Yorks; in private possession. See Andersen)
Holdgate (Shropshire)
Kilpeck (Herefordshire)
Llandrindod (Radnor) (*Plate 60*)
Lower Swell (Glos)
Oaksey (Wilts)
Oxford (Oxon)
Penmon (Anglesey)
St Ives (Cambs; in private possession)
Stoke-sub-Hamdon (Somerset)
Tugford (two figures) (Shropshire)
Whittlesford (Cambs)

Plate 61 Birr (Type III). (Photo: Nat. Museum of Ireland, Dublin)

Remarks

To the above figures we add some new, as yet unpublished figures, with some remarks about a few of the above:

Bugthorpe (E. Yorks)	Sitting among abstract forms of 'beakhead' (see Chapter 10) on the south respond of the Norman chancel arch is a very typical sheela; witness the head, eyes, nose, herculean shoulders, position of arms and knees. It has passed unnoticed until now because at some time in the past the 'offending' parts have been filled in with plaster, and then the whole church interior has been covered in thick whitewash. It is an important figure for reasons given in the next chapter.
Buncton (Sussex)	Drawn to our attention by G. Zarnecki, it is situated on the north impost of the Romanesque chancel arch, and is much 'rubbed' in the genital area.
Cirencester (Glos)	In the Corinium Museum are two very crudely-made carvings, one male, one female. The latter consists of one disc on top of the other to represent head and body, with pits for eyes, and a pit for a vulva. It has no known provenance, is about 30cm (12in) high, and is known as C.2748 from the Cripps Collection. Cripps was an antiquarian, as was Bathurst from whose collection comes the second figure (B.997) – about 38cm (15in) high, with an obliterated face and a vague bulge for the penis. It is now known that many crude artefacts were passed off on to late nineteenth-century collectors (see Jerman, Glos 1981). Is it possible that these two figures, said to be 'Romano-Celtic', are forgeries?

Egremont (Cumbria) and Pennington (Cumbria)	Both of these were published long ago, but have been ignored by Hutchinson, Andersen and others. They have been 'rediscovered' and republished by Bailey (Bailey 1983).
Ely Cathedral (Cambs)	Reported to us by Professor Zarnecki, it is high up on a roof corbel, not visible from the ground.
Lammas (Norfolk)	Part of a circular plaque (fourteenth-century?) with a boy in shallow relief. His penis has been hacked off and a rough vulva substituted. Privately-owned (Jerman 1982).
Devizes (Wilts)	In the Museum (Brooke Collection) is a bogus rock-chalk sheela probably sold to, or made for, Joshua Brooke (who was shown to be somewhat unscrupulous rather than ingenuous in his collecting) (Jerman, Glos 1981).
Rochester (Kent) (*Fig. 13*)	The woman holding fish on the central lunette of the cathedral façade has been mutilated but was once undoubtedly exhibitionist.
Elkstone (Glos)	On the corbel table stands a figure with its lower half cut away. What is left is very reminiscent of the Kilpeck sheela.
Studland (Dorset)	On a corbel is a female pulling at her vulva with one hand (there are many other interesting corbels, illustrated in the inventory of the Royal Commission for Historic Monuments, Dorset).

Plate 62 Seir Kieran. (Photo: Nat. Museum of Ireland, Dublin)

Plate 63 Lavey Old Church. (Photo: Nat. Museum of Ireland, Dublin)

LIST B IRELAND

Since many are in private hands or museums, we indicate P, M or NM for private, museum or National Museum Dublin respectively. We give first the published figures, then append a list of recent discoveries, not listed by Andersen:

Abbeylara (Longford)
Athlone (Westmeath) (M)
Ballinderry (Galway)
Ballyfinboy (Tipperary)
Ballylarkin (Kilkenny) (NM)
Ballynacarriga (Cork)
Ballyportry (Clare) (NM)
Berrymount (Cavan)
Birr (Offaly) (NM) (*Plate 61*)
Blackhall (Kildare)
Bunratty (Clare) (*Plate 65*)
Burgesbeg (Tipperary) (NM)
Caherelly (Limerick) (P)
Carne (Westmeath) (NM)
Castle Widenham (Cork) (P)
Cavan (Cavan) (NM)
Clenagh (Clare) (*Plate 69*)
Cloghan (Roscommon)
Clomantagh (Kilkenny)
Clonmacnois (Offaly)
Clonmel (Tipperary) (NM)
Cullahill (Laois)
Doon (Offaly)
Dowth (Meath)

Drogheda (Louth) (M)
Dunnaman (Limerick) (*Plate 66*)
Errigal Keeroge (Tyrone) (M)
Fethard Wall (Tipperary) (*Plate 64*)
Fethard Abbey (Tipperary)
Garry (Offaly) (P)
Lavey (Cavan) (NM) (*Plate 63*)
Liathmore (Tipperary)
Lixnaw (Kerry) (NM)
Malahide (Dublin)
Moate (Westmeath)
Moycarky (Tipperary) (now disappeared)
Newton Lennan (Tipperary) (NM)
Rahan (Offaly)
Rattoo (Kerry) (a cast in NM)
Rochestown (Tipperary) (now disappeared)
Seir Kieran (Offaly) (NM & a cast in British Museum) (*Plate 62*)
Stepaside (Dublin) – a doubtful sheela.
Swords (Dublin) (NM)
Tinnakill (Laois) (two figures, both now disappeared. Photographs in *MAN* 1932)
Tracton (Cork) (disappeared)
Tullavin (Limerick)

Plate 64 Fethard Wall (Type I (?)).

Plate 65 Bunratty Castle.

Plate 66 Dunnaman Castle.

Remarks

Additional to the above are the following, not in Andersen:

Ballaghmore Castle (Laois)	Published by Feehan and Cunningham in *Journal* of *Royal Society of Antiquaries of Ireland* 1978.
Killua (Westmeath)	Known as 'Chloran' and reported by Andersen. Now found in the British Museum Witt Collection.
Garry Castle (Offaly)	Published by Weir in Murtagh 1980.
Glendalough (Wicklow)	*La femme aux serpents* found by Weir on the south jamb of the Romanesque east window of St Saviour's Church, in a small triangular panel. The vulva is indicated by a small gash.
Knockarley (Offaly)	Published by Feehan in *Antiquity* 1979.
Cooliagh (Kilkenny)	(or Kyle) Published by O'Doherty in *Old Kilkenny Review* 1979.
Moygara Castle (Sligo)	The figure listed by Andersen seems to be a dancer or acrobat, but on a fallen voussoir is a coital pair, illustrated in Weir 1980.
Redwood Castle (Tipperary)	A crude figure with a large head pulls at a big pendent vulva with one hand.

LIST C FRANCE

(See *Fig. 58* for general distribution.)

Squatting or splay-legged

Aillas
Bonnesvalyn
Corme-Ecluse
Courpière
Guéron
Manéglise
Nonac
Saint-Hilaire-des-Loges

Saint-Martin-d'Ary
Saint-Martin-de-Sescas
Saint-Pierre-de-Pensac
Saint-Quantin-de-Rançannes
Saint-Vallier
Tollevast
Vouvant

Feet-to-ears acrobats

Allas-Bocage
Archingeay
Assouste
Audignon
Béceleuf
Bonnesvalyn
Bors-de-Baignes
Bruyères-Montbérault
Champagnolles
Chauvigny
Le Cher
Echillais
Givrezac
Guéron
Guitinières
Jouers
Lescar

Marignac
Massac
Montbron
Montfrin
Montmorillon
Saint-Coutant-le-Grand
Saint-Germain-de-Vibrac
Saint-Loup-Hors
Saint-Martial-lès-Coivert
Saint-Pierre d'Excideuil
Saint-Quantin-de-Rançannes
Saint-Sauvant
Saint-Savin
Saint-Séver
Vandré
Villenave-d'Ornon

Vulva-pulling

Beaulieu
Charmant
Civray
Guéron

Sainte-Radegonde, Poitiers (clothed, another
    figure almost identical but not displaying
    nearby, bare breasted. A very explicit
    figure.)
Sévignac-Thèze (but filled-in with cement)

Acrobatic vulva-pullers

Bruyères-Montbérault
Chauvigny

Chouday
Echillais

Thorn-pullers

(i) *Female* (all discussed in the text)
     Béceleuf
     Foussais
     Limoges

(ii) *Male*
      Bignay
      Merlévenez
      Poitiers
      Le Puy
      Saint-Léger-en-Pons
      Saint-Léonard-de-Noblat
      Vézelay

Plate 67 Buckland, Bucks. Much rubbed (?).
(Photo: J. & C. Bord)

Plate 68 Mens, La Coruña.

Fig. 51 Sainte-Radegonde, Poitiers: a most explicit exhibitionist.

LIST D SPAIN

(See *Fig. 56* for general distribution.)

Squatting or splay-legged

Cervatos
Corullón
Echano (hermitage)
Frómista
Jubia
Lomilla de Aguilar
Olóriz
Pecharromán

Perorrubio
San Cebrián de Muda
San Martín de Unx
San Pedro de Tejada (two with males)
Santa Marta del Cerro
Sangüesa
Santiago (chapel of San Bartolomé)
Villanueva de Cangas

Feet-to-ears acrobats

Cervatos
Corullón (San Esteban)
Frómista

San Cebrián de Muda
Valdenoceda

Vulva-pulling

Monterrey (with two males)

Villaviciosa (with a male)

Acrobatic vulva-puller

Revilla de Santullán

Thorn-pullers

Leyre
Matalbaniega

Monterrey
Segovia (San Millán)

The foregoing lists are not exhaustive. Even with strong binoculars one cannot always make out figures at a height. There are many anomalous figures, like those on the crossing ribs at Agonges. Some discreetly display their sexual parts as they fall prey to monsters (e.g. at Saint-Palais, Biota, Estella and Villanueva de Cangas), but since the organs are not dramatically exaggerated the didactic message is not emphatically sexual. It would take an age to scour all the corbel tables in France and Spain. We have followed the guidance of the Zodiaque series in many cases, always seeking out buildings whose corbels have received mention. In any case, the purpose of the lists is not to furnish a complete guide to the monuments but to demonstrate the weight of evidence supporting our contention that sheela-na-gigs are not an insular phenomenon, but most likely an off-shoot of the Continental flowering. How the transmission took place is the subject of the next chapter.

Plate 69 Clenagh Castle.

11 The distribution of sexual carvings

On a transept capital at Saint-Pierre d'Aulnay in Saintonge is a squatting figure with his feet on the necking ring of the pier (*Plate 70*). He has passed his arms under his knees, and is pulling down his mouth, full of sharp teeth with his hands. Between his hands there issue from his mouth two snakes which curl down to his nether region, there to open wide jaws. From the top of his head two other snakes stream out under the abacus, then turn their heads with open jaws and snarl at him. A few miles to the south, at Matha Saint-Hérie, a south window capital has been carved by the same sculptor or his atelier.

Over a thousand miles away at Kilpeck in Herefordshire, the famous south door has a capital consisting of a mask from whose mouth foliage (a vinescroll terminating in leaves and a bunch of fruit) emerges (*Fig. 52*). The face is like

that of the Aulnay and Matha figures. On the archivolt there are some human heads. From the mouth of one, snakes emerge to curl up and over and snarl at each other; from the mouth of the other, two snakes curl down below and turn and snarl (*Fig. 53*). The Kilpeck carver seems to have taken elements of the French carvings and shared them out among his three figures.

The question is – did the Kilpeck carver know of the French carvings? We shall see that there are many other similarities between Kilpeck, the other churches of the 'Herefordshire School of Sculpture', and churches in France and Spain. We have quoted the above figures because no one, to our knowledge, has drawn attention to these very precise details. Indeed, the window at Matha Saint-Hérie has on the opposite capital a monster with a curly tail just like that of Kilpeck's other door capital; the abaci have identical patterning of quirks and star-diapers or nailhead; the arch carving is top-

Plate 70 Mouth-puller at Aulnay. (Photo: J.A. Jerman)

Fig. 52 Kilpeck foliage-spewer.

Fig. 53 Kilpeck beakhead carvings exhibiting elements based on the Aulnay and Matha, Saint-Hérie figures).

heavy and the abaci continue well beyond strict necessity, as at Kilpeck.

Jónsdóttir (Jónsdóttir 1950) has established most of the details which characterise the 'Herefordshire School', and we can recognise the carvings of that atelier and those of its imitators in Shropshire, Worcestershire and Gloucestershire. Zarnecki (Zarnecki 1953) went further and showed how the inspiration for the tympana at Brinsop and Stretton Sugwas is to be found at Parthenay-le-Vieux. One clinching detail is that the horseman (known in France as 'le chevalier Constantin', from a mistaken impression that this equestrian statue, modelled on that of Marcus Aurelius in Rome, was that of the Emperor Constantine) in both the French and the Herefordshire carvings carries a hawk. The French carving had, in addition to the Constantine details, acquired those of a local knight, active on the Church's behalf, one Guillaume Larchevêque. The other tympanum, in both cases, is of Samson slaying the lion.

Many other links also exist. The voussoirs of Brinsop around the tympanum and in the vestry are cut in a way that is reminiscent of Saintonge voussoirs; saints standing on each other's heads at Kilpeck are found at Corme-Royal (which has outer archivolts of a watch-spring design found

at Shobdon), and in many other churches the figures are arranged round the arch. Column-swallowers found in Saintonge form the boss joining the ribs in Kilpeck's apse; the long claws of lions and other animals which are typical of the Herefordshire atelier are found at Parthenay-le-Vieux; the tetramorph (signs of the evangelists – the Angel of St Matthew, lion of St Mark, ox of St Luke and the eagle of St John) and the Battle of Vices and Virtues, which figure on fonts of the School, are everywhere common in Saintonge, and derive from *Beatus* and *Psychomachia* manuscripts; the conical caps or 'Phrygian hats' worn by a number of Herefordshire angels and soldiers, or the concentrically-ringed hairstyles, and the parallel folds of garments, can also be found abroad; the medallions joined by masks at Brinsop, Leominster, on a number of fonts in Shropshire, and on the archivolt of Kilpeck (and Iffley in Oxfordshire) occur on the south porch of Aulnay. There are many other resemblances, for instance the incidence of sexual exhibitionists, the types of acanthus foliage, the masks on corbels, the Agnus Dei carvings, carvings of wrestlers, musicians and acrobats (is it a coincidence that at Kilpeck a clutching couple, a musician and an acrobat occur in exactly the same order as at Massac and other places?) and so on. This is not the place to develop this parallelism fully; suffice to say that one can be left in no doubt that the Herefordshire School was strongly influenced by Continental models, even without the support of some extraordinary documentary evidence to which we shall turn shortly.

The resemblance of the Holdgate and Kilpeck sheelas with those of Guitinières, Champagnolles and many others has already been noted. There are many more similarities, whose cumulative testimony is too bulky to ignore, for which a few examples must suffice:

males at Studland look like the males of Champagnolles, which look like the males of Barahona;

coupling couples, clutching pairs, 'wrestlers' in Spain, Saintonge, Kilpeck and Shobdon, all have affinities;

la femme aux serpents in France is the same in Spain, and the torments of the damned, including those of the miser, are common in France and Spain, and we find them at Lincoln;

the Egremont sheela, holding sheep-shears to her lower abdomen, has affinities with a carving in Milan, the Porta Tosa woman;

peasants warming themselves, with lifted garments, occur in Navarra and in one French manuscript, and there is a similar scene involving a boy at Lammas in Norfolk;

the curious head which sprouts arms at Canterbury also occurs at Cunault, at Berrymount;

animal and human masks on corbels are everywhere indistinguishable one from another. One particular carving known as 'beakhead' will be the subject of further discussion; it is found alongside sexual exhibitionists in many places;

acrobatic figures and musicians at Kilpeck can be found abroad, and there is, for instance, an obvious relation between acrobats at Saint-Martin-de-Sescas, Sablonceaux, Saint-Michel-d'Entraygues and Grey Abbey;

the triangular head, slit mouth, long nose, herculean shoulders, posture and gesture of Irish and English sheelas have their foreign counterparts, e.g. at Marienhafe, Germany.

Of course some resemblances are fortuitous, but it is unlikely that they all are. When one considers geometric, zoomorphic and vegetal designs as well (without taking into consideration the all-too-obvious architectural similarities), then it is apparent that, whether through the passing-on of pattern books and plans, the travels of monks, or the mediation of itinerant workmen and their ateliers, architectural and iconographical ideas were swiftly dispensed throughout the Romanesque world. It is a remarkable phenomenon that within some 50 years, from AD 1100 to 1150, Romanesque churches and their decoration were everywhere to develop along the same lines and bear the same characteristics, distinguishing this art form from any other which preceded it.

It is equally remarkable that, if one concentrates attention upon the spread of sexual exhibitionists, a pattern of distribution emerges. It becomes clear that these unusual carvings are not random. We shall be more precise later, but, roughly speaking, they are to be found in the northern provinces of Spain, the west side of France, Auvergne and Normandy, and the British Isles. Outside these areas very few sheela-like figures are to be found.

Fig. 54 Map I
Map of Ireland showing the distribution of
exhibitionists and allied figures

Legend (for further information about this
taxonomy see Jerman 1981, Dundalk)

1 Sheela-na-gigs with both hands passed below the thighs from behind, fingers inserted in the vulva
2 Figures with only one hand passed behind
3a Figures with both hands passed in front to touch the pudenda
3b Figures with both hands only indicating the pudenda
4 Figures with one hand either touching or indicating the pudenda
5 Anomalous figures, with sheela-like characteristics but too eroded or damaged to be accurately ascribed to a class
6 Horses' heads biting a roll-moulding or billet
7 *La femme aux serpents*
8 Male figures

Locations

1 Errigal Keeroge
2 Cavan
3 Lavey
4 Drogheda
5 Killua
6 Cloghan
7 Swords
8 Ballinderry
9 Carne
10 Moate
11 Stepaside
12 Garry
13 Birr
14 Tinnakill
15 Blackhall
16 Killinaboy
17 Ballyportry
18 Ballyfinboy
19 Seir Kieran
20 Ballaghmore
21 Burgesbeg
22 Cullahill
23 Clenagh
24 Killaloe
25 Liathmore
26 Clomantagh
27 Ballylarkin
28 Moycarky
29 Bunratty
30 Redwood
31 Ballynahinch
32 Caherelly
33 Rattoo
34 Dunnaman
35 Tullavin
36 Fethard (Abbey)
37 Cooliagh (Kyle)
38 Lixnaw
39 Fethard (wall)
40 Kiltinane (church)
41 Newton Lennan
42 Clonmel
43 Rochestown
44 Castle Widenham
45 Athlone
46 Ballynacarriga
47 Doon
48 Knockarley
49 Clonmacnois
50 Dowth
51 Abbeylara
52 Malahide
53 Rahan
54 Tracton (Abbey)
55 Tomregan (Berrymount)
56 Clonfert
57 Dysart O'Dea
58 Glendalough
59 Grey Abbey
60 Ballycloghduff

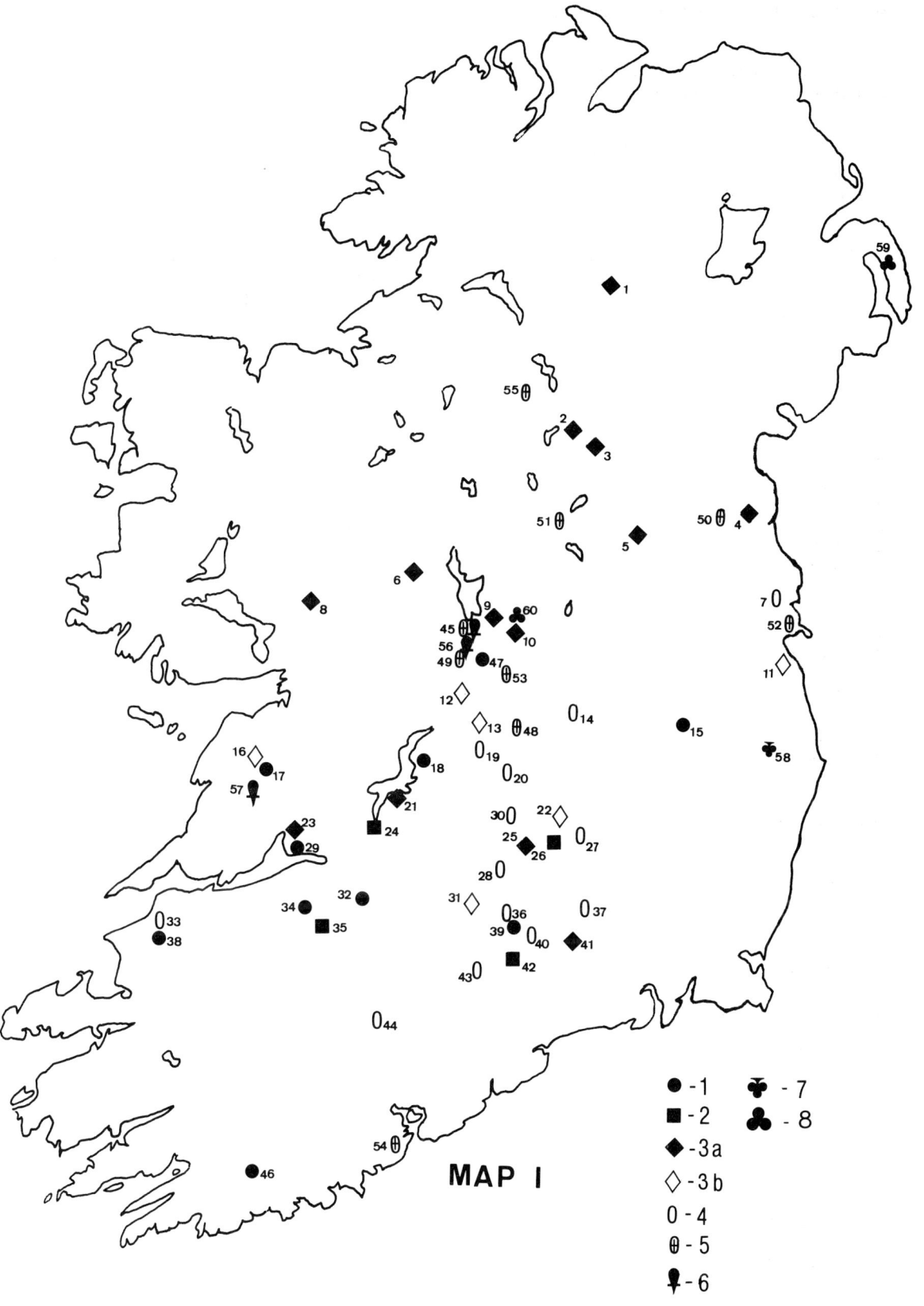

MAP I

- ● -1
- ■ -2
- ◆ -3a
- ◇ -3b
- 0 -4
- ⬧ -5
- ⬨ -6
- ⬥ -7
- ♣ -8

127

Fig. 55 Map II

Map of England and Wales showing location of exhibitionist figures

Legend

As for Map I (Ireland), though it is to be noted that much less significance can be attached to the groupings of the carvings in Britain.

The Rochester lunette figure was once undoubtedly exhibitionist but has been disfigured.

Locations

1	Binstead, I.O.W.	15	Austerfield
2	Bridlington	16	Egremont
3	Bilton-in-Ainsty	17	Buncton
4	Holdgate	18	Copgrove
5	Tugford (2)	19	Penmon
6	Church Stretton	20	Croft-on-Tees
7	Kilpeck	21	St Ives
8	Oxford	22	Buckland
9	Whittlesford	23	Ely
10	Easthorpe	24	Bugthorpe (requires restoration)
11	Ampney St Peter	25	Haddon Hall (late 17th-century)
12	Oaksey	26	Lincoln
13	Llandrindod		
14	Pennington		

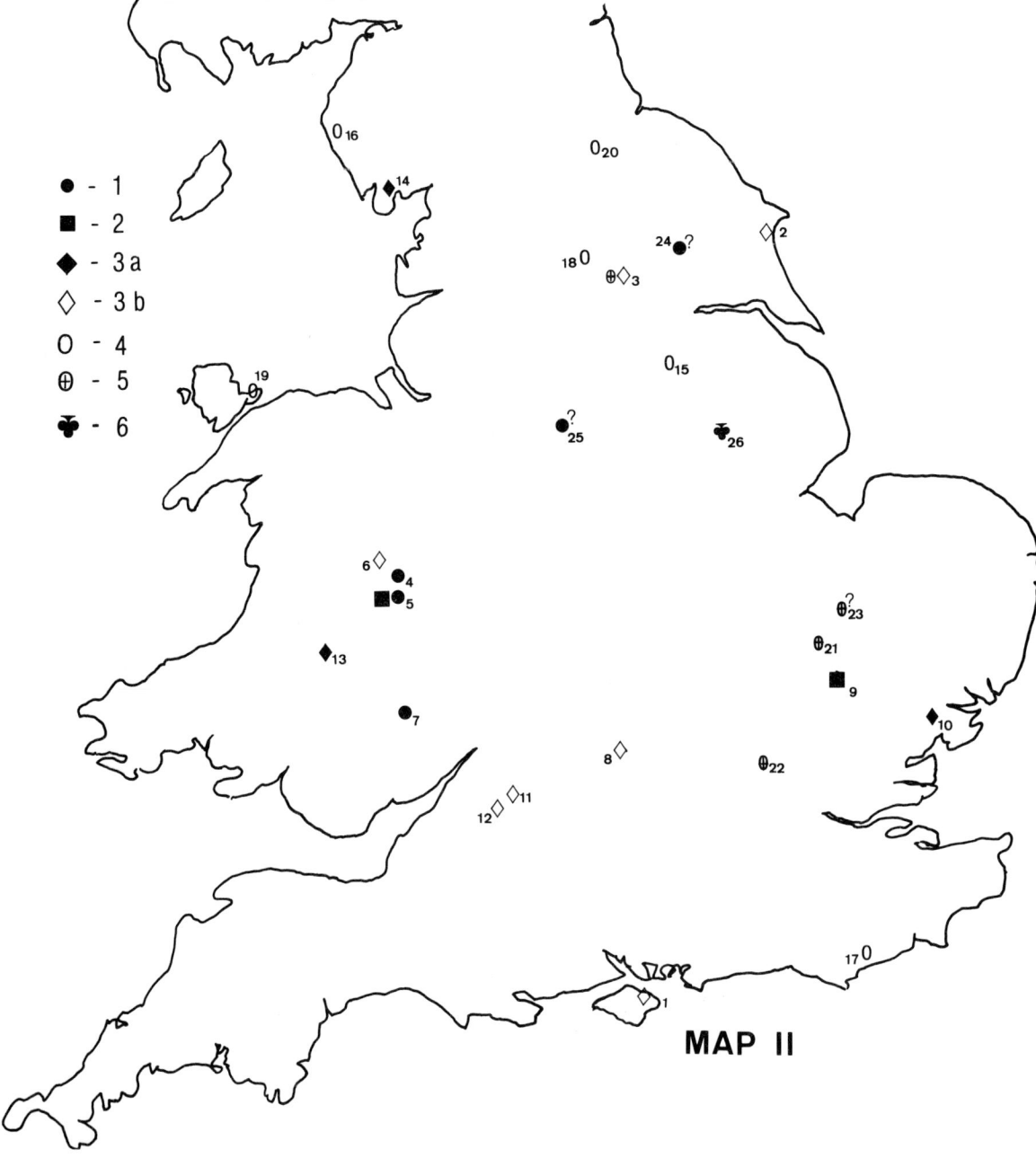

MAP II

Fig. 56 Map III
Map of northern Spain

Legend
1 Spinario (thorn-puller)
2 *La femme aux serpents*
3 The miser
4 Beakhead decoration
5 Female exhibitionist
6 Coital or exhibiting couples
7 *L'homme aux serpents*
8 Anus-shower

Examples

 1 Santiago de Compostela
 2 Mens
 3 La Coruña
 4 Jubia
 5 San Martín de Mondoñedo
 6 Orense
 7 Monterrey
 8 Corullón
 9 León
10 Aramíl
11 Villaviciosa
12 Amandi
13 Villanueva de Cangas
14 Revilla de Santullán
15 Cervatos
16 Lomilla de Aguilar
17 Matalbaniega
18 Valdenoceda
19 Frómista
20 San Quirce
21 Tejada
22 Miranda de Ebro
23 Estella
24 Olóriz
25 Echano (hermitage)
26 San Martín de Unx
27 Tudela
28 Leyre
29 Sangüesa
30 Sos del Rey Católico
31 Huesca
32 San Juan de la Peña
33 Gerona
34 Fuentidueña
35 Segovia
36 Perorrubio
37 Vallejo
38 Santa Marta del Cerro
39 Biota
40 Maranges
41 Olopte
42 Marzán
43 Sequera
44 Pecharromán
45 San Cebrián de Muda
46 Uncastillo
47 Agüero

Geographical locations

a Madrid
b Salamanca
c Zamora
d Oviedo
e Santillana del Mar
f Santander
g León
h Soria
i Logroño
j Jaca
k Saragossa (Zaragoza)
m Puenta la Reina
n Roncevaux
o Bayonne
p St Jean-Pied-de-Port
q Lescar
r La Seu d'Urgell (Seo de Urgel)
s Sahagún
t Lérida
u Santo Domingo de Silos
v Barahona
w Lugo

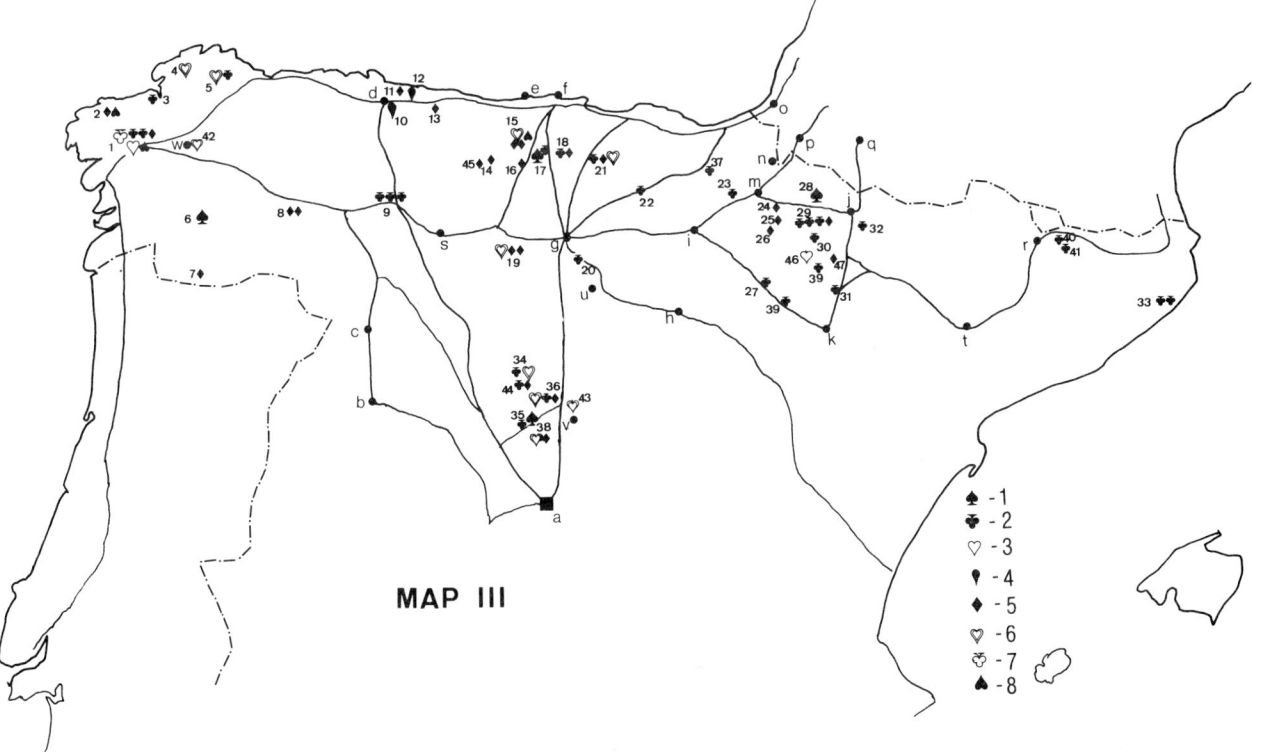

MAP III

- 1
- 2
- 3
- 4
- 5
- 6
- 7
- 8

Fig. 57 Map IV

Map of France showing distribution of *femmes aux serpents*, *hommes aux serpents*, misers (male and female, including Dives, *le mauvais riche*)

Legend

1 *La femme aux serpents*
2 *L'homme aux serpents*
3 Misers (male)
4 Misers (female)

Examples
Misers

1 Marolles-sur-Ourcq
2 Maringues
3 Ennezat
4 Clermont-Ferrand Notre-Dame-du-Port
5 Orcival
6 Saint-Nectaire
7 Besse-en-Chandesse
8 Nonette
9 Mailhat
10 Blesle
11 Brioude
12 La Graulière
13 Lavaudieu
14 Beaulieu
15 Conques
16 Chanteuges
17 Moissac
18 Bordeaux Sainte-Croix
19 Ingrandes
20 Dinan
21 Saint-Fort-sur-Gironde
85 Migron
87 Lucheux

La femme/L'homme aux serpents

22 Angers
23 Vézelay
24 Semur-en-Auxois
25 Thouars
26 Saint-Léger-de-Montbrillais
27 Saint-Jouin-de-Marnes

28 Preuilly-sur-Claise
29 Ardentes
30 Sémelay
31 Vouvant
32 Parthenay-le-Vieux, Parthenay, Notre-Dame-la-Couldre
33 Montmorillon
34 Cluny
35 Semur-en-Brionnais
36 Saint-André-de-Bagé
37 Deyrançon
38 La Jarne
39 Melle
40 Archingeay
41 Aulnay
42 Bénévent l'Abbaye
43 Charlieu
44 Champagne
45 Aujac
46 Cognac
47 Foussignac
48 Vienne
49 Biron
50 Marignac
51 Guitinières
52 Barret
53 Cressac
54 Blesle
55 Saint-Palais
56 Brive
57 Riom-ès-Montagnes

58 Bourg-Argental
59 Bordeaux Sainte-Croix
60 Saint-Christophe-de-Bardes
61 Targon
62 Gourdon
63 Valence
64 Mouchan
65 Lescure
66 Toulouse
67 Roquesérière
68 Lescar
69 Saint-Séver-de-Rustan
70 Ôo (also spelt Oô)
71 Saint-Pons
72 La-Charité-sur-Loire
73 Tournus
74 Limalonges
75 Thiers
76 Courpière
77 Riom-ès-Montagnes
78 Maurice
79 Romans
80 Solignac
81 Rodez
82 Bozouls
83 Saint-Georges-de-Montagne
84 Beaulieu
86 Lavaudieu
88 Urcel
89 Arthous

Geographical locations

a Paris
b Orléans
c Tours
d Mont-Saint-Michel
e Poitiers
f Saintes
g Blaye

h Arles
i Troyes
j Bayonne
k Le Puy
m Clermont-Ferrand
n Cluny
o Limoges

p Périgueux
q Saint-Séver
r Saint-Jean-d'Angély
s Nantes
t Caen
u Rouen
v Saulieu

w Autun
x Langres
y Chartres
z Liesse

Routes

Some of the main pilgrimage routes to Compostela are shown. Irish pilgrims probably sailed either direct to La Coruña, or to other northern Spanish ports, or to ports in western France. Some pilgrims sailed from Blaye in the Gironde estuary to Spain, or simply across the Gironde to follow the coastal route via Mimizan from Soulac-sur-Mer.

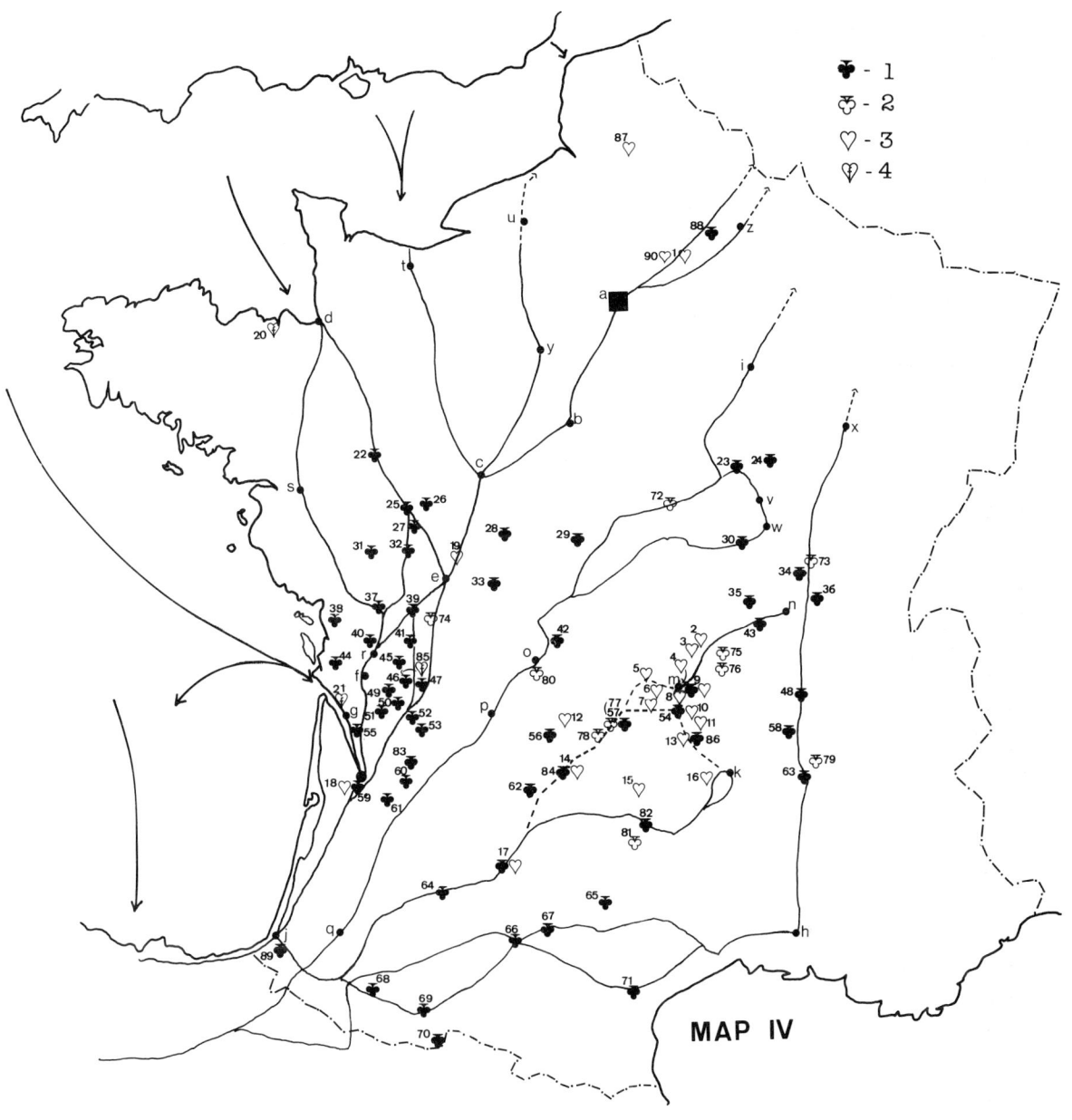

MAP IV

Fig. 58 Map V
Map of France showing distribution of female
exhibitionists, including female thorn-pullers
(Spinariae); in addition, male thorn-pullers are
indicated

Legend
1 Female exhibitionists   3 Male thorn-pullers
2 Female thorn-pullers

Sites

1 Saint-Hilaire-des-Loges	21 Allas-Bocage	41 Audignon
2 Vouvant	22 Saint-Martin-d'Ary	42 Chauvigny
3 Foussais	23 Montmoreau	43 Vandré
4 Béceleuf	24 Nonac	44 Asnières
5 Poitiers, Sainte-Radegonde	25 Charmant	45 Briantes
6 Le Cher	26 Saint-Vallier	46 Chouday
7 Saint-Coutant-le-Grand	27 Saint-Germain-de-Vibrac	47 Montfrin
8 Archingeay	28 Civray	48 Villenave-d'Ornon
9 Saint-Martial-les-Coivert	29 Limoges	49 Jouers
10 Massac	30 Courpière	50 Aillas
11 Bors-de-Baignes	31 Beaulieu	51 Merlévenez
12 Echillais	32 Saint-Séver	52 Poitiers
13 Saint-Sauvant	33 Lescar	53 Melle
14 Corme-Ecluse	34 Assouste	54 Bignay
15 Givrezac	35 Guéron	55 Saint-Léger-en-Pons
16 Saint-Quantin-de-Rançannes	36 Saint-Loup-Hors	56 Audignon
17 Champagnolles	37 Manéglise	57 Saint-Léonard-de-Noblat
18 Montbron	38 Bruyères-Montbérault	58 Vézelay
19 Marignac	39 Marolles-sur-Ourcq	59 Le Puy
20 Guitinières	40 Bonnesvalyn	60 Fontaines d'Ozillac

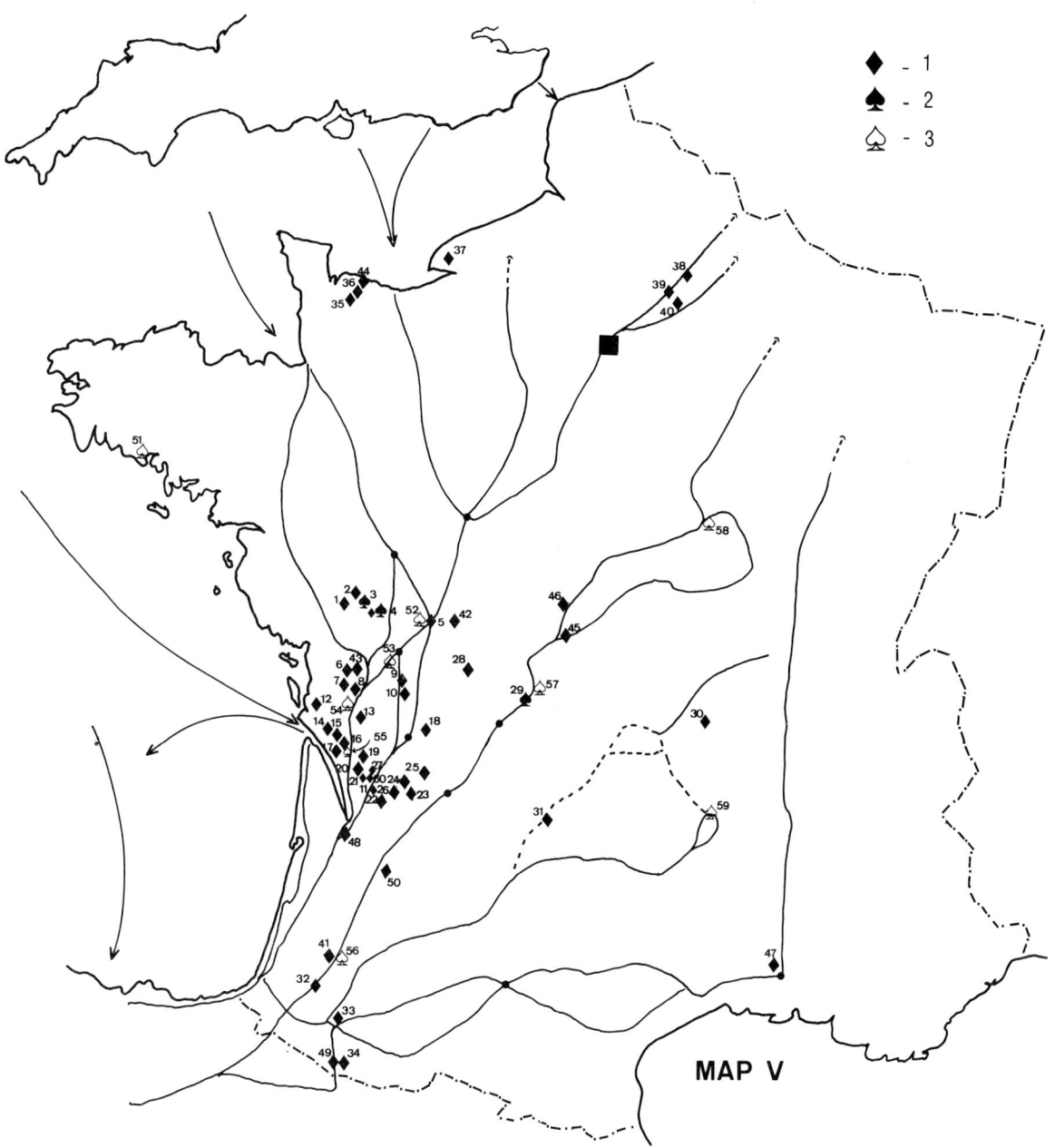

MAP V

Fig. 59 Map VI
Map of France showing distribution of beakhead
decoration and exhibitionist pairs. The
distribution of beakheads should also be compared
with that of female exhibitionists (Map V)

Legend

1 Coital couples in X-position
2 Couples exhibiting
3 Couples embracing

4 Horses' heads biting a billet
5 Monsters' heads biting a billet
6 Beakheads, of birdbeak type

Examples

1 Beaulieu
2 Carennac
3 Vaux-sur-Mer
4 Corme-Ecluse (2 pairs)
5 Nieul-le-Virouil
6 Melle, Saint Savinien
7 Fontaines d'Ozillac
8 Pérignac
9 Marignac
10 Studland, Dorset
11 Cénac
12 Passirac
13 Marthon
14 Audignon
15 Béceleuf
16 Saint-Hilaire-des-Loges
17 Echillais
18 Reignac
19 Saint-Loup
20 Saint-Trojan
21 Sévignac-Thèze
22 Savignac-d'Auros
23 Loctudy

24 Guimiliau
25 Arthous
26 Saint-Front-sur-Nizonne
27 Aulnay
28 Matha Marestay
29 Avallon
30 Maillezais
31 Sainte-Ouenne
32 Saint-Quentin-le-Baron
33 Mouthiers
34 Vitrac
35 La Chaise-le-Vicomte (La-
   Chaize-le-Vicomte)
36 Anzy-le-Duc
37 Poitiers
38 Saint-Jouin-de-Marnes
39 Angers, Saint-Aubin
40 Parçay-sur-Vienne
41 Mesland
42 Fresnay-sur-Sarthe
43 Beaumont-sur-Sarthe
44 Cuvergnon
45 Marizy-Sainte-Geneviève

46 Neuilly-Saint-Front
47 Bonnesvalyn
48 Epaux-Bézu
49 Marolles-sur-Ourcq
50 Brucheville
51 Asnières
52 Guéron
53 Saint-Loup-Hors
54 Nonant
55 La Fontaine-Henry
56 Douvres
57 Ouistreham
58 Bretteville
59 Norrey
60 Rots
61 Authie
62 Saint-Contest
63 Bayeux
64 Saint-Quantin-de-Rançannes
65 Saint-Germain-du-Seudre
66 Saint-Fort-sur-Gironde

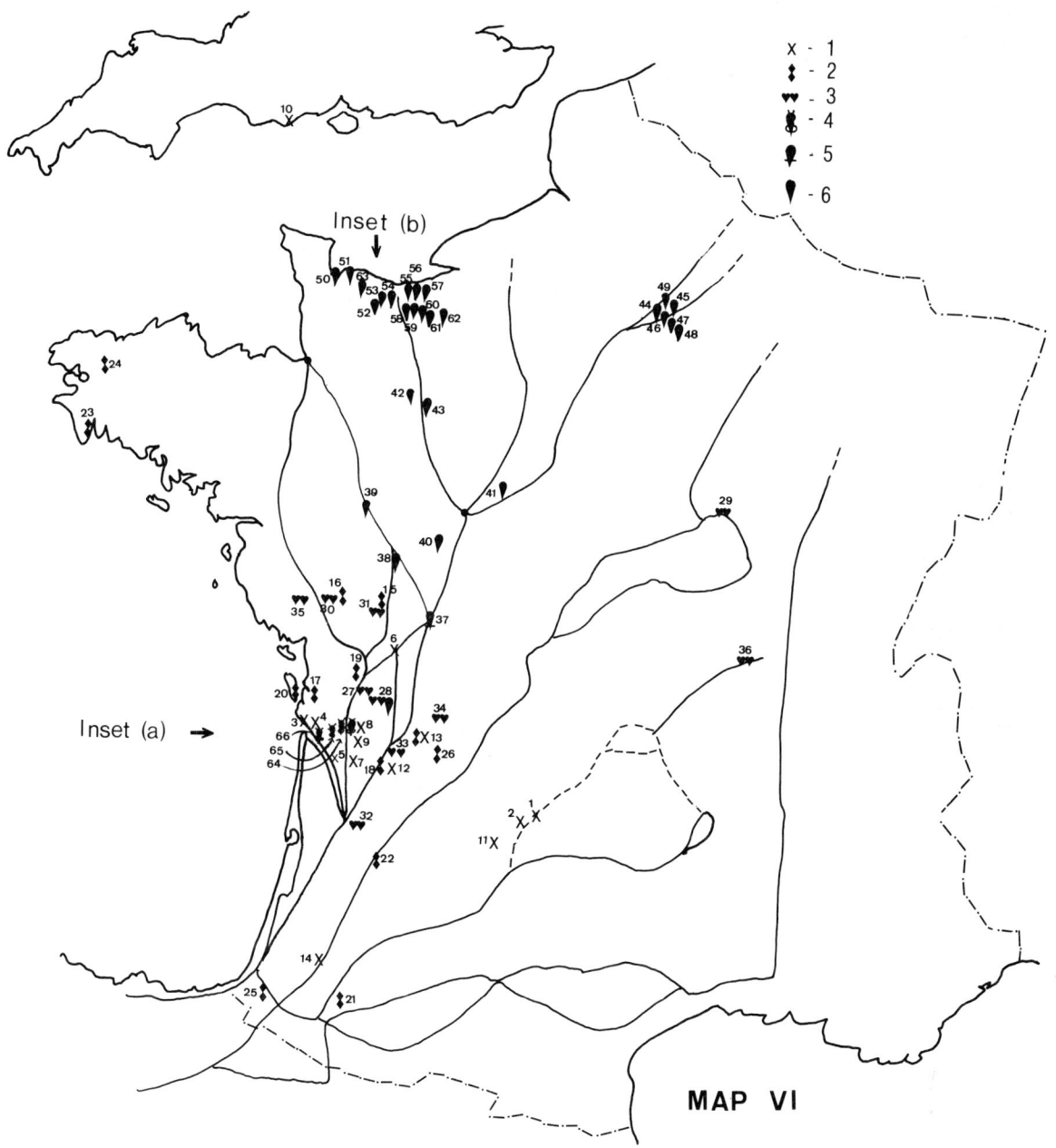

Inset (b)

Inset (a) →

x - 1
♦ - 2
▼▼ - 3
♣ - 4
♠ - 5
♦ - 6

MAP VI

Fig. 60 Map VI (*Inset a*) Detailed map of Saintonge

Legend

1 Female exhibitionist
2 *La femme aux serpents*
3 Male thorn-pullers
4 Female misers
5 Coital couples in the X-position
6 Clinging lovers
7 Exhibiting pairs
8 Anus-showers
9 Horses' heads biting a billet or moulding
10 Human heads, prototype of beakhead

Sites (geographical land-marks in italics)

1 La Jarne
2 Vandré
3 Saint-Martial-lès-Coivert
4 Aulnay
5 Saint-Loup
6 Saint-Coutant-le-Grand
7 Archingeay
8 Bignay
9 Echillais
10 Matha-Marestay
11 Champagne
12 Aujac
13 Migron
14 Mornac
15 Sablonceaux
16 *Saintes*

17 Saint-Sauvant
18 Vaux-sur-Mer
19 Corme-Ecluse
20 Cognac
21 Saint-Léger-en-Pons
22 Pérignac
23 Biron
24 Givrezac
25 Saint-Quantin-de-Rançannes
26 Marignac
27 Saint-Germain-du-Seudre (restoration)
28 Champagnolles
29 Saint-Fort-sur-Gironde
30 Guitinières
31 Saint-Germain-de-Vibrac

32 Nieuil-le-Virouil
33 Allas-Bocage
34 Fontaines-d'Ozillac
35 Saint-Palais
36 Reignac
37 Saint-Martin-d'Ary
38 *Blaye*
39 *Pons*
40 Saint-Trojan
41 Le Cher
42 *Talmont*
43 *Soulac-sur-Mer*
44 *Saint-Jean-d'Angély*
45 *Rochefort*
46 *La Rochelle*

Fig. 61 Map VI (*Inset b*)
Map of Normandy showing beakheads and exhibitionists

Sites

1 Brucheville
2 Asnières
3 Bayeux
4 Saint-Loup-Hors
5 Guéron
6 Nonant
7 Fontaine-Henry
8 Douvres
9 Ouistreham
10 Bretteville
11 Norrey
12 Rots
13 Authie
14 Saint-Contest
15 Thury-Harcourt

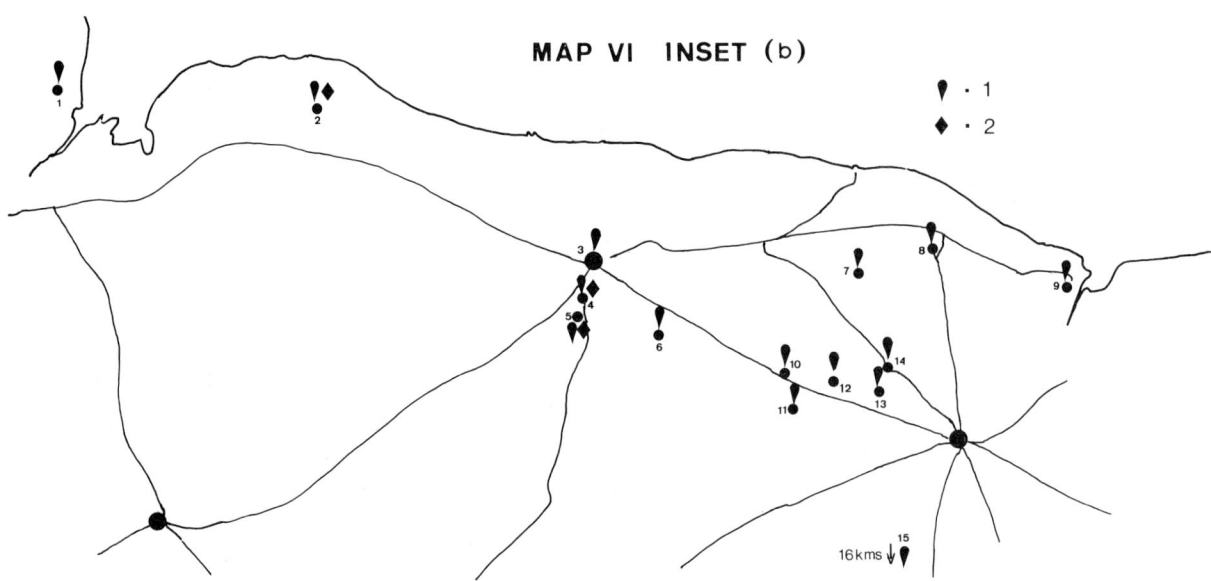

MAP VI INSET (b)

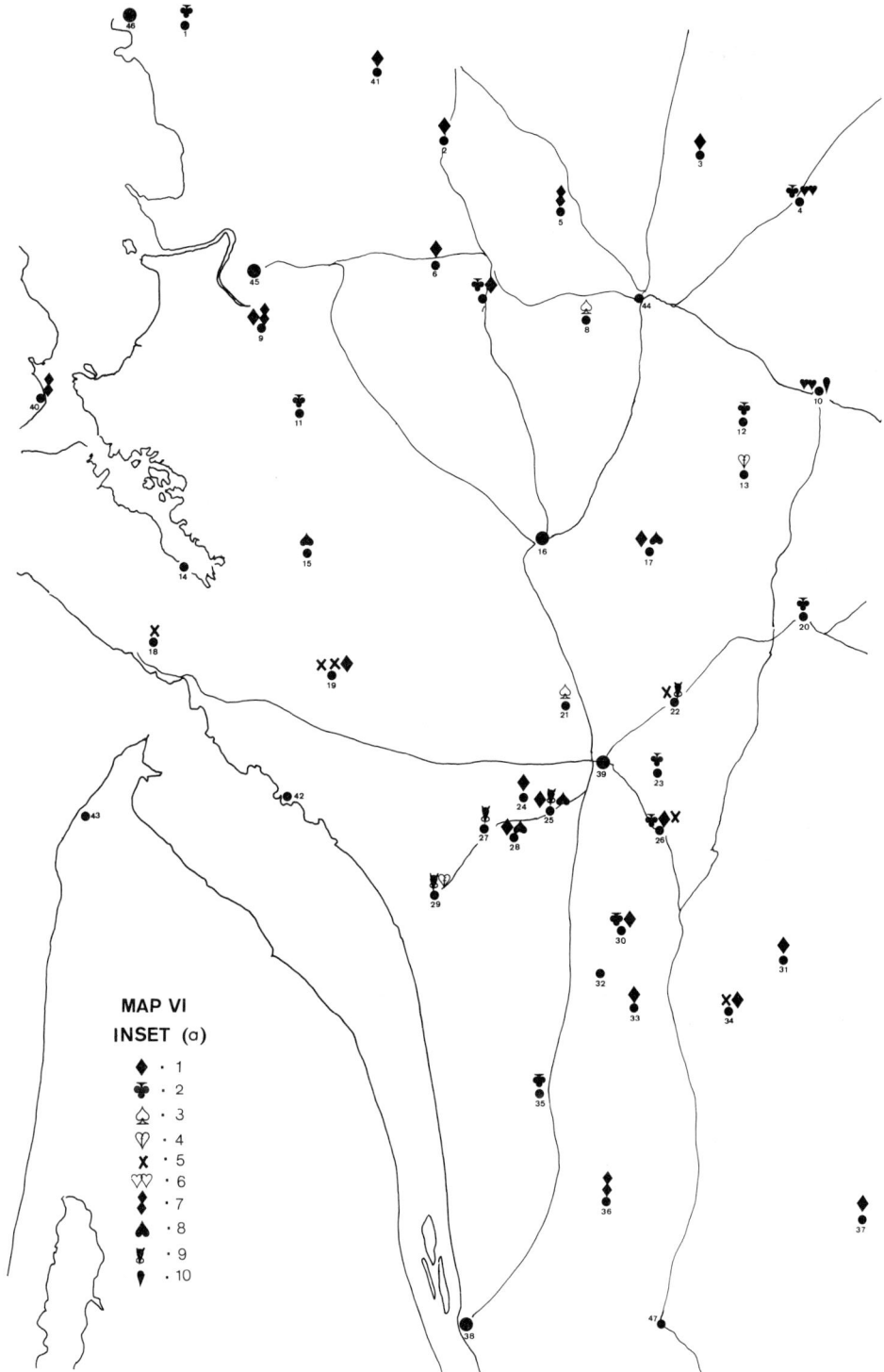

MAP VI

INSET (a)

Many ports in the Gironde estuary have silted up. Irish pilgrims (and English pilgrims coming to Saintonge by sea) would have landed at a number of ports from La Rochelle down to Blaye. From the latter port, other pilgrims sailed to Spain or were ferried across the Gironde to follow the coastal route on foot. The area contains many shrines visited by pilgrims – relics of saints at Poitiers (Saint-Hilaire), Saint-Jean-d'Angély (head of John the Baptist), Saintes (Saint-Eutrope), Blaye (Saint-Romain) and also the body of Roland, whose ivory horn lies in Bordeaux. Oliver's body lies in the Landes at Belin. All these shrines are mentioned by Aimery Picaud, author of the twelfth-century *Pilgrim's Guide*.

Evidently there was much coming and going throughout western Europe (quite apart from military operations) and the communication of art forms was rapid and easy. Travel in the Middle Ages continued to be as vigorous as it had been in previous centuries, when Celtic monks established Irish monasteries in Italy, Germany and Switzerland, when Anglo-Saxon bishops and abbots made their way to Rome, often more than once, and when the Vikings forayed deep into Russia and the Mediterranean. The route to Rome was well established by bishops going to seek the *pallium*, by plaintiffs and defendants engaged in canon law suits, or by pilgrims wishing to see the site of Paul's death and Peter's church. The Crusades took pilgrim-soldiers even further afield. Pilgrimages began in the eighth century, if not before, attracting those who could combine devotion with ecclesiastical or legal business. Irish lords, for instance, are known to have made the journey to Rome in the tenth century.

The pilgrimage which attracted the greater number of travellers, however, was that to St James of Compostela. Based on the strange and apocryphal legend of St James' burial in Spain after he had carried out his mission there, a rumour apparently started by Theodemir, Bishop of Iria in about AD 830, pilgrimages soon began. A French manuscript (*Martyrologie d'Adon*) of AD 860 states that St James was buried in Spain 'not far from the sea'. It is clear that when Gotescalc, Abbot of Le Puy, made his pilgrimage in AD 951, the route was well-established; he stopped at Albelda to have a copy made of a *Beatus* apocalypse, about which he must have known.

The pilgrimage to Compostela had special appeal because it was not cut off by Saracens, as the Holy Land was to be, and because it was as arduous as a voyage to Palestine, as remote, and as challenging – at any rate once the Pyrenees were reached and crossed, and the hard journey over the arid lands of Castile (pluvious and cold in some seasons) undertaken. The traffic became enormous. On February 26th, 1189, just as Frederick Barbarossa was coming to terms with the Pope, some 10,000 German pilgrims were reported to have left for Compostela by sea (where they tried without success to carry off the head of the statue of St James). One of St James' hands had somehow or other already come into the possession of the Emperor Henry V, whose wife Mathilda brought it to England, to become a precious relic at Henry I's foundation of Reading. A fleet of some 300 ships full of pilgrims is reputed to have stood outside Corunna waiting to dock at some date during the thirteenth century; and earlier, at the beginning of the twelfth century, 1000 new pilgrims arrived in Santiago each day. There was so much traffic that special hospices and hospitals, mortuary chapels, churches and shrines were built all along the principal routes. Thousands of masons, carpenters, architects, goldsmiths and other artisans moved along the pilgrim roads (significantly known in Spain as 'el camino francés' or in French as 'la route d'Espagne').

The Benedictine Order, and especially the Cluniac, organised a vast building programme (in which, paradoxically, lay the spearhead of the destruction of monasticism, for the building of churches to accommodate pilgrims was the first step towards a secular Church). The great churches of Saint-Martin at Tours (destroyed), Conques, Le Puy, Vézelay, Frómista, Santiago and others, with their ambulatories and side chapels, designed to allow floods of pilgrims to circulate inside, were all built at much the same time. Scholars argue about which came first, whether French influence was stronger than Spanish influence – did Saint Sernin, Toulouse, furnish elements of Santiago, or was it the other way about? – but the fact is that, whatever the case, dozens of major churches and hundreds of smaller ones were constructed in an unparalleled building boom. It is not to be marvelled at that similar ideas and motifs were transmitted and eagerly seized upon by enthusiastic patrons and masons. The pilgrim roads became the source of trade and wealth; churches sought the patronage of wealthy, pious pilgrims. The introduction of the Cluniac Benedictines into England was the result of an abortive pilgrimage to Rome by William de Warennes, kinsman of the Conqueror, and his wife Gundrada. They had to stop at Cluny, where they were much impressed, and became benefactors, as did Henry I (who paid for a new refectory) and Roger de Montgomery.

Emile Mâle and Kingsley Porter have made admirable studies of the art and architecture of the pilgrimage roads, tracing the source and development of ideas, and it becomes apparent that the Cluniacs seized the opportunity of the pilgrim roads to invest heavily in building and administration. Moissac was Cluniac by 1047 and, by the end of the eleventh century, nearly all the bishops and secular clergy along the Spanish route were French Cluniacs. The transfer of ideas both ways across the Pyrenees, an almost impenetrable mountain frontier, was facilitated. It is important to note that traffic in iconographic ideas moved in both directions.

Into Spain, the northern part of which was Mozarabic Christian, with a long history of architecture and sculpture, may have travelled ideas from Moissac and Toulouse. What is certain is that the pattern-books ultimately derived from *Beatus* and *Psychomachia* manuscripts (both of which came from Spain) gave us the sculpture of south-west France; Moorish influences can be traced in the polylobed arches of places as far afield as Le Puy, Thouars, and Montréal in Burgundy, or in the use of multi-coloured stone at Vézelay and Le Puy.

> Les pèlerins de Saint Jacques n'en étaient pas à un détour près en se rendant à Notre-Dame du Puy ou à Conques . . . ils passaient volontiers par Brioude, Clermont, Saint-Nectaire ou Aurillac
> Craplet 1972

(The pilgrims of St James did not mind detours when they went to Notre-dame at Le Puy or to Conques . . . they would willingly go through Brioude, Clermont, Saint Nectaire or Aurillac)

What was true for Auvergne was true for other places. One has the impression from reading Aimery Picaud's 'Guide du pèlerin' (an impression reinforced by many modern writers) that there were only four pilgrim roads in France and one in Spain. There were, in fact, many tributary and alternative roads, apart, of course, from the sea-routes used by the wine traders, among others, to Bordeaux and other Saintonge ports, or to Bilbao, Santander and La Coruña. In Spain there was a coast road running from Saint-Jean-de-Luz to La Coruña, with turn-offs to join the main inland road at Bilbao and Santander. This explains the sculptures of remote churches like Cervatos or Tejada (one of the carvings of San Pedro de Tejada is of a pilgrim with his staff). Santillana had stopping places for pilgrims, and Bishop Martin of Orzendjan of Armenia passed through in about 1390, leaving an account of his pilgrimage. In

France it is clear that churches like Orcival, Issoire and Brioude, with their ambulatories, were places of pilgrimage. Brioude indeed was the church of Saint Julien, a saint revered in France second only to Saint Martin. But small remote churches like Mailhat have left sculptural evidence that they, too, were on pilgrim routes.

The attraction of the road to Santiago was enhanced by the knowledge that Charlemagne and his peers had trodden part of the path. Perhaps the 'chansons de geste' began here, the 'Chanson de Roland' certainly did; and part of the pilgrimage was to places renowned for their connection with Charlemagne. The pilgrims stopped at Roncevalles, scene of the last rearguard stand of Oliver, Turpin and Roland and their friends; at Blaye and Belun, where were the bodies of Roland, Oliver and others, and at Bordeaux to see Roland's horn in the church of Saint-Seurin.

Picaud tells us of famous shrines – the tomb of Saint Eutropius at Saintes (with its other famous churches), the alleged head of John the Baptist at Saint-Jean-d'Angély. To the north the west road passed through Orléans, where were kept pieces of the Cross at Sainte-Croix, or the knife used at the Last Supper at Saint Samson. The pilgrim roads were dotted with obligatory stops and detours. The churches along the route are of the typical pilgrimage design.

Yet it cannot be said that there was a distinctive 'Pilgrimage Roads School of Sculpture'. What is true of architecture is not true of decoration. Motifs and iconographical details were passed along, but it remained a matter to be decided by local patrons, clergy and the masons they employed what actually took place in the matter of decoration; finance was obviously the operative factor. Thus we find a great similarity in the Soria churches of Fuentesauco, Omeñaca and Tozalmoros; indeed the masons' marks tell us that the same workmen were involved in them. They have very similar doorways, carved with human-headed, serpent-tailed bird-sirens entwined with serpents, but only at Tozalmoros are the corbels carved (perhaps by the man who left distinctive masons' marks not found at the other two churches). It seems that carved corbels were not part of the contract at Fuentesauco and Omeñaca. The size of the

Fig. 62 A page from the Escorial *Beatus* showing Satan in a sheela Type III position.

church and the extent of its ornamentation were matters for local purses and predilections.

Local styles prevailed in many areas. Crozet has shown how Saintonge influenced Poitou, and how these in turn passed ideas to surrounding areas and as far north as Brittany and Normandy; Jónsdóttir has shown these influences at work in Herefordshire. What is interesting, however, is the transfer of ideas across these main local spheres of influence.

One such idea is 'beakhead' decoration (*Fig. 63*). The word 'beakhead' was coined in the nineteenth century, perhaps under the impulse of the common English form which shows the head of a bird with a long pointed beak. In France 'têtes plates' refer to human and animal faces whose chin, tongue or beard lap over a moulding of an arch. An important article (Zarnecki & Henry 1958) traces the development of this motif from Saintonge northwards to the Loire, thence into Normandy and across the Channel. Norman influence in the Aisne-Oise area was strong, and beakheads are found there also (Lefèvre-Pontalis 1906; Prache 1981, 1983). In Normandy and England it became a

birdhead after the mid-twelfth century and flourished in the areas of the Cotswolds, Gloucestershire, Oxfordshire and Herefordshire, and was very popular in Yorkshire (Salmon 1946). Whether or not its popularity had something to do with a residual penchant for Danish/Viking ideas cannot be argued here, though because of a lack of examples in Scandinavia it can be affirmed that it did not start there. When introduced into England, however, it may have elicited some response traceable in part to Anglo-Viking ideas. Zarnecki proposed a looking-back to pre-anarchy times and hence to pre-anarchy motifs.

The distribution of churches with beakhead decoration in France follows very closely that of sexual exhibitionists. Even when beakhead made its way, through Norman influence, into the Aisne-Oise area, sexual exhibitionists accompanied it (Marolles-sur-Ourcq has two exhibitionists and a miser on the transept pier capitals; Bonnesvalyn has six exhibitionists. Others can be found at Chelles, Villers-Saint-Paul, Montigny-Lengrain, Saint Vaast de Longmont). Even in England this incidence is to be noted: Kilpeck and Holdgate have the only beakhead in Shropshire; Bilton and Austerfield have beakhead, as well as sheelas. The argument here is not that beakhead has any sort of sexual significance but that its congruence with exhibi-

Fig. 63 Continental beakheads at Cuvergnon and Argenton (after Lefèvre-Pontalis).

Fig. 64 Beakhead at Bugthorpe, and a beakhead which on closer inspection is a sheela whose lower portions have been hidden by plaster or cement.

tionists suggests that they were contemporaneous, and, since beakhead in England and France dates from about the mid-twelfth century, we have further evidence for dating exhibitionists to the same period (Jerman, Dundalk 1981).

The most telling piece of evidence is at St Andrews, Bugthorpe, just east of York (*Fig. 64*). The responds of the Norman chancel arch have abstract beakheads. On the north jamb there is an actual beakhead among these. On the south jamb, her lower portions filled-in crudely with plaster, is a sheela – to judge by the features of the head, shoulders, arms and knees. The whole church has been daubed with thick whitewash which, while lending a certain clean bright look to the interior, has succeeded in obliterating much of the carved detail of beakheads and capital carvings (among which seems to be an anguipede). Bishop Wilton church, not far away, has beakhead, and a late male exhibitionist.

There is one other conclusion to be drawn. In Ireland there are very few beakheads (there are some at Dysart O'Dea), but instead there are horses' heads, the mouth gripping a piece of roll-moulding (if the heads are placed next to each other the moulding then becomes continuous). Henry showed that in only one other area

in Europe were such heads to be found, at Pérignac, Saint Quantin de Rançannes, Saint-Fort-sur-Gironde (and Saint-Germain-du-Seudre), i.e. in Saintonge, not far from the ports at which Irish pilgrims landed, on their way to join the throngs at Saintes, Saint-Jean d'Angély, and thence to Spain. So the horseshead motif is likely to be one introduced into Ireland by returning pilgrims.

We then find that the Aisne-Oise carvings are on a pilgrim route north-east of Paris, to Liesse, a shrine frequented by French kings and Joan of Arc among others, and thence towards Aachen and Germany, a road which northern pilgrims would have taken in reverse direction, on their way to Santiago (*Fig. 65*).

We also find that sexual exhibitionists and beakhead decoration are along well-marked pilgrim routes and, indeed, are rarely to be found more than 8 to 16km (5 to 10 miles) away from such routes; strangely, though, they are only on rural churches. The miser is found on main pilgrim churches, as is *la femme aux serpents*, but exhibitionists feature on the smaller establishments. Why this is so is a matter requiring further research.

As to why the miser, the *homme/femme aux serpents* and exhibitionists should be found near or on pilgrim routes, an obvious answer can be given. Aimery Picaud tells us of the merchants ready to sell pilgrim pouches, scallop shells and the like, in the church square at Santiago. It is not hard to imagine all the other folk who made a living out of the pilgrimages – the entertainers and buskers, jugglers and magicians, acrobats and dancers, con-men, wine-sellers and innkeepers. The Church itself did well out of all this piety, yet must have looked askance at the commercialism that flourished in the streets, (and upper rooms and cellars). It was, in any case, not entirely blameless. Prostitution accompanied the pilgrimages as it had done the Crusades, and the Church drew up regulations to control it; but it also drew revenue from it in some places (McCall 1979). What it could do, and did, was to preach against low standards of morality among the pilgrims and their entourage, all of them far from home, kith and kin, and with the promise of forgiveness for their sins at the end of the journey.

This resulted, in our view, in the didacticism that is so prevalent in the sculpture of the

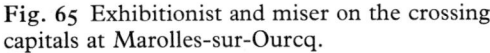

Fig. 65 Exhibitionist and miser on the crossing capitals at Marolles-sur-Ourcq.

pilgrim road churches; and the close connection between the roads and the exhibitionists. Is there other evidence to support our thesis?

Dugdale (*Monasticon*) and Wright (*History of Ludlow*) both published partial accounts of a missing document, the history of Wigmore Abbey in Shropshire. The *Chronicle* was rediscovered in the University of Chicago Library in 1929. It tells the fascinating story of Oliver de Merlimont, seneschal to Hugh de Mortimer, Lord of Wigmore, who made the pilgrimage to St James of Compostela (for details see Zarnecki 1953; Dickinson & Ricketts 1969). Before leaving he set about rebuilding a little church at Shobdon, and, while on his pilgrimage 'always mindful of the undertaking at Shobdon', he made note of all he saw (no doubt one of his retinue made drawings for him). On his return the designs he had noted were incorporated in his church. Unfortunately the church was pulled down in the eighteenth century and only parts remain, re-erected as a 'Romantick Ruin'. But from the vestiges it is possible to see how a local atelier, the 'Herefordshire School of Sculpture' began. On his way back from Compostela, Merlimont stayed at the

Abbey of Saint-Victor in Paris, and, after some difficulty, succeeded in getting Victorine monks to come over to Shobdon to serve his church, the first Victorine house in England. Robert de Bethune, Bishop of Hereford, dedicated the church and, after falling out with his lord, Miles of Gloucester, took refuge at Shobdon. Miles died in 1143, and the quarrel took place before then. By calculating how long it took to build the little monastery, to get the monks there from Paris, and so on, it is possible to suggest that Merlimont's pilgrimage took place in about 1138. The tympana of Brinsop and Stretton Sugwas; the fonts of Eardisley, Castle Frome and Stottesdon; the churches of Rowlestone and Fownhope, and Kilpeck cannot be much later than 1150–60.

It is a fascinating study to take all the elements of the 'Herefordshire School' and, using these, to trace Merlimont's journey, outwards and inwards. Parthenay he must have seen, then Saint-Jouin-de Marnes to the south, on the way to Aulnay. (Did he sleep the night there like other pilgrims, in the north transept, away from the west and south doors to be out of the draught? And is that where he saw the figure described at the beginning of this chapter? And did he then go to Matha, and see the window that furnished a design for Kilpeck?) We must remember in all this that we have focused our attention on one man, Oliver de Merlimont, but of course there were other pilgrims from Herefordshire who followed in his footsteps, or at least there were masons and monks who came to Shobdon during its early days, bringing ideas for sculpture.

We must also recall the tremendous ferment of intellectual activity going on in France which must have impressed pilgrims like Merlimont. The Abbey of Saint-Victor was already famous for its teachers and pupils – William de Champeaux, Peter Abelard, Saint Bernard – and its library, ridiculed by Rabelais, was extensive. Another of its pupils, Robert de Bethune, became Bishop of Hereford. Reputed to be one of the foremost theologians of his day, he was only one of three English clerics permitted by Stephen to attend the inquisition of Gilbert de la Porrée at Rheims. Here Robert died, attended by bishops, archbishops and even the Pope. A humble, unassuming man, he had worked while a monk at Llanthony Priory *as a mason*, on the conventual buildings at Weobley. A staunch friend of Merlimont, he approved of his venture at Shobdon, and it was through his good offices that Gilduin of Saint Victor consented to send monks to serve the little monastery. An indefatigable dedicator of churches throughout his diocese, he had personal experience of architecture, and a letter from him to Abbot Suger, builder of Saint-Denis, survives.

It was no wonder that Merlimont was impressed by his stay in Paris. Equally he would have been impressed by the artistic activity in Poitiers through which he must have passed on his return. It was here that William IX, the 'troubadour' duke of Aquitaine, Count of Poitiers, had held his court of brilliant young men and women, poets and jongleurs and entertainers, following the lead of their artistic lord whose own poetry, at times near-pornographic, could rise to heights of elegance. Here throve 'courtly love', much to the chagrin of the Church which considered it adulterous. A light-hearted social diversion, it was also a defiance of Christian teaching by the urbane and cultivated nobility, and very much at odds with St Augustine's teachings. Concubinage in Aquitaine, a province noted for the 'looseness of its women and the lustiness of its men' was rife among the lax, uneducated, ignorant country clergy as well as among the aristocracy. Both hunted and hawked, drank and over-ate, borrowed and lent money, and fornicated at will. Duke William himself was excommunicated for abandoning his wife in favour of his mistress. His wife was widow of Sancho-Ramirez of Aragon; the house of Aquitaine had long been related to the dynasties of Aragon and Navarra, a matter of no little importance for the establishment under royal protection of a safe pilgrimage route along the 'camino francés'. William's son,

Plate 71 Exhibitionist at Bonnesvalyn.

William X, after a stormy encounter with St Bernard, died on the pilgrimage to Compostela and was buried there in 1137. His daughter, Eleanor, was to bring all south-western France to the Norman possessions when she married Henry II of England, after her first annulled marriage to Louis VII of France, making the Angevin empire the biggest since Charlemagne. In 1170, when she was banished to Poitiers for protesting against her husband's liaison with the 'fair Rosamund', she established a court that became the chief academy in Europe for the arts of 'courtoisie' and her ladies become the arbiters of a small glittering society of young men who came to joust and tourney and seek brides or mistresses.

Poitiers, then, was a centre of courtly love (as were Provence and Languedoc) and therefore a centre also for the Church's attack against what Orderic Vitalis called 'les libertines qui s'étudient à plaire aux femmes par toutes sortes de lâchetés' (libertines who study the art of pleasing women by every manner of immorality). Evidence so far collected suggests that the first exhibitionist motif appeared here at Saint-Hilaire and at Melle Saint-Savinien, perhaps not surprisingly. The Saint-Hilaire frieze dates from about 1055. Some ten years later an exhibitionist ape appeared on a capital of the Panteón de los Reyes at León. Exhibitionist sculptures spread in those areas most influenced by Aquitainian figure-carving. In two areas which have been investigated, just under 50 out of 500 churches in Saintonge have exhibitionists, and just over 25 have coupling couples; in Palencia some 12 churches out of 120 have exhibitionists, and half a dozen have coupling couples. The proportions are similar – the numbers differing because Saintonge is larger and has a greater number of churches.

In Spain exhibitionists are concentrated in western and northern Galicia, Asturias, Palencia and Santander, Segóvia and Soría, and Navarra (Fig. 54). The coastal areas have an abundance of acrobatic figures. These are all regions where carved corbels are found and where motifs seem to be derived from Aquitaine. It goes without saying that all these provinces are along the camino francés to Compostela, with another by-pilgrimage to León, to the tomb of San Isidoro; along the road arose magnificent churches like Frómista,

which was to influence so many smaller churches.

Motifs we have studied, like Avaritia and la femme aux serpents, are to be found along, or in the close vicinity of, the four main pilgrimage roads of France; but only the westernmost, from Compostela, along the northern provinces of Spain, into Aquitaine, Poitou, the Vendée, Brittany and Normandy (with a tributary north-east of Paris to Liesse), thence to the British Isles, has sexual exhibitionists in significant numbers. Along that route are the sisters and brothers, as it were, of the Irish and English sheelas (Maps IV, V). Alongside the exhibitionists is beakhead decoration (Map VI); it even features in later Romanesque Spanish churches at Aramil and Amandi, and it is thought that the design was an importation from the north. It is also thought that beakhead in Normandy was an importation from England. (The whole question of beakhead decoration is in need of research.)

The association of beakhead decoration and sexual exhibitionists gives dating evidence which suggests that Poitou-Saintonge is the area where these were first elaborated, and that these motifs spread out along the main western pilgrim and trade routes, including direct sea links with Ireland. Both designs were exclusive to churches, which points to a re-use of exhibitionists in Ireland on castles and towers for a purpose not originally in the minds of the men who carved them.

A recurring theory about the function of British sheelas proposes a talismanic, protective role, rather than the minatory or didactic one which we have put forward. It hinges on the fact that in both the ancient world and parts of the modern one, phallic symbols are used to ward off the Evil Eye or the effects of bad luck. We examine this theory in the next chapter, pre-empting the argument a little by repeating that we do not know of any attribution of prophylactic or apotropaic power to the Continental figures we have reviewed. It does seem as if only in the British Isles is this folkloric theory held. Our own findings incline us to suppose that the Romanesque figures were first introduced into our islands, and at some later date folklore began to invest them with popular notions of magic.

12 Exhibitionists and folklore

These figures were probably intended as fetishes or charms to keep off the evil eye or its influence, and consequently they are found placed over doors . . .
Mr Clibborn addressing the Royal Irish Academy
1844

A two-fingered gesture of derision and insult, of unknown origin but undoubted rudeness, in impolite use among Anglo-Saxons at moments of stress was used with great effect during public appearances in World War II by Winston Churchill. Presenting the palm side of his hand with two fingers extended, he made a 'V for Victory' sign which cheered the onlookers all the more for the piquant *double-entendre* of the gesture, for a simple twist of his hand would have presented the dorsal side in a mocking snub to the common enemy. This simple stratagem, enjoyed by all, was his reply to the Hitlerian salute, though very few who savoured its slightly risqué character would be able to explain why the gesture was, in its commonly used form, indecent.

Originally it was a sexual gesture, of very ancient lineage, known to the races of the Classical world, in a variant of the sign which is still in use among Latin peoples from Italy to South America. Perhaps the Romans brought it to these islands. They certainly decorated their horse-trappings and buildings here with it, in the form now known as the *fica*. The sign is made by extending the first two fingers, placing the thumb between them, then closing the hand so that the thumb protrudes. It becomes the game played by adults with children when they pretend to 'pull their nose off' then show the thumb between the fingers (all sexual significance set aside). In Italy (Milan especially it is claimed) it is insulting to make this gesture. Etymological dictionaries explain *fica* as the outcome of Barbarossa's punishment for the

citizens of Milan, who had paraded his wife nude on horse-back during his absence. He made them remove with their mouths a fig placed in the anus of a mule and then replace it. A refusal meant instant death. But the Italian for fig is *fico*, masculine, so it is difficult to justify this derivation. In any case, the fica sign was in existence many centuries before Frederick Barbarossa.

The dictionary makers were right in one respect, though: the sign is coarse and of a sexual nature. Its appearance on Roman artefacts makes this clear. For instance, a stone from Roman Wroxeter (Uriconium) in Shropshire, as yet unpublished, depicts a large wheeled phallus, with a fica sign and a bundle of phalloi (*Fig 66a*); horse bronzes illustrated by Turnbull and Johns (Turnbull 1978, Johns 1982) show a crescentic pendant, one horn of which is an erect penis, the other a fica, while in between is a microphallic penis, scrotum and pubic hair. Such amulets made up of phalloi were popular among the Romans, and a *bulla*, such as were worn by children round their necks, is in the Rowley House Museum in

Fig. 66a Wheeled (and winged?) phallus in the Museum at Viroconium (Wroxeter), with a *fica* and a bundle of phalloi.

Fig. 66b Phallus on the bridge abutment at Chesters.

Shrewsbury; it shows a stylised penis peeping out from neat ringlets of pubic hair. A number of buildings were 'protected' by phalloi, e.g. the *colonia* wall at Lincoln, the fort at Maryport on Hadrian's Wall, and, further east along the Wall, the principia (*Plate 72*) and bath-house at Chesters, and the bridge abutment on the Tyne (*Fig. 66b*). A child was buried at Catterick with a necklace, probably of leather, on which were affixed half a dozen phallic charms, and at Brough-on-Humber a disc, on which was inscribed a jumble of words representing in all probability a curse, had a penis on one side and a vulva on the other. The Maryport stone also seems to have a vulva.

No doubt the origin of the use of phalloi as protective devices stems from the life-giving function of the phallus, from which follows the idea that phalloi could be used symbolically to combat the forces of death and destruction. The Lamb and Cross, or Agnus Dei, was used with similar protective force in the Middle Ages on Christian buildings. The important thing to note, however, is that the female emblem, the vulva, is very rare indeed in this role, perhaps because it plays a receptive, passive part in comparison with the male organ. It has been proposed by folkloric writers that the sheela-na-gig is an apotropaic carving, designed to defend a building against the onslaughts of the Evil Eye of Satan, in spite of the rarity of female amulets in European cultures. To what extent can this position be supported?

Andersen's very last illustration is an engraving by Charles Eisen for an edition of La Fontaine's *Fables*. A demon is repulsed by a young woman who lifts her skirts and shows her nakedness to him, an action echoed in the *Irish Times* of September 23rd 1977. In it Walter Mahon-Smith wrote:

> In a townland near where I lived, a deadly feud had continued for generations between the families of two small farmers. One day, before the first World War, when the men of one of the families, armed with pitchforks and heavy blackthorn sticks, attacked the home of their enemy, the woman-of-the-house came to the door of her cottage, and in full sight of all (including my father and myself, who happened to be passing by) lifted her skirt and underclothes high above her head, displaying her naked genitals. The enemy of her and her family fled in terror.

It stretches credulity, in spite of Mahon-Smith's personal testimony, Freudian 'castration complex' theories, and North American Indian beliefs in a frightening 'vagina dentata' ready to bit off men's genitals, to accept that a mob of angry men could lose the name of action on being presented with such a spectacle. One

Plate 72 Phallus outside the headquarters building at Chesters. (Photo: J. & C. Bord)

young inexperienced lad, repulsed by the deed of an older, brazen woman, could well fall back in dismay, but a collective effect on several grown men is unlikely, though no doubt the unexpected action might stop them in their tracks for an instant. After a moment's hesitation they would be more inclined to smile in the way an audience does at the impudent last gesture of the can-can dancer. The story, which is not isolated in folklore, echoes the La Fontaine illustration, and keeps up the articles of belief in a fear-provoking effect of the naked female genitalia, as potent in their magical power as the male signs used apotropaically.

Two exhibitionist carvings from Cumbria – one from Pennington, the other from Egremont – have recently been republished (Bailey 1983). Neither is listed by Andersen or the Hutchinsons, though the first was published in 1929 (Fell 1929, and in the *Barrow News*) and the second in 1902 (Parker). Both are female sheela-na-gigs, but the Egremont figure is, in addition, holding a pair of shears aimed at the vulva (the stone has disappeared, and only a photograph remains). The interest of this stone, apart from its intrinsic curiosity, is that it recalls an Italian figure now in the Museum (Castello Sforcesca Collection) at Milan, of a clothed woman, raising her garment in order to hold shears to her pubic hair. The stone is described by an Italian folklorist (Antonucci 1933), as being the act of depilation, presumably in order to lay bare the vulva for greater effect ('che si depila . . . per mettere più a nudo le pudende'). This figure, popularly supposed to be the wife of Frederick Barbarossa (the recipient of the insult which is erroneously given as the source of the fica punishment meted out to the Milanese), once stood on the medieval Porta Tosa gateway into the city, and is dated to the twelfth century. The word *Porta* is inscribed over it. There was a companion piece dated to the same period on the Porta Romana, traditionally thought to be of Barbarossa himself, showing him with his left hand covering his genital area. Bailey states that it is generally agreed that the female figure in its original setting had an apotropaic function, and so deduces that the Egremont sheela played a similar role.

Skirt-raisers receive mention from Pansa in his study of phallic rites and customs in the Abruzzi (Pansa 1924, reprinted 1970). In this

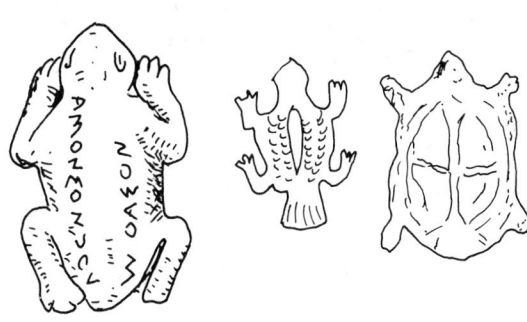

Fig. 67 Modern votive toads and wax turtle from Munich, Austria, Austrian Alps (after Gimbutas).

area of Italy throve a number of rites, blessed by the clergy, involving, for instance, the offering of votive phallic candles at the sanctuary of SS Cosma and Damian; to restore husbands' virility, matrons offered up, with pious prayers, wax phalloi of all sizes, sold with accessories by the canons. Talismanic objects, such as the frog-brooch (*Fig. 67*) splay-legged *ranochielle*, were common. One is reminded of the accounts by Witkowski and others of the phalloi borne in procession on Palm Sunday in Saintonge, the phallic Corpus Christi cakes, the Diana charm bracelets of Sicily, and the vulva-shaped *miches* or baps made in Auvergne – all examples quoted in the early literature of sheela-na-gig investigations, and all suggesting that phallic objects continued to be revered into modern times on account of their potency (*Fig. 68*).

Phallic emblems were still being carved in the seventeenth century on granite fireplaces in parts of Normandy (information supplied by members of the 1981 annual meeting of the Normandy Folklore Society), and Williams reports them in at least two farmhouses in Wales (Williams 1978). A half-timbered house at Le Mans has an exterior beam decorated with ithyphallic males. Perhaps one of the most curious discoveries ever to be made occurred when Professor Geoffrey Webb, as Secretary of the Royal Commission on Historical Monuments, was surveying ruined churches after World War II with a view to restoration. When he looked inside an altar whose lid had been blown off by a bomb blast, he found a male organ carved in stone. This led him to look into other altars and to reach a conclusion that phalloi could be found inside the altars of 90 per cent of churches built up to the time of the Black Death (Harrison *The roots of Witchcraft*, reported by Wilson in *Mysteries* 1978).

There is a late sheela-na-gig over the seventeenth-century stables of Haddon Hall in Derbyshire. It would seem to be a 'learned' piece of carving by a mason with knowledge of such objects, who believed that they had apotropaic power. The Smithstown phallus is also a 'learned' piece (*Plate 73*).

It would seem reasonable to suppose, therefore, that there has survived from ancient times a belief in the apotropaic power of phallic symbols among the common people, and that they have, in some areas, supposed that female exhibitionists were such prophylactic instruments; and that some post-Romanesque sheelas were carved expressly with this notion in mind. There is no proof of this, but certain features of sheela-na-gigs do lend themselves to such an interpretation, as we shall see shortly (*Plate 74*).

In the meantime, it is to be noted that they do not appear on misericords, where, being out of sight most of the time, one might have expected to find them. What we do find here are tongue-stickers and foliage-spewers. We have argued that these, by association, have some sexual connotations, but one cannot dismiss the proposition that some are Jack in the Green representations, carved by carpenters who had the May Day festival in mind rather than apotropaic devices. Green Men on bench-ends, roof bosses, misericords and other woodwork are post-Romanesque, and may have been influenced by the earlier foliage-spewers or foliate masks. At Linley in Shropshire a twelfth-century weather-worn typanum depicts a figure, arms akimbo, legs widely-splayed, surrounded by greenery, some of which sprouts from him. He is a cross between an exhibitionist and a Green Man, and, being in an area which, to judge by fonts and other carvings, was very much swayed by the atelier of the 'Herefordshire School', it is likely that his origin lies in the foliage mask on the Kilpeck portal. One view of such masks is that they had an apotropaic, tutelary function:

> de tels masques extérieurs sont la comme pour défendre et exorciser l'entrée. Ils ont une valeur prophylactique.
>
> Beigbeder 1970

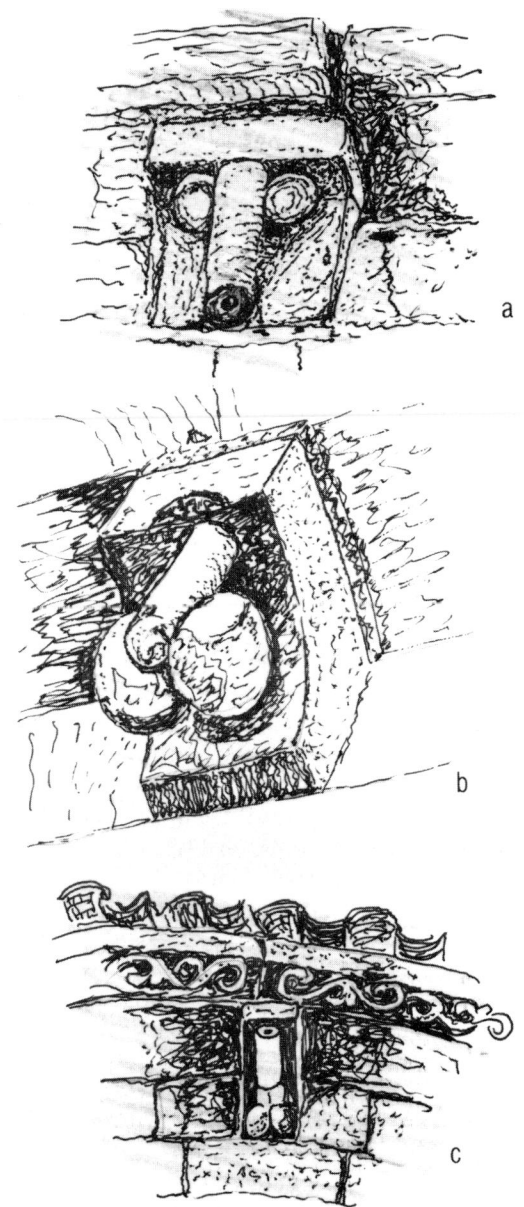

Fig. 68 Phalloi as corbels at (a) Vandré, (b) Sainte-Colombe and (c) Artaíz.

(such exterior masks are there as if to defend and exorcise the entrance. They have a prophylactic function.)

It is as well to note the use of the word *comme* (as if), for there is no certain proof that these masks played the role ascribed to them. The statement suggests that masks, and perhaps, therefore, foliate masks, are not only minatory but talismanic.

Plate 73 Smithstown Castle, Clare: a medieval use of the phallus (as a protective device?).

We can accept the possibility of a combination of purposes only in some carvings. Romanesque foliage-spewers, Jack in the Green images, tutelary carvings and fertility symbols could easily merge under the stimulus of folk ideas, especially in post-Romanesque manifestations. The figures like the squatter on the north and south portals of Melbourne church, from whose extremities foliage grows, and which reflect the linguistic passage from 'luxuria' to 'luxuriance', mark a development from the end of the twelfth century onwards, in which exhibitionism is blurred by vegetation, until it finally disappears. Jacobean plaster ceilings show a return to Classical triton-like figures, sprouting *rinceaux* of foliage, who, though bare-breasted, are devoid of sexual symbolism. By the thirteenth century, popular notions of fertility figures might well be represented in the foliate masks of Southwell Minster, which look like 'wood spirits, tree sprites'. Some protrude a tongue, others sprout leaves and tendrils. They may symbolise renaissance – life growing out of dead matter – but equally they may not, for Kathleen Basford has commented on one noticeable aspect: they are evil-looking. Not one could be described as a smiling figure. The spring festival of rebirth ought to generate happy faces; the Green Man, if he heralds new life and growth, should bear a smiling countenance, yet most Green Men and foliate masks have a menacing look about them. They seem to be dwelling on solemn thoughts of sin, death and decay rather than on the joys of resurrection. In other words, they recall the minatory nature of Romanesque foliage-spewers and masks. We are not entirely convinced about 'fertility figures' and agree with Andersen, who rejected suggestions that exhibitionists were such.

Ever since the nineteenth-century discussions of sheela-na-gigs, it has been difficult to counter a lingering tendency to see in them 'old fetish idols', vestigial gods and goddesses of the Old Religion of pre-Christian days. Branston tried to make out a case for sheelas on south walls being Earth Mothers awaiting the embrace of the Sky Father, tracing them back to Scandinavian religions (Branston 1957). Those who propose such ascriptions point to the admoni-

Plate 74 Ballinderry Castle: a damaged sheela with triskele, triquetra, rose and marigold (with tressed hair?). Carved as a voussoir or key-stone, suggesting apotropaic use.

tions of authorities like Pope Gregory, who exhorted Mellitus by no means to destroy the heathen temples but only the idols – the temples themselves were to be aspersed with holy water then turned to Christian use (Bede's *Ecclesiastical History*); or Theodore of Canterbury, who forbade idolatry, worship of demons, the cult of the dead, the worship of trees, fire, stones, and the practice of witchcraft, sorcery, augury, divination and astrology in his *Penitential*. The people, notwithstanding, continued in these practices, and King Edgar had to reiterate much the same thing (he included well-worshipping and necromancy), and King Cnut in 1035 forbade all forms of barbarous worship, itemising them in the same way. There is no doubt that the Church found it extremely difficult to nullify the lingering ideas of the Old Religion, and there are those today, imbued with the belief that witchcraft never died out in country districts, who seek evidence of a continuance of pagan practices. They point to fertility rites performed by barren women on the Cerne Abbas Giant; to sheelas which bear marks of 'rubbing' (Buckland in Buckinghamshire, Buncton in Sussex); to tales of priests placing sheelas out of reach to prevent such happenings, and they instance the survival of phallic tree worhsip in the maypole dance, and of fertility magic in well-dressing and tree-decking, horn-dancing, and so on.

More seriously, from the point of view of this book, it could be argued that many insular exhibitionists are mere graffiti, scratched on flat blocks of stone which have no architectural function such as corbels have; that they are so crude in their technical execution as to be unworthy of any serious mason; that only a popular belief in their supernatural efficacy could have ensured their survival, and that they must, therefore, be apotropaic devices. If their purpose is not to teach morality but to scare away the Devil, then the roughest botched-up caricature will serve the purpose.

There is no way of countering this argument; indeed there may be some truth in the proposition – who is to know? We can only produce our evidence for saying that we believe that the source of inspiration for the twelfth-century insular exhibitionists is to be found abroad, in the area of the Continent roughly demarcated by the pilgrimage routes, along which Roman-

esque sculpture developed. Here are hundreds of sexual carvings, many of which could be deemed the direct model for our sheelas, all forming part of a huge campaign against sin, mounted in the first instance by the celibate monks and clergy who built the churches and manned the pilgrimage undertakings. We have not found the slightest suspicion that there entered into any of these works an element of fertility worship – unless the foliage-spewers are construed as showing life springing forth from dead skulls – or any sign of apotropaic magic. We have not met any folkloric accounts suggesting that they are pre-Christian vestigial idols.

Powerful images they were, though; powerful enough to have impressed themselves on the minds of pilgrims. Those rich enough to endow churches in recognition of their safe return from Compostela were pleased to see them attached to the edifice. They were powerful enough, too, to have exerted a sort of spell in the folk mind, long after their primary purpose had been fulfilled.

Epilogue

That carving, Sir? Why, that's the last man (sic) to be hanged on Hangman's Hill.
> Sexton of Holdgate Church, verbatim, to Colin and Janet Bord, 1980

The majority of sheela-na-gigs were apparently either warnings of immoral behaviour, or Schandbilder, denouncing local women of ill-repute.
> Ellen Ettlinger, *FOLKLORE* 1974

Sheela-na-gig: an obscene female figure of uncertain significance.
> Lord Killanin and M.V. Duignan, *Shell Guide to Ireland* 1967

Sheela-na-gig: the Irish Goddess of Creation.
> Barry Cunliffe, *The Celtic World* 1979

Probably the remains of a fertility cult.
> Margaret Murray, *MAN* 1923

Sheela-na-gig: the actual representation of the Great Goddess Earth Mother on English soil.
> Brian Branston, *The Lost Gods of England* 1974

The portrayal of the Celtic goddess of creation and destruction, the sheela-na-gig at Kilpeck offers wordless instruction in the art of self-delivery.
> S.C. Stanford, *Archaeology of the Welsh Marches*, 1980

Sheila-na-gig: fertility figure, usually with legs wide open.
> N. Pevsner, *Buildings of England*, glossary (various dates)

(Sheela-na-gigs) portray the territorial or war-goddess in her hag-like aspect.
> Ann Ross, *Divine Hag of the Pagan Celts*, ed. Newall 1973

Sheela-na-gig: female exhibitionist figure, one of the many representations of Lust in Romansque carving.
> A. Weir, *Early Ireland, a Field Guide* 1980

The defensive nature of the exposed vulva is even clearer in Ireland in the Sheila-na-gig representations of women exposing themselves.
> *Encyclopedia of World Art*, 1966

This list of discrepant opinions is by no means exhaustive. One finds many more in the literature about female exhibitionists. Andersen said: 'Sheelas have proved elusive figures to the archaeologist as well as to the art historian, and the encounter with them can be a baffling experience'. We hope fervently that the reader is by now in a position to make an informed judgment, hopefully more in accordance with the Weir quotation given above than with any of the others.

There is a divergence of opinion among the authors writing in the *Zodiaque* series as to the significance of Romanesque iconography. Craplet, speaking of Notre Dame des Miracles at Mauriac (Craplet 1972) states:

> Les corbeaux qui soutiennent cette corniche, assez espacés, offrent un grand intérêt . . . Pleins de verve et de vie, ils n'ont aucune prétention symbolique ou didactique. On y voit des têtes humaines mélancoliques ou hilares, des oiseaux, des animaux ou même des hommes dans des postures acrobatiques, parfois obscènes. Le vieil esprit gaulois entraîne si loin nos vieux sculpteurs que certains de leurs sujets ne sauraient se décrire, sauf peut-être en latin, comme faisait jadis Mérimée dans ses rapports au ministre quand il se trouvait devant des cas semblables. Mais qui aujourd'hui comprendrait le latin?

> (The corbels supporting this cornice, widely spaced, offer much interest. Full of verve and life, they have no symbolic or didactic meaning whatsoever. There are human heads, sad or mirthful, birds, animals, or even men in acrobatic postures at times obscene. The old *esprit gaulois* carried away our ancient stone-carvers so far as to make their work indescribable except perhaps in Latin. Merimée, in his reports to the minister used Latin when he found himself face to face with such objects. But who would understand Latin today?)

Mérimée was Inspector of Ancient Monuments in the nineteenth century, and he was evidently taken aback by some of the sculptures he had to list. He would, like Craplet, have found the Mauriac carvings indeed curious in their grossness. We have already made note of the scrotum-showers, anus-displayers and penis-swallowers on the exterior corbels of this church. Craplet, a scholar who has made a particular study of Auvergne, does not discern any moralising intent in these corbels but puts them down to the mordant, earthy humour that characterises Gallic wit.

By contrast, Lojendio (Lojendio 1966), in describing the Spanish church San Quirce, has no hesitation in speaking of 'des scènes moralisatrices' (moral scenes). He says:

> Le contenu des ces chapiteaux et en général de toute la décoration de cette église révèle un but intentionellement didactique et catéchétique qui étonne un peu dans un monastère se trouvant en marge des rassemblements populaires. La femme aux serpents doit être une représentation de la luxure ... Outre son intérêt artistique et iconographique, qui est grand, il est utile de souligner pour toute la sculpture de San Quirce, son orientation didactique précise. Les représentations bibliques ont un sens nettement déterminé.

> (The subject matter of these capitals, and in general of all the ornamentation of this church shows an intentionally didactic and catechetical aim, surprising in a monastery which stands away from passing crowds. The woman with snakes must be a symbol of Lust ... Apart from its artistic and iconographical interest, which is considerable, what ought to be underlined for all the sculpture of San Quirce is its precise didactic orientation. The Biblical scenes have a precise significance.)

The anonymous author of the little *Zodiaque* booklet describing Saint-Pierre-d'Aulnay concurs with the above sentiments:

> A tout cet ensemble on ne peut s'empêcher de trouver surtout un air maléfique. La bêtise le dispute à la méchanceté. La figure humaine, si elle apparaît en quelques monstres, paraît submergée dans la bestialité . . . Est-il possible que toute cette faune inscrite à la porte d'une église soit sans intention moralisatrice?

> (One cannot but be struck by the baleful aura of this assemblage wherein evil vies with folly. When a human face appears on one of these monstrous beings it seems invested with bestiality. Surely all this fauna attached to a church door cannot be without a moral purpose?)

It is to the question which ends this quotation that we have addressed ourselves in this book. We find that the weight of testimony is overwhelmingly in favour of didacticism as the mainspring of Romanesque carving. In the face of cumulative evidence we find it impossible to believe that medieval carvers could adorn religious edifices with every manner of lewd designs unless they had had the approval of their ecclesiastical patrons. The Church *must* have been in consonance with the masons, and vice versa, and both worked with a view to showing mankind the error of its ways.

We may marvel at the preoccupation with sexual matters in the sculptures of the early Middle Ages, but some light has been cast on the question by Spanish historical scholars who have suddenly become aware of the vast amount of 'obscene' carving in their northern churches. Montejo, in her study of lewd carvings in rural churches of northern Spain (Montejo 1978), enlists the help of historians (our translations):

> Indecent carvings give some idea of the brutal harshness of the times.
>
> Perez Carmona

> When medieval carvers criticised the sins and vices of men they did so in a very natural, almost brutal manner, with sincerity and force as at Cervatos, in detail which beggars description.
>
> Serrano Fatigati

> León lived close to the earth, with no other spur than sensuality, no other spiritual preoccupation than a deep and burning devotion. Mystic and sensual, rustic and warring, the city divided its time between prayer and agriculture, love and war. The secular grasped the sword to fight the infidel or the plough to till the land; the monks took up the hoe to work the orchards or the pen to copy out the Scriptures. All, or nearly all, prayed . . . and made love.
>
> Sancho Albornoz

> Such indecorous figures place before the view of rough medieval folk all the horrors of sin, not in a symbolic way which would not be understood by the illiterate, but in an obvious and realistic one. For us twentieth-century folk the result may be a bit strong, but that is not how it struck people in the twelfth century. Nor must we be surprised if the priests did not appear to be offended.
>
> Lamperez y Romea

So, as Montejo puts it, there flourished an iconography which may seem to us to surpass the limits of a strictly adequate and modest necessity, but is explainable in terms of the harsh reality of life in those days. She describes medieval life as a dichotomy between periods of extreme strictness and bouts of equally extreme laxity. The protests of clergy when ordered to put away their concubines, the songs of wandering scholars whose theme was that sensual pleasures are the only compensation for a life lived in hardship and constant fear of divine retribution – all indicate that carnal joys were probably the only solace to which they could have recourse. The Church recognised the need for the release from tension by turning a blind eye to the excesses of carnival and similar occasions, which allowed men a glimpse of another world in which all men would be equal, all would be fed and all would share the same happiness. It was noted that, in any case, after all the licence and debauchery, men returned to the service of God with renewed zeal and contrition.

The view we have just put forward about the extraordinary part played in the lives of medieval people by sexual matters seems to be supported by an unusually interesting archaeological discovery made late in 1983 at Gloucester, on the site of the first motte-and-bailey castle. Excavators (directed by Ian Stewart) uncovered, below a sealed layer giving a date prior to AD 1100, the almost complete remains of a backgammon or 'tables' set. The bone inlays have survived, together with a complete set of 30 carved counters. At present all are being treated by conservators but even without extensive cleaning (and some of the counters scarcely need it), it is possible to pick out the deeply cut designs on the 5cm (2in) 'tablemen'. They comprise a number of motifs commonly found on Romanesque corbel tables, such as quadrupeds, affronted birds, a centaur, a centaur-sagittarius, a rebec player, a harpist, an archer, a falconer, men with shields, a crowned head, two nudes, a serpent, a copulating pair, a nude holding large rings, Samson and the lion, a hair-puller (perhaps another also), a possible glutton, a frog or toad, and . . . a probable sheela-na-gig. The latter is almost certainly exhibitionist, showing a nude squatting figure with hands under the thighs. One of the sets was undoubtedly coloured at one time, but even without colouring it might be possible to suggest that two sets could be made up by subject matter. The discovery is shortly to be published

and will prove one of the most exciting finds in recent years, giving further proof of the part played by small objects in the modelling of architectural compositions. Most fascinating of all, in the context of this book, is the evidence of the pervasiveness of sexual interests in the early Middle Ages, even appearing in gaming counters.

We set out to investigate the sexual symbolism implicit and explicit in early medieval carving, and to draw attention to a fact which has been overlooked in histories of the Romanesque period, namely that a great deal of this sculpture is devoted to sexual themes of one kind or another. When one begins to look for it, one realises that it is there in superabundance. We have, in this book, produced evidence to support our thesis; nevertheless, the reader is encouraged to take heed of the words of Rabelais quoted in Chapter 5:

> Si ces discours ne satisfont à l'incrédulité de vos seigneuries, visitez Lusignan, Partenay, Vovant etc . . . là trouverez tesmoings . . .

Substantial testimony of the kind instanced by Rabelais can be found in the areas we have shown on the maps. In Spain, at the collegiate church of San Pedro de Cervatos, south of Santander, for instance, among the 95 corbels can be found (over the south door, from right to left) interlocked beasts; a female exhibitionist with a person on her back; a megaphallic male; a squatting ape; an exhibitionist ape with the right hand between its legs and the left hand in its mouth; an anal exhibitionist beast; a male exhibitionist beast holding a bar over its head; a ram; a pair of males (sodomising?); a squatting figure with a large mouth; a harpist and an acrobat. On the nave and chevet are an anal exhibitionist ape; squatting figures; an exhibitionist male whose buttocks are being parted by another man; pigs, goats, rams and apes; a squatting, beast-headed figure pulling its jaws open; acrobatic beasts, one with a protruding tongue; an upside-down female with her head between her legs; a megaphallic male with one hand on his belly, the other holding his testicles; female feet-to-ears exhibitionists, and an upside-down man with his head between his legs; a pair of males sodomising; a male with large testicles, feet in his mouth; two men carrying barrels; harpists; a man with a large penis in his mouth; a male exhibitionist (genitalia of normal size) holding a disc, and a female holding her breasts. Finally (on window capitals) are found an acrobatic feet-to-ears female exhibitionist illustrated in the text (*Plate 41a and Fig. 6*), a megaphallic male (opposite her), and other megaphallic males; and on the tower, on a capital, is a centaur-sagittarius.

In France, north-east of Paris, at Villers-Saint-Paul, near Creil, there is an interesting church which alternates corbels with long metopes. These both show a man struggling with a monster; a foliage-spewer; a tongue-sticking foliage-spewer; a single-tailed mermaid; another tongue-sticker; a megaphallic toothy devil trampling with glee on a soul; two naked figures lying sideways, interlocked groin to groin, one of them male and bearded; a grinning devil with a purse; an acrobat peering out from under his legs; a beast-head sprouting foliage from either side; a mask with flaming hair; a rebec or vielle; bearded naked figures lying sideways; a figure playing a shawm or similar instrument; horses' heads; a lobster, and a mask spewing a foliate wolf's head.

Mauriac, on the western border of Auvergne, is a splendid church for the study of acrobatic exhibitionists – testicle-showers, penis-swallowers and other bizarre items. The south-western region of France is especially rich in such carvings.

To us, nowadays, these carvings may seem to be just grotesque pieces which express the irreverent, impish, impudent, whimsical humour of the stonemason, but there can be little doubt that they once served a useful purpose in the moral education of the unlettered folk of the Middle Ages. Today their minatory or instructive character passes us by. Immersed in our materialistic world of unprecedented wealth and comfort, we either ignore or view with indifference the amazing art of the eleventh and twelfth centuries. Modern psychology has taught us to see them through secular, unpoetic eyes. Our relatively simplistic world, in which things are real or unreal, true or false, has few gradations in moral matters. We no longer regard avarice, gluttony, luxury, greed, pride, ambition, vainglory and envy as sins, much less as mortal sins. We set no store by the tale of Dives and Lazarus, we no longer fear the wrath to come on Judgment Day, and we consider

ourselves more or less unaccountable. The only sin we have to any extent retained is the one which is least life-denying, yet the most life-denying to deny – the sin of concupiscence. True to our Christian heritage we have not only retained it, but, like the twelfth-century monks, we have become obsessed with it. We do not call it *Luxuria* any more – we call it sex; and it permeates our lives, from the Vatican Council down to the TV commercial for lager. Our fascination with it is perhaps our only tenuous link with the visionary world of the Romanesque, which saw *Luxuria* and *Avaritia* everywhere threatening God's kingdom on earth.

It is an irony that it is through our different but equally morbid approach to sexuality that we can best enter the imaginative world of medieval man, with its landscape and ecology of mystical, symbolic sculptures, even though we still find it difficult to recapture the tense atmosphere of doom and the struggle for salvation. Over our heads the menace still ominously lours, if we but deign to glance up at it. In the twelfth century, men and women raised their eyes to Heaven and, like as not, saw images of Hell.

Bibliography

Readers should consult the very full bibliography supplied by Andersen for the study of sheela-na-gig carvings. We have, in addition, consulted the works appended. We give short titles and, as far as possible, the latest edition. Books published by the Abbey of La-Pierre-qui-Vire at Saint Léger-Vauban, Yonne, are indicated by the designation *Zodiaque*.

Adéline, J. & C. *Les sculptures grotesques et symboliques*, Augé, Rouen 1879

Adhémar, J. *Les influences antiques dans l'art du moyen âge français*, Warburg Institute, London 1939

Alexander, J.J.G. *Insular Manuscripts, sixth to ninth centuries*, H. Miller, London 1978

Andersen, J. *The Witch on the Wall*, Allen & Unwin, London 1977; Rosenkilde & Bagger, Copenhagen

— At holde Kirken oppe *Der Iconographiske Post*, Copenhagen 1978

— Temptation in Kilkea *Journal of Kildare Archaeol. Soc.*, Kildare 1973–4

Andersson, A. *L'art scandinave*, Zodiaque, L.P.Q.V. 1968

— *The art of Scandinavia* (translation), Hamlyn, London 1970

Andrade, J.M.P. La iglesia románica de Santo Tomé de Serantes *Estudios Gallegos*, Santiago 1947

Anthony, E.W. *Romanesque frescoes*, Princetown University Press, Princeton 1951

Antonucci, G. Temi fallici nell'iconografia medievale *Il Folklore italiano*, Catania 1933

Aubert, M. *Romanesque cathedrals & abbeys of France*, Vane, London 1966

Avery, M. *The Exultet Rolls of S. Italy*, Princetown University Press and O.U.P., London 1936

Bailey, R. Apotropaic figures in Milan and NW England *Folklore*, London 1983

Baltrušaitis, J. *Le Moyen Age fantastique*, Colin, Paris 1955

— *La Stylistique ornementale*, Leroux, Paris 1931

— *Art sumérien, art roman*, Leroux, Paris 1934

Barbadillo, J.L. & Martinez, J. & M. *See* Martini for Spanish version

Barret, P. & Gurgaud, J.N. *Priez pour nous à Compostelle*, Hachette, Paris 1978

Basford, K. *The Green Man*, D.S. Brewer, Ipswich 1978

Beigbeder, O. *Forez-Velay roman*, Zodiaque, La-Pierre-qui-Vire 1962

— *Lexique des Symboles*, Zodiaque, L.P.Q.V. 1969

— *Le Masque de la Terre*, Zodiaque (*Quarterly Review*), L.P.Q.V. 1970

Bloch, R. *The Etruscans*, Thames & Hudson, London 1961

Bloomfield, M.W. *The Seven Deadly Sins*, Michigan State Univ. Press, Michigan 1967

Boardman, J. & La Rocca, E. *Eros in Greece*, John Murray, London 1978

Boardman, J. *Greek Art*, Thames & Hudson, London 1973

Bock, E. *Schwäbische romanik*, Verlag Urachhaus, Stuttgart 1973

Böckler, A. *Der Regensburg-Prüfeninger Buchmalerei des XII und XIII Jahrhunderts*. A. Reusch, Munich 1924

Bonner, G. *St. Augustine de Hippo*, S.C.M. Press, London 1963

Bord, C. & J. *Earth Rites*, Granada, London 1982

— *Mysterious Britain*, Granada, London 1974

— *The Secret Country*, Granada, London 1978

Boswell, J. *Christianity, Social Tolerance and Homosexuality*, Chicago U.P., Chicago 1980

Boulanger, C. *Le mobilier funéraire gallo-romain*, Charles Foulard, Paris 1902–3

Branston, B. *The Lost Gods of England*, Thames & Hudson, London 1957

Bréhier, L. *Le style roman*, Larousse, Paris 1941

Lehmann-Brockhaus, O. Die Kanseln des Abruzzen im XII und XIII Jahrhunderts, *Romisches Jahrbuch*, Rome 1942–4

Brøndsted, J. *Early English ornament*, Hachette, London 1924; Levin & Munksgaard, Copenhagen

Brooke, C. *The twelfth century renaissance*, Thames & Hudson, London 1969

Budde, R. *Deutsche romanische Skulptur*, Hirmer, Munich 1979

Cabanot, J. *Gascogne romane*, Zodiaque, L.P.Q.V. 1979

Carlsson, F. *The iconology of tectonics in Romanesque art*, Am Tryck, Hässleholm 1976

Cave, C.J.P. *Roof-bosses in medieval churches*, C.U.P., London 1948

Chambers, E.K. *The medieval stage*, O.U.P., Oxford 1903

Champeaux, G. de *Introduction au monde des symboles*, Zodiaque, L.P.Q.V. 1972

Chierici, S. *Lombardie romane*, Zodiaque, L.P.Q.V. 1978

— *Piémont-Ligurie roman*, Zodiaque, L.P.Q.V. 1979

Cirlot, J.E. *A dictionary of symbols*, Routledge & Kegan Paul, London 1962

Cocagnac, A.-M. *Le Jugement dernier dans l'art*, Editions du Cerf, Paris 1955

Cohn, N.F.C. *Europe's inner demons*, Basic Books, New York 1975; Chatto & Windus, London 1975; Heinemann for Univ. of Sussex Press

Conant, K.J. *Cluny – les églises*, Medieval Academy of America, Cambridge (Mass.); Protat Frères, Macon 1968

Cook, A.B. *Zeus* (vol 2), C.U.P., Cambridge 1925
— (addenda), C.U.P., Cambridge 1940

Cooper, J.C. *An illustrated encyclopedia of traditional symbols*, Thames & Hudson, London 1978

Corish, P.J. *The Catholic community in the 17th and 18th centuries*, Helicon, Dublin 1981

Craplet, B. *Auvergne romane*, Zodiaque, L.P.Q.V. 1972

Crichton, G.H. *Romanesque sculpture in Italy*, Routledge & Kegan Paul, London 1954

Crozet, R. *L'art roman en Saintonge*, A. & J. Picard, Paris 1971
— *L'art roman en Poitou*, Bibliothèque d'Erudition artistique, Paris 1948

Coulton, G.G. *Life in the Middle Ages*, C.U.P., Cambridge 1928–30

Daras, C. *Angoumois roman*, Zodiaque, L.P.Q.V. 1961

Davidson, H.R.E. *Scandinavian mythology*, Hamlyn, London 1969

Davison, E.S. *Forerunners of St. Francis*, Cape, London 1928

Déonna, W. *Le symbolisme de l'acrobatie antique*, Collection Latomus, Brussels 1953

Deschamps, P. *French sculpture of the Romanesque period*, Hacker Art Books, New York 1972

Dickinson, J.C. & Ricketts, P.T. The Anglo-Norman Chronicle of Wigmore Abbey, *Woolhope Naturalists' Field Club* Stroud 1969

Dillange, M. *Vendée romane*, Zodiaque, L.P.Q.V. 1976

Dobson, D.P. Primitive figures on churches, *Man*, London 1940

Dodwell, C.R. *The Canterbury school of illumination*, C.U.P., Cambridge 1954

— *Painting in Europe 800–1200 AD*, Harmondsworth, London 1971

Druce, G.C. Medieval Bestiaries and their influence on medieval decorative art, *Journal of British Archaeol. Ass.*, London 1919–20

Duff, E.G. *The dialogue of Solomon and Marcolphus*, Lawrence & Bullen, London 1892

Dupont, J. Nivernais-Bourbonnais roman, Zodiaque, L.P.Q.V. 1976

Durdik, J. et al *The pictorial encyclopedia of antiques*, Hamlyn, London 1970

Durliat, M. *Pyrénées romanes*, Zodiaque, L.P.Q.V. 1969
— The pilgrimage roads revisited? *Bulletin Monumental*, Paris 1971
— *Haut-Languedoc roman*, Zodiaque, L.P.Q.V. 1978

Erickson, C. *The medieval vision*, O.U.P., 1976

Eygun, F. *Saintonge romane*, Zodiaque, L.P.Q.V. 1970

Faral, E. *Les jongleurs en France au Moyen Age*, Champion, Paris 1910
— La queue de poisson des sirènes, *Romania*, 1953

Favière, J. *Berry roman*, Zodiaque, L.P.Q.V. 1976

Fell, A. *A Furness manor*, Kitchin & Co., Ulverston 1929

Firth, R. *Symbols – public and private*, Allen & Unwin, London 1973

Focillon, H. Apôtres et jongleurs, *Revue de l'Art*, Paris 1929
— *The art of the West in the Middle Ages*, Phaidon, New York 1980

Fontaine, J. *L'art préroman hispanique*, Zodiaque, L.P.Q.V. 1973

Frere, S. *Britannia*, Routledge & Kegan Paul, London 1967

García Guinea, M.A., El Arte Románico en Palencia, El Arte Románico en Santander, 1961

Gimbutas, M. *Gods, goddesses of Old Europe*, Thames & Hudson, London 1974

Goddard, E.R. *Women's costume in French texts of the 11th and 12th Centuries*, John Hopkins Press, Baltimore 1927; Presses Universitaires de France, Paris 1927

Goff, J. le *La civilisation de l'occident médiéval*, Arthaud, Paris 1964

Goldschmidt, A. *Die Elfenbeinskulpturen aus der Zeit der Karolingischen und Sächsichen Kaiser*, Deutscher Verlag für Kunstwissenschaft, Berlin 1969

Gombrich, E.R. *Symbolic images*. Phaidon, London 1972

Gonzales, A.V. *Leon roman*, Zodiaque, L.P.Q.V. 1972

Grandmaison, C. de *Tours archéologique*, Champion, Paris 1879

Graves, R. *The Greek myths*, Cassell, London 1955

Grivot, D. Images de l'Apocalypse, *Zodiaque*, L.P.Q.V. 1977

Grivot, D. & Zarnecki, G. *Gislebertus, sculptor of Autun*, Collins, London 1961; Trianon Press, Paris 1961

Hahnloser, H.R. *Villard de Honnecourt*, Akadem, Graz 1972

Harbison, P. Some medieval sculpture in Kerry, *Kerry Archaeol. and Hist. Soc. Journal*, Tralee 1973

— Temptation in Kilkea again, *Kildare Archaeol. Soc. Journal*, Kildare 1977

Harrison, M. Roots of witchcraft, in Wilson, C. *Mysteries*, Hodder & Stoughton, London 1978

Hawkes, J. *et al* The Finglesham man, *Antiquity*, London 1965

Hayes, R. Ireland's links with Compostela, *Studies*, Dublin 1948

Heer, F. *The medieval world*, Weidenfeld & Nicolson, London 1974

Henry, F. *Art irlandais*, Cultural Relations Committee of Ireland, Dublin 1962

— *L'Art irlandais*, Zodiaque, L.P.Q.V. 1964

— *Irish High Crosses*, Cultural Relations Committee of Ireland, Dublin 1964

— *Irish art in the Romanesque period*, Methuen, London 1970

— *Irish art during the Viking invasions*, Methuen, London 1976

Hickey, H. *Images of stone*, Blackstaff Press, Belfast 1976

Hughes, P. *Witchcraft*, Penguin, Harmondsworth, London 1965

Hunt, J. *Irish medieval figure sculpture*, Irish University Press, Dublin 1974; Sotheby Parke Bernet, London

Hurry, J.B. The shrine of St James at Reading Abbey, *Antiquary*, London 1915

Hutchinson, A.L. & G.E. The 'Idol' or sheela-na-gig at Binstead, *Proc. I.O.W. Nat. Hist. & Archaeol. Soc.*, Newport 1969

Jalabert, D. De l'art oriental antique à l'art roman, *Bulletin Monumental*, Paris 1936

Janson, H.W. *Apes and ape-lore in the Middle Ages*, Warburg Institute, London 1952

Jerman, J.A. The 'sheela-na-gig' carvings of the Br. Isles, *Co. Louth Archaeol. and Hist. Soc. Journal*, Dundalk 1981

— Simulation or dissimulation? *Wiltshire Archaeol. and Nat. Hist. Magazine*, Gloucester 1981

— Linguistics and sculpture at Melbourne Church, *Derbyshire Miscellany*, Derby 1981

— An exhibitionist figure from Lammas, *Council for Brit. Archaeol. Gp. 6 Bulletin*, Norwich 1982

Johns, C. *Sex or symbol?* British Museum Publica tions, London 1982

Johnson, P.M. Romanesque ornament in England, *Journal of Brit. Archaeol. Assoc.*, London 1924

Jónsdóttir, S. The portal of Kilpeck Church, *Art Bulletin*, New York 1950

Leclercq-Kadaner, J. De la Terre-Mère à la Luxure, *Cahiers de civilisation médiévale*, Poitiers 1975

Katzenellenbogen, A. *Allegories of the Vices and Virtues*, Warburg Institute, London 1939

Kauffmann, C.M. *Romanesque manuscripts*, Harvey Miller, London 1975

Kraus, D. & H. *The hidden world of misericords*, G. Braziller, New York 1975; Joseph, London 1976

Kraus, H. *The living theatre of medieval art*, Thames & Hudson, London 1967; Indiana Univ. Press

Krenkel, W.A. Exhibitionismus und Skopophilie in der Antike, *Wissenschaftliche Zeitschrift*, Univ. of Rostock 1952

Nancke-Krogh, S. Træ-Kvinden, *ICO Den iconographiske Post*, Copenhagen 1974

Lamas, M.C. *et al* Galice romane, *Zodiaque*, L.P.Q.V. 1973

Langlois, E. *Mélanges de l'Ecole de Rome*, L'Ecole française de Rome, Rome 1886

Leach, E. Magical hair, *Journal of Royal Anthropological Institute*, London 1958

Leach, E.R. *Culture and communication*, C.U.P. Cambridge 1976

Durand-Lefebvre *Art gallo-romain et sculpture romane*, G. Durassié, Paris 1937

Lewis G.R. *Illustrations of Kilpeck*, London 1842

— *The ancient church of Shobdon*, London 1852

Lojendio, L.-M. *Navarre romane*, Zodiaque, L.P.Q.V. 1967

— *Castile romane*, Zodiaque, L.P.Q.V. 1966

Lopez, Barbadillo, J. & Martinez J. & M. *see* Martini for Spanish version

Canellas-López *Aragon roman*, Zodiaque, L.P.Q.V. 1971

Lyman, T.W. The pilgrimage roads revisited, *Gesta*, New York 1969

McCall, A. *The medieval underworld*, Hamish Hamilton, London 1979

Maeterlinck, L. *Le genre satirique, fantastique et licencieux dans la sculpture flamande*, J. Schemit, Paris 1910

Bretz-Mahler, D. *Rosheim*, Zodiaque, L.P.Q.V. 1979

Labande-Mailfert, Y. *Poitou roman*, Zodiaque, L.P.Q.V. 1962

Maillard, E. *Les sculptures de la cathédrale de St. Pierre à Poitiers*, Societé des Antiquaires de l'Ouest, Poitiers 1921

— Les sculptures romanes de l'église de Foussais, *Gazette des Beaux-Arts*, Paris 1930

Mâle, E. *L'art religieux au XII siècle*, Colin, Paris 1966

— *Religious art of the 12thC* (translation), Princetown Univ. Press, Princeton 1978

Marle, R. van *L'iconographie de l'art profane*, La Haye, Nijhoff 1931

Martini, G.L. *Il gabinetto segreto del museo nazionale di Napoli*, R. Aprile, Torino 1971

Mason, E. *Aucassin et Nicolette and other medieval romances and legends*, Dutton, New York 1910, Dent, London

Maury, J. *Limousin roman*, Zodiaque, L.P.Q.V. 1974

Meaney, A.L. *Anglo-Saxon amulets and curing stones*, B.A.R., London 1981

Megaw, J.V.S. *Art of the European Iron Age*, Adams & Dart, Bath 1970

Mendell, E.L. *Romanesque art in Saintonge*, Yale Univ. Press, New Haven 1940; O.U.P.

Meyer, P. La descente de Saint-Paul en enfer, *Romania*, Paris 1974

Micheli, G. *L'enluminure du haut moyen âge*, Editions de la Connaissance, Brussels 1939

Millingen, J. Baubo, *Annali del Instituto*, Rome 1843

Montejo, M.I.R. La temática obscena en la iconografía del románico rural, *Goya*, Madrid 1978

Moorey, P.R.S. *Ancient Persian bronzes in the Ashmolean*, Clarendon O.U.P., Oxford 1971

— *Ancient Persian bronzes in the Adam Collection*, Faber & Faber, London 1974

Moralejo, S. *Actas del XIII congreso internacional de historia del arte*, Granada 1976

— *Cahiers de Saint-Michel de Cuxa*, Abbey of Saint Michel de Cuxa, Prades-Codalet 1977

— *Marcolfo, el espinario, Priapo etc.*, Primera Reunión Gallega de Estudios Clasicos, Santiago 1981

Gomez-Moreno, M. *El arte románico español*, Blass, Madrid 1934

Morey, C.R. *Medieval art*, W.W. Norton, New York 1942

Mullins, E. *The pilgrimage to Santiago*, Secker & Warburg, London 1974

Murray, M. Female fertility figures, *Journal of Royal Anthropological Institute*, London 1934

Musset, L. *Normandie romane*, Zodiaque, L.P.Q.V. 1974

Mylonas, G.E. *Eleusis and the Eleusinian mysteries*, Princeton University Press, Princeton 1961

Neale, J.M. & Webb, B. *Symbolism of churches and church ornaments*, Gibbings & Co., London 1906

Nebolsine, G. *Journey into Romanesque*, Weidenfeld & Nicolson, London 1969

Nelli, R. *L'érotique des troubadours*, Union générale d'éditions, Paris 1974; E. Privat, Toulouse 1963

Jean-Nesmy, C. Bestiaire roman, *Zodiaque*, L.P.Q.V. 1977

Dubourg-Noves, P. & Lefrancq, P. Saint-Pierre de Passirac, *Bulletin Mensuel de la Société Archaeologique et Historique de la Charente*, Angoulême 1978

Oursel, R. *Living architecture – Romanesque*, Oldbourne, London 1967

— *Haut-Poitou roman*, Zodiaque, L.P.Q.V. 1975

Pansa, G. *Miti, leggende e superstizioni dell'Abruzzo*, Caroselli, Sulmona 1929; Forni, Bologna 1970

Parga, V. *et al. Las peregrinaciones a Santiago de Compostela*, Consejo superior de investigaciones scientíficas, Escuela de estudios medievales, Madrid 1948–9

Parker, C.W. Early sculptured stones at Egremont, *Transactions Cumb. & Westm. Antiquarian & Archaeol. Society*, Kendal 1902

Turville-Petre E.O.G. *Myth and religion of the north*, Weidenfeld & Nicolson, London 1964

Phillips, J. *Grey Abbey*, William H. Greer, Bookseller, Belfast 1874

Picard, C. L'épisode de Baubô dans les mystères d'Eleusis, *Revue de l'histoire des religions*, Paris 1920

Lefèvre-Pontalis, E. *L'architecture religieuse dans l'ancien diocèse de Soissons*, Plon/Nourrit et Cie, Paris 1896

— Les influences normandes au XI et XII siècles dans le nord de la France, *Bulletin Monumental*, Paris 1906

Porter, A.K. *Spanish Romanesque sculpture*, Pantheon, Florence 1928

— *The Romanesque sculpture of the pilgrimage roads*, Marshall Jones, Boston 1969

Prache, A. *Champagne romane*, Zodiaque, L.P.Q.V. 1981

— *Ile de France romane*, Zodiaque, L.P.Q.V. 1983

Randall, L.M.C. *Images in the margin of Gothic manuscripts*, Univ. of California Press, Berkeley/ Los Angeles 1966

Rawson, P. (ed.) *Primitive erotic art*, Weidenfeld & Nicolson, London 1973

Réau, L. *L'iconographie dans l'art chrétien*, Presses Universitaires de France, Paris 1955

Reinach, S. Le rire rituel, *Cultes, mythes et religions*, Paris 1922

Remnant, G.L. *A catalogue of misericords in G.B.*, Clarendon, Oxford 1969

Rivère, G. *Saint-Gaudens*, Zodiaque, L.P.Q.V. 1979

Rodriguez, A. *Castille romane*, Zodiaque, L.P.Q.V. 1966

Ross, A. The Divine Hag of the pagan Celts, in Newall, V. (ed.) *The Witch Figure*, Routledge & Kegan Paul, London 1973

— *Pagan Celtic Britain*, Routledge & Kegan Paul, London 1974

Rowland, B. *Animals with human faces*, Allen & Unwin, Tennessee 1973

Rushforth, G. Magister Gregorius de mirabilibus urbis Romae, *Journal of Roman Studies*, London 1919

Salin, E. *La civilisation mérovingienne*, Picard, Paris 1959

Salmon, J. Beakhead ornament in Norman architecture, *Yorkshire Archaeological Journal*, London 1946

Saxl, F. *English sculpture of the 12th century*, Faber & Faber, London 1954

Schapiro, M. On the aesthetic attitude in Romanesque art, *Essays in honour of Dr Coomaraswamy*, Luzac, London 1947

Schapiro, M. *Romanesque art*, Chatto & Windus, New York 1977

Scott, G.R. *Phallic worship*, Luxor Press, London 1970

Secret, J. *Périgord roman*, Zodiaque, L.P.Q.V. 1968

Seidl, L. Romanesque sculpture in American collections, *Gesta*, New York 1972

Sheridan, R. & Ross, A. *Grotesques and gargoyles*, David & Charles, Newton Abbot 1975

Southern, R.W. *The making of the Middle Ages*, Hutchinson, London 1953

Sperber, D. *Rethinking symbolism*, C.U.P., Cambridge 1975

Stalley, R. *Architecture and sculpture in Ireland*, Macmillan, London 1971

Stoll, R. *Architecture and sculpture in early Britain*, Thames & Hudson, London 1967

Svanberg, J. *Gycklarmotiv i romansk konst*, *Antikvariskt Archiv*, Stockholm 1970

Swarzenski, H. *Monuments of Romanesque art*, Faber & Faber, London 1974

Świechowski, Z. *Sculpture romane d'Auvergne*, E. de Bussac, Clermont-Ferrand 1973

Tannahill, R. *Sex in history*, Hamish Hamilton, London 1980

Temple, E. *Anglo-Saxon manuscripts 900–1066*, Harvey Miller, London 1976

Tristram, E.W. *English medieval wall-painting, 12th century* O.U.P. (Pilgrim Trust), London 1944

Turnbull, P. Phallic art in Roman Britain, *London University Inst. of Archaeol. Bulletin*, London 1978

Turner, V.W. *The forest of symbols*, Cornell Univ. Press, London 1970

Valin, J.C. *et al*, *Joi – poèmes de troubadours*, Editions de l'ORAC (Château-Larcher), Vienne 1976

Vidal, M. *Quercy roman*, Zodiaque, L.P.Q.V. 1969

Vieillard, J. *Le guide du pèlerin de St Jacques de Compostelle*, Macon 1978

Villermont, Comtesse de *Histoire de la coiffure féminine*, A. Mertens, Brussels 1981; Société Belge de Librairie 1892

Viollet-le-Duc, E. *Dictionnaire du mobilier français*, A. Morel et Cie, Paris 1872–5

Wacher, J. *Roman Britain*, Dent, London, 1978

Wackernagel, M. *Die Plastik des XII und XIII Jahrhunderts in Apulien*, K.W. Hiersemann, Leipzig 1911

Walsh, P.G. *Courtly love in the* Carmina Burana, Univ. of Edinburgh, Edinburgh 1971

Weir, A. Three carved figures in County Louth, *Co. Louth Archaeol. and Hist. Soc. Journal*, Dundalk 1977

— Exhibitionists and related carvings in the Irish Midlands, *Irish Midland Studies* (Murtagh ed.) Old Athlone Society, Athlone 1980

— *Early Ireland – a field guide*, Blackstaff Press, Belfast 1980

Welsford E. *The Fool – his social and literary history*, Faber & Faber, London 1935

Wessel, K. *Coptic art*, Thames & Hudson, London 1965

White, T.H. *The book of beasts*, Putnams, New York 1960

William, E. The protection of the house, *Folklore*, London 1978

Williams, J. *Early Spanish manuscript illumination*, Chatto & Windus, London 1977

Wilson, C. *Mysteries*, Hodder & Stoughton, London 1978

Witkowski, G.J. *L'art profane à l'église*, Schemit, Paris 1908

Wormald, F. Decorated initials in English manuscripts, *Archaeologia*, London 1945

Yarza, J. El infierno del *Beato* de Silos, *Pro Arte*, Barcelona 1979

Zarnecki, G. *English Romanesque sculpture*, Tiranti, London 1951

— *Later English Romanesque sculpture*, Tiranti, London 1953

— *The early sculpture of Ely Cathedral*, Tiranti, London 1958

— *Art of the medieval world*, Abrams, New York 1975

— *Romanesque sculpture at Lincoln Cathedral*, Friends of Lincoln Cathedral, London 1979

— *Studies in Romanesque sculpture*, Dorian, London 1979

Zarnecki, G. & Henry, F. Romanesque arches decorated with human and animal heads, *Journal of British Archaeological Assoc.*, London 1958

Gazetteer

Places and sites in the British Isles, France and Spain are classified by county, *département* or *provincia*; for the convenience of students who consult the Pevsner *Buildings of England* series, we have kept the old nomenclature of English counties. In other cases the country is also shown.

Aachen	Rhineland, Germany
Abbeylara	Longford
Abillé	Indre-et-Loire
Abson	Avon
Adel	Leeds, Yorkshire WR
Agen	Lot et Garonne
Aghalurcher	Fermanagh
Agonges	Allier
Agüero	Huesca
Aibar	Navarra
Aillas	Gironde
Albignac	Corrèze
Allas-Bocage	Charente-Maritime
Alloué	Vienne
Alquezar	Huesca
Amandi	Oviedo
Amboise	Indre-et-Loire
Amiens	Somme
Ampney St Peter	Gloucestershire
Angers	Maine-et-Loire
Angoulême	Charente
Annaghdown	Galway
Anzy-le-Duc	Saône-et-Loire
Aramil	Oviedo
Arboe	Tyrone
Arce	Navarra
Archingeay	Charente-Maritime
Ardentes	Indre
Ardfert	Kerry
Ardillières	Charente-Maritime
Arezzo	Tuscany, Italy
Argenton-Château	Deux-Sèvres
Arles	Bouches-du-Rhône
Ars-sur-le-Né	Charente
Artaíz	Navarra
Arthous	Landes
Asnières	Calvados
Assouste	Pyrénées-Atlantiques
Astureses	Orense
Athlone	Westmeath
Audignon	Landes
Aujac	Charente-Maritime
Aulnay	Charente-Maritime
Aurillac	Cantal
Austerfield	Yorkshire WR
Authie	Calvados
Autun	Saône-et-Loire
Auzon	Haute-Loire

Ávallon	Yonne
Ávila	Ávila
Avy-en-Pons	Charente-Maritime
Ballaghmore	Laois
Ballinderry	Galway
Ballycloghduff	Westmeath
Ballyfinboy	Tipperary
Ballylarkin	Kilkenny
Ballynacarriga	Cork
Ballynahinch	Tipperary
Ballyportry	Clare
Balrothery	Dublin
Barahona	Segóvia
Barbadelo	Lugo
Barfreston	Kent
Bari	Apulia, Italy
Barletta	Apulia, Italy
Barret	Charente
Bayeux	Calvados
Bayonne	Pyrénées-Atlantiques
Beaulieu-sur-Dordogne	Corrèze
Beaumont-sur-Sarthe	Sarthe
Béceleuf	Deux-Sèvres
Bénévent-l'Abbaye	Creuse
Benevento	Campania, Italy
Bernay	Eure
Berrioplano	Navarra
Berrymount	Cavan
Besse	Dordogne
Besse-en-Chandesse	Puy-de-Dôme
Bignay	Charente-Maritime
Bilbao	Viscaya
Bilton-in-Ainsty	Yorkshire WR
Binstead	Isle of Wight
Biota	Aragon
Biron	Charente-Maritime
Birr	Offaly
Blackhall	Kildare
Blaignac	Gironde
Blaye	Gironde
Blesle	Haute-Loire
Boa Island	Fermanagh
Bonnesvalyn	Aisne
Bordeaux	Gironde
Bords	Charente-Maritime
Bors-de-Baigne	Charente
Bouresse	Vienne
Bourg-Argental	Loire
Boyle Abbey	Roscommon
Bozouls	Aveyron
Bråby	Sydsjælland, Denmark
Brañosera	Palencia
Brem-sur-Mer	Vendée
Brescia	Lombardy, Italy
Bresdon	Charente
Bretteville	Calvados
Briantes	Indre
Bridge Sollers	Herefordshire
Bridlington	Yorkshire ER
Brindisi	Apulia, Italy
Brinsop	Herefordshire
Brioude	Haute-Loire

Brive	Corrèze	Covet	Lérida
Broadford	Clare	Cressac	Charente
Brough-on-Humber	Yorkshire ER	Croft-on-Tees	Yorkshire NR
Brucheville	Manche	Cugnoli	Abruzzi, Italy
Bruyères-et-Montbérault	Aisne	Cullahill	Laois
Buckland	Buckinghamshire	Cunault	Maine-et-Loire
Bugthorpe	Yorkshire ER	Cuvergnon	Aisne
Buncton	Sussex	Cuxhagen	Saxony, Germany
Bunratty	Clare		
Burgesbeg	Tipperary	La Daurade	Tarn-et-Garonne
Bussière-Badil	Dordogne	Devizes	Wiltshire
		Deyrançon	Deux-Sèvres
Caherelly	Limerick	Dinan	Côtes-du-Nord
Cahors	Lot	Doon	Offaly
Cambes	Gironde	Douvres	Calvados
Canterbury	Kent	Dowth	Louth
Carennac	Lot	Drakestown	Meath
Carne	Westmeath	Drogheda	Louth
Cashel	Tipperary	Droiturier	Allier
Castledermot	Kildare	Dublin	Dublin
Castle Frome	Herefordshire	Dunnaman	Limerick
Castletown	Louth	Dysert O Dea	Clare
Castle Widenham	Cork		
Catterick	Yorkshire NR	Eardisley	Herefordshire
Caunay	Deux-Sèvres	Easthorpe	Essex
Cavan	Cavan	Echano (hermitage)	Navarra
Cénac	Dordogne	Echillais	Charente-Maritime
Cerne Abbas	Dorset	Egremont	Cumbria
Cervatos	Santander	Elkstone	Gloucestershire
Chadenac	Charente-Maritime	Ely	Cambridge
La-Chaize-le-Vicomte	Vendée	Ennezat	Puy-de-Dôme
Chaldon	Surrey	Epaux-Bézu	Aisne
Champagne	Charente-Maritime	Epinal	Vosges
Champagnolles	Charente-Maritime	Errigal Keeroge	Tyrone
Chanteuges	Haute-Loire	L'Estany	Barcelona
La Charité-sur-Loire	Nièvre	Estella	Navarra
Charlieu	Loire		
Charmant	Charente	Faurndau	Baden-Württemberg,
Chartres	Eure-et-Loire		Germany
Châteaumeillant	Cher	Faye-la-Vineuse	Vienne
Chauriat	Puy-de-Dôme	Fénioux	Charente-Maritime
Chauvigny	Vienne	Fethard	Tipperary
Cheb	W. Bohemia, Czechoslovakia	Fole	Gotland, Sweden
Chelles	Aisne	La Fontaine-Henry	Calvados
Le Cher	Charente-Maritime	Fontaines-d'Ozillac	Charente-Maritime
Chermignac	Charente-Maritime	Fontevrault	Maine-et-Loire
Chouday	Indre	Foussais	Vendée
Church Stretton	Shropshire	Foussignac	Charente
Civray	Vienne	Fownhope	Herefordshire
Claverley	Shropshire	Freiberg	Saxony, Germany
Clenagh	Clare	Fresnay-sur-Sarthe	Sarthe
Clermont-Ferrand	Puy-de-Dôme	Frómista	Palencia
Cloghan	Roscommon	Fuentesáuco	Soria
Clomantagh	Kilkenny	Fuentidueña	Segóvia
Clonca	Donegal		
Clonfert	Galway	Garry Castle	Offaly
Clonmacnois	Offaly	Germigny-les-Prés	Nièvre
Clonmel	Tipperary	Gerona (Girona)	Gerona
Cluny	Saône-et-Loire	Gisors	Eure
Cognac	Charente-Maritime	Givrezac	Charente-Maritime
Colombiers	Charente-Maritime	Glaine-Montaigut	Puy-de-Dôme
Combronde	Puy-de-Dôme	Glendalough	Wicklow
Como	Lombardy, Italy	Gloucester	Gloucestershire
Compostela	see Santiago	Gosmer	Østjælland, Denmark
Conzac	Charente	Gotland	Sweden
Cooliagh	see Kyle	Gourdon	Lot
Copgrove	Yorkshire WR	Grandson	Switzerland
Conques	Aveyron	La Graulière	Corrèze
Corme-Ecluse	Charente-Maritime	Grey Abbey	Down
Corme-Royal	Charente-Maritime	Guarbecque	Pas-de-Calais
Corsiguano	Tuscany, Italy	Guardo	Palencia
Corullón	León	Guéron	Calvados
La Coruña	La Coruña	Guimiliau	Finistère
Courpière	Puy-de-Dôme		

Guitinières	Charente-Maritime
Haddon Hall	Derbyshire
Haux	Gironde
Hellifield	N. Yorkshire
Hérent	Belgium
Hexham	Northumberland
Holdgate	Shropshire
Hook Norton	Oxfordshire
Huesca	Huesca
Iffley	Oxfordshire
Ingrandes	Vienne
Irache	Navarra
Issoire	Puy-de-Dôme
Jaca	Huesca
la Jarne	Charente-Maritime
Jouers	Pyrénées-Atlantiques
Jubia	La Coruña
Jugazan	Gironde
Kells	Meath
Kilkea	Kildare
Killaloe	Clare
Killinaboy	Clare
Killua	Westmeath
Kilpeck	Herefordshire
Kilteel	Kildare
Kiltinane	Tipperary
Knockarley	Offaly
Kyle (Cooliagh)	Kilkenny
Lacommande	Pyrénées-Atlantiques
Lammas	Norfolk
Larumbe	Navarra
Lautenbach	Haut-Rhin
Lavaudieu	Haute-Loire
Lavey	Cavan
Leominster	Herefordshire
León	León
Lérida	Lérida
Lescar	Pyrénées-Atlantiques
Lescure	Tarn
Lestiac	Gironde
Letnitsa	Lovech, Bulgaria
Leyre	Navarra
Liathmore	Tipperary
Lichères	Charente
(Liébana)	(Santander)
Liesse	Aisne
Limalonges	Charente
Limburg-am-Lahn	Hesse, Germany
Limoges	Haute-Vienne
Lincoln	Lincolnshire
Linley	Shropshire
Lixnaw	Kerry
Llandrindod	Radnor
Loarre	Huesca
Loctudy	Finistère
Logroño	Logroño
Lomilla de Aguilar	Palencia
Loughborough	Leicestershire
Loupiac	Gironde
Lucca	Tuscany, Italy
Lucheux	Somme
Ludlow	Shropshire
Lugo	Lugo
Lusignan	Vienne
Lussac-les-Châteaux	Vienne
Macqueville	Charente-Maritime
Madrid	Madrid
Maen Achwyfan	Clwyd
Mailhat	Puy-de-Dôme
Maillezais	Vendée
Malahide	Dublin
Manéglise	Seine-Maritime
Maranges	Gerona
Margam	Glamorgan
Marienhafe	Ost-Friesland, Germany
Marignac	Charente-Maritime
Maringues	Puy-de-Dôme
Marizy-Sainte-Geneviève	Aisne
Marolles-sur-Ourcq	Aisne
Marthon	Charente
Maryport	Cumberland
Marzan	Lugo
Massac	Charente-Maritime
Matalbaniega	Palencia
Matha	Charente-Maritime
Maubourguet	Hautes-Pyrénées
Mauriac	Cantal
Meigle	Perthshire
Melbourne	Derbyshire
Melle	Deux-Sèvres
Mens	La Coruña
Merlévenez	Morbihan
(Mervent	Vendée)
Mesland	Loir-et-Cher
Migron	Charente-Maritime
Milan	Lombardy, Italy
Millstadt	Austria
Miranda de Ebro	Gerona
Mirepoix	Ariège
Moate	Westmeath
Modena	Emilia, Italy
Moissac	Tarn-et-Garonne
Monasterboice	Louth
Montbron	Charente
Monte Cassino	Campania, Italy
Monterrey	Orense
Montfrin	Gard
Montigny-Lengrain	Aisne
Montils	Charente-Maritime
Montmorillon	Vienne
Montréal	Yonne
Mont-Saint-Michel	Manche
Moone	Kildare
Morláas	Pyrénées-Atlantiques
Mornac	Charente-Maritime
Moscufo	Abruzzi, Italy
Mosnac	Charente-Maritime
Mouchan	Gers
Mount Athos	Greece
Mouthiers	Charente
Moycarky	Tipperary
Moygara	Sligo
Mozac	Puy-de-Dôme
Murato	Corsica
Nantes	Loire-Atlantique
Navascués	Navarra
Nerbis	Landes
Neuilly-Saint-Front	Aisne
Newton Lennan	Tipperary
Nieul-le-Virouil	Charente
Nohant-Vicq	Indre
Nonac	Charente
Nonant	Calvados
Nonette	Puy-de-Dôme
Norrey	Calvados
Oaksey	Wiltshire
Olcóz	Navarra
Olopte	Gerona
Olóriz	Navarra
Omeñaca	Soria

Oô (Ôo)	Haute-Garonne
Orange	Vaucluse
Orcival	Puy-de-Dôme
Orense	Orense
Orisoain	Navarra
Orléans	Loiret
Ouistreham	Calvados
Oviedo	Oviedo
Oxford	Oxfordshire
Parçay-sur-Vienne	Indre-et-Loire
Parthenay	Deux-Sèvres
Parthenay-le-Vieux	Deux-Sèvres
Passirac	Charente
Patrixbourne	Kent
Paulinzella	Thüringen, Germany
Pavia	Lombardy, Italy
Pecharromán	Segóvia
Penmon	Anglesey
Pennington	Cumberland
Pérignac	Charente-Maritime
Perorrubio	Segóvia
Perros-Guirec	Côtes-du-Nord
Pienza	Tuscany, Italy
Plaisance-sur-Gartempe	Vienne
Pleinigen	Baden-Württemberg, Germany
Poitiers	Vienne
Pons	Charente-Maritime
Pont-l'Abbé-d'Arnoult	Charente-Maritime
Pouzauges	Vendée
Preuilly-sur-Claize	Indre-et-Loire
Puente la Reina	Navarra
Le Puy	Haute-Loire
Puypéroux	Charente
Queniborough	Leicestershire
Rahan	Offaly
Rath (Blathmaic)	Clare
Rattoo	Kerry
Ravenna	Emilia, Italy
Rebordanes	Galicia
Redwood Castle	Tipperary
Regensburg	Bavaria, Germany
Reignac	Charente
Reinheim	Saarland, Germany
Revilla de Santullán	Palencia
Reims	Marne
Riom	Puy-de-Dôme
Riom-ès-Montagnes	Cantal
Rio Mau	Portugal
Rochefort	Charente-Maritime
La Rochelle	Charente-Maritime
Rochester	Kent
Rochestown	Tipperary
Rodez	Aveyron
Romans	Drôme
(Rome	Italy)
Roncevalles (Roncevaux)	Navarra
Roquesérière	Tarn-et-Garonne
Rosheim	Bas-Rhin
Rots	Calvados
Rouen	Seine-Maritime
Rowlestone	Herefordshire
Rubiães	Portugal
Sablonceaux	Charente-Maritime
Sahagún	León
Saint-André-de-Bagé	Ain
Saint-Antonin	Tarn-et-Garonne
San Cebrián de Muda	Palencia
Saint-Christophe-de-Bardes	Gironde
Saint-Claude	Jura
Saint-Contest	Calvados
Saint-Coutant-le-Grand	Charente-Maritime
Saint-Dier	Puy-de-Dôme
Santo Domingo de Silos	Burgos
Saint-Fort-sur-Gironde	Charente-Maritime
Saint-Front-sur-Nizonne	Dordogne
Saint-Gaudens	Haute-Garonne
Saint-Genès-de Lombaud	Gironde
Saint-Genou	Indre
Saint-Georges-de Boscherville	Seine-Maritime
Saint-Georges-de Montagne	Gironde
Saint-Germain-de Vibrac	Charente-Maritime
Saint-Germain-du Seudre	Charente-Maritime
San Giovanni in Borgo	Lombardy, Italy
Saint-Hilaire (Poitiers)	Vienne
Saint-Hilaire-des-Loges	Vendée
Saint Ives	Cambridgeshire
Saint-Jean-d'Angély	Charente-Maritime
Saint-Jean-de-Luz	Pyrénées-Atlantiques
Sant Joan de les Abadesses	Gerona
Saint-Jouin-de-Marnes	Vienne
San Juan de la Peña	Huesca
Saint-Léger-de-Montbrillais	Vienne
Saint-Léger-en-Pons	Charente-Maritime
Saint-Léonard-de-Noblat	Haute-Vienne
Saint-Loup	Charente-Maritime
Saint-Loups-Hors	Calvados
Saint-Martial-lès-Coivert	Charente-Maritime
Saint-Martin-d'Ary	Charente-Maritime
San Martín-de Mondoñedo	Lugo
Saint-Martin-de-Sescas	Gironde
San Martín de Unx	Navarra
Saint-Michel-d'Aiguilh	Haute-Loire (Le Puy)
Saint-Michel-d'Entraygues	Charente
San Miguel de Lillo	Oviedo
Saint-Nectaire	Puy-de-Dôme
Saint-Palais	Gironde
Saint-Parize-le-Châtel	Nièvre
Saint-Paul-lès-Dax	Landes
San Pedro de Tejada	Burgos
Saint-Pierre-de-Pensac	Dordogne
Saint-Pierre-d'Excideuil (Civray)	Vienne
Saint-Pons	Herault
Saint-Quentin-de-Rançannes	Charente-Maritime
Saint-Quentin-de-Baron	Gironde
San Quirce	Burgos
San Quirce de Rio Pisuerga	Palencia
Saint-Rémy	Bouches-du-Rhône
Saint-Roman-lès-Melle	Deux-Sèvres
Saint-Sauvant	Charente-Maritime
Saint-Savin	Vienne
Saint-Séver	Landes
Saint-Séver-de-Rustan	Hautes-Pyrénées
Saint-Sulpice-de-Mareuil	Dordogne
Saint-Symphorien-de-Broue	Charente-Maritime
Saint-Trojan	Charente-Maritime
Saint-Vaast-de-Longmont	Oise
Saint-Vallier	Charente
Saint-Wandrille	Seine-Maritime
Sainte-Colombe	Charente
Sainte-Engrâce	Pyrénées-Atlantiques
Sainte-Marie d'Oloron	Pyrénées-Atlantiques
Sainte-Ouenne	Deux-Sèvres
Saintes	Charente-Maritime
Salamanca	Salamanca
Sangüesa	Navarra
Santa Cruz de Seros	Huesca
Santa Maria del Sar	La Coruña
Santa Marta del Cerro	Segóvia
Santander	Santander
Santiago de Compostela	La Coruña
Santillana de Mar	Santander

Saragossa (Zaragoza)	Zaragoza	Verona	Veneto, Italy
Saujon	Charente-Maritime	Vester Egede	Sydsjælland, Denmark
Saulieu	Côte-d'Or	Vézelay	Yonne
La Sauve	Gironde	Vielle-Tursan	Landes
La Sauve-Majeure	Gironde	(Vienna	Austria)
Savignac-d'Auros	Gironde	Vienne	Isère
Segóvia	Segóvia	Villanueva de Cangas	Oviedo
Seir Kieran	Offaly	Villanueva de Pisuergo	Palencia
Sémelay	Nièvre	Villaviciosa	Oviedo
Semur-en-Auxois	Côte-d'Or	Villedieu-du-Clain	Vienne
Semur-en-Brionnais	Saône-et-Loire	Villenave-d'Ornon	Gironde
Sequera	Segóvia	Villers-Saint-Paul	Oise
Sessa Arunca	Campania (Naples) Italy	Viterbo	Tuscany, Italy
Serantes	Orense	Vitrac	Charente
Sérigné	Vendée	Vouvant	Vendée
La Seu d'Urgell	Lérida		
Sevignacq-Thèze	Pyrénées-Orientales	Wells	Somerset
Shobdon	Herefordshire	Whittlesford	Cambridgeshire
Smithstown	Clare	Willingham	Cambridgeshire
Soest	N. Rhineland, Germany	Winchester	Hampshire
Solignac	Haute-Vienne	Worcester	Worcestershire
Somogyvar	Hungary	Wroxeter	Shropshire
Soria	Soria		
Sos del Rey Católico	Navarra	Zamora	Zamora
Souillac	Lot	Zurbano	Álava
Soulac-sur-Mer	Charente-Maritime		
Stepaside	Dublin		
Stottesdon	Shropshire		
Strasbourg	Bas-Rhin		
Stretton Sugwas	Herefordshire		
Studland	Dorset		
Surgères	Charente-Maritime		
Swords	Dublin		
Talmont	Charente-Maritime		
Targon	Gironde		
Taüll	Barcelona		
Tavant	Indre-et-Loire		
Thiers	Puy-de-Dôme		
Thouars	Deux-Sèvres		
Thuret	Puy-de-Dôme		
Thury-Harcourt	Calvados		
Tibberaghny	Kilkenny		
Tingstäde	Gotland, Sweden		
Tinnakill	Laois		
Tollevast	Manche		
Tomregan (Toomregan)	see Berrymount		
Toulouse	Tarn-et-Garonne		
Tournus	Saône-et-Loire		
Tozalmoros	Soria		
Tracton Abbey	Cork		
Trévières	Calvados		
Trogir	Yugoslavia		
Troyes	Aube		
Tudela	Navarra		
Tugford	Shropshire		
Tullavin	Limerick		
Turin	Piedmont, Italy		
Turoe	Galway		
Uncastillo	Navarra		
Urcel	Aisne		
Uriconium	see Wroxeter		
Valbona de les Monges	Lérida		
Valdenoceda	Burgos		
Valdeomillos	Palencia		
Valence	Drôme		
Vallejo	Burgos		
Vandré	Charente-Maritime		
Vannes	Morbihan		
Väte	Sweden		
Vaux-sur-Mer	Charente-Maritime		
Venice	Veneto, Italy		

Index